LANGUAGE, THOUGHT, AND EXPERIENCE

ANGUAGE, THOUGHT, AND EXPERIENCE

A Tapestry of the Dimensions of Meaning

William G. Hardy, Ph.D.
The Johns Hopkins University

University Park Press
Baltimore

UNIVERSITY PARK PRESS
International Publishers in Science and Medicine
233 East Redwood Street
Baltimore, Maryland 21202

Typeset by American Graphic Arts Corporation and Alpha Graphic, Inc.
Manufactured in the United States of America by
The Maple Press Company.

Library of Congress Cataloging in Publication Data:

Hardy, William G.
Language, thought, and experience.

Bibliography: p.
Includes index.
1. Meaning (Philosophy)   2. Semantics
(Philosophy)   3. Semiotics.   4. Languages—
Philosophy.   I. Title.

B105.M4H37   121   77-28163
ISBN 0-8391-1213-0

Contents

Preface

A friend to whose scholarship and wisdom I have recurrently turned in putting this book together once wrote some prefatory remarks in one of his own books that have always interested me. "This is not a book for scholars," he wrote, "but is intended for the half-mythical 'general reader.' He will excuse my avoiding long preliminary explanations and apologies but will judge the book upon what he gets out of it, not by what he thinks I should have put into it." This was written by George Boas a fair number of years ago about a book on some of the major traditions of philosophy. There are frequent references to this book in the present work.

The book you now have in your hand refers to some principal studies of the dimensions of meaning (or of the meaning of meaning, or of a broad background of semantic theory—you may choose the terms that seem to be most appropriate; there are many of them). Some of this has to do with philosophical systems and trends, because philosophy has to do in large part with meanings. Let us say, then, that this book is designed for students of meaning. They may be scholars or interested readers. My professional concerns have for many years been related to human communication and to disorders of communication. The nature and the dimensions of meaning are very much a part of all aspects of this very confusing part of the complex of human behavior.

Years ago I undertook a doctoral dissertation on this topic. This early work was perhaps somewhat premature, so far as public awareness was concerned, and it was interrupted by World War II and several years of work with the then very profound problems of communication that came from the results of naval engagements. Then followed thirty years of clinical concerns that centered around attitudes and procedures that we all had to learn. This involved something quite different from academic thoughts.

Now, with time to rethink in a variety of ways, it has been possible to go back over the early material on the dimensions of meaning, put it into some reasonably modern order with a clear effort to retain historical perspective.

All the intellectual or otherwise social digging in reference here has required much aid and support from my wife and close associates, particularly from my assistant, Jeanette Fino, and from colleagues and students—which I acknowledge freely and for which I am profoundly grateful. This is at least a major part of the warmth of a system of meanings in human communication.

Introduction

It has long been a twentieth-century commonplace that the natures of meaning and communication are subjects for both speculation and hard thinking. Recurrently through the course of long periods of history, there have been periods of special attention to theories of meaning, possibly as one result of some of the cycles of highs and lows in the human state. Enough of importance has happened for good or ill that a critical review is in order. This often involves special attention to meanings that have emerged and that must be accounted for.

The general concept of a critical study of theories of meaning in communication is, then, an integral part of the history of ideas. A person's use of audible and visible symbols can very clearly reflect his thinking about the nature of reality, of which a sense of communicated meanings is probably a principal focus. In a broad sense, critical attention to the field of meanings may be circumscribed as the study of methods of interpreting experience. Its subject matter is the relation that obtains among language, thought, and experience. The student of meaning seeks to untangle in some sort of practical terms the web of words that has been spun about the analysis of human intelligence. He is interested in the problems of simplifying and systematizing an understanding of interpretative activities.

The modern mind is apt to be empirical. It is characterizable by the presumption that knowledge arises in, and must be confirmed by, experience. The apprehension and organization of experience into clearly articulated beliefs of whatever sort or extent is mainly an interpretative process, and in large part a communicative process. It then follows that the world of existence is very much a world of meanings. There are in this world divergent social forces and varying perspectives. This brings about a strong conviction that truth-values are not absolutes, but functions of meanings, relative to the things known, the habits of the knower, and the medium that connects them. This medium is usually some aspect of language, and we become critical of the fact that the awareness of environment that we call intelligence is a product of our symbolic habits. In several ways, a

1

theory of knowledge is a theory of communication. No matter whether one chooses to orient one's existence on a faith based upon aesthetics, science, religion, or practical efficiency—according to systemic dogma, systemless skepticism, or any stage intermediate—one acts in a realm of meanings (Langer, 1942). The empirical mind is led inevitably to consider communication by signs, of which the verbal-symbolic must obviously be most important, the sine qua non of both personal reflection and impersonal knowledge. In his study of the meaning process—of the relations which seem to obtain among language, thought, and experience—the student of meaning seeks a means for putting his world in order.

He shares the conviction, persistent in the history of ideas, that civilization is a derivative of man's capacity to use symbols, that the human mind cannot be divorced from its symbolic functions, that symbol-making is its fundamental process (Dewey, 1930; Ritchie, 1936; Langer, 1942). This predilection has a long history. It is without doubt "one of the most characteristic accompaniments of the various manifestations of empiricism" (Morris, 1937). Today, possibly to a greater extent than ever before, there is a vital concern with sign usage. The burgeoning of computerization from the cradle to the grave is affecting all of us. Even our identities reflect the numbers game of a very modern version of Neo-Pythagoreanism. There is an acute consciousness, in terms other than social security, of the need to re-examine our meaning-communicative activities. This continues to bring forward a torrent of evidence and speculation about human affairs, an exposure of the commonplace and the obscure the like of which customarily attends our efforts to understand the nature of reality, whether the focus be foreign policy or the cost of a new refrigerator. This concern seems to reappear in waves every thirty or forty years, but with a constant undertow always apparent.

This general interest has become a communal phenomenon of the twentieth century. Investigators in almost every field of endeavor, from theoretical physics and metaphysics to propaganda analysis and the study of merchandising techniques and people's rights, are studying sign usage. Nor is this limited to the philosopher, the politician, or the interested specialist. In our propaganda- and advertising-conscious age, not much different from what it was forty years ago, the analytical interpretation of events is the property of the man(woman) in the street. There is an intensive awareness of the purposive direction of ideas and the use of things. "The meaning of . . ." is a favorite lead for every kind of writing and doing, from adjurations in the pulpit to remarks in the analysis of the news. On the assumption that a person's intentions are not always what they seem, an assumption that is supported by our "curriculum" of social studies in the street and an apparent lack of realization that most of all this has happened before, the modern person is well on his way to becoming suspicious of all ideas, including his own. He is a student—not always apt, and frequently unable to recognize and evaluate that which he seeks, but nonetheless a student—of meaning.

Several postulates are derivable from current theoretical essays and descriptions: that meaning is a referential process in a broad sense, that it is equatable with knowing (even including intuition), that it may well be described in terms of the interaction among the components of reference (and therefore must involve performance as well as competence), and that the knowing process is structurally similar to communicative activity. Perhaps the most notable aspects of descriptive semantics involve the reduction of the study of meaning to a fairly simple formula of sign analysis, and the emphasis upon the variability of value-judgments according to twentieth-century voluntarism.

In discussing what are considered important and contributory theories in the study of meaning, I have adopted no fixed order of topics and no precise critical scheme. As with most tapestry that has withstood the marks of time, whether aging or enduring, there emerges a pastiche with a form that outlines the dimensions of meaning that have been interwoven over the centuries. For this reason it seems better to vary the critical tone according to the sense and intention of the ideas under consideration. This is an important aspect of communication. It is in agreement with a basic attitude of criticism, to the effect that judgments in terms of intelligibility, probability, and utility come close to answering most of the questions that can be asked of reasoned discourse (MacKaye, 1939). This book approaches the evaluative problem with these criteria in mind.

For better or worse, the analysis of meaning in all its aspects is in the air. It is also in the headlines: "Negotiations break down because of semantic misunderstanding!" The level of cerebration in such circumstances is not always high, but it is with us daily. In some ways the cry of "semantic differences" is simply a euphemism employed to avoid calling the other fellow a liar. Semantics has become a major interest at all levels—for instance in daily conversations (as with some recurrent discussions of "people's rights"), and on national and international levels, (as in Presidential opinions and off-the-cuff interviews with the man-in-the-street on television). Some of the disquisitions are exceedingly obscure. It would be an impossible task to survey the entire field of this interest, or to trace the full history of the analysis of meanings. Only a critical interpretation of some current theories and attitudes about semantics, especially verbal-symbolic meanings, is attempted here. Many of the principal topics, old and new, are, thus, I hope, exposed to view. The subject is confused and confusing, and its pursuit takes us into ranges of metaphysics and epistemology, logic and linguistics, psychology and sociology, rhetoric and poetics, and much more than a little way into consideration of the "communicative chain," wherein at least two unique nervous systems are connected through a verbal-symbolic system that is language in action (Hardy, 1976).

Regardless of the value judgments involved, one must recognize in the mid- and latter part of the twentieth century the prevalence of the belief in economic determinism. This way of interpreting reality emerged from the activities of the social reformers and humanitarians of the nineteenth century, who worked on the theory that man is a product of his environment. It has received its fullest philosophical formulation from Karl Marx and Friedrich Engels in the doctrine of dialectical materialism. Perhaps basic in this doctrine is what Sidney Hook calls "the social interpretation of categories"—the belief that the modes of economic production determine the modes of social behavior and that "in this behavior are formed ideas, attitudes and habits which express themselves in other fields of culture" (1937). This is what Dewey has called the theory of "occupational psychoses." Whatever the political status of Marxian ideas may be, there can be no doubt that a significant aspect of the modern attitude is a keen awareness of social forces operating in terms of "the mode of production." This is an attitude that forces us to think in terms of meaning, for the fundamental notion of economic determinism—the social interpretation of categories, e.g., management and worker—expresses relations of external conditions to the apparatus of thought, and thus is a semantic theory in itself. In broader terms, the encompassing modern concept of *the social* steadily forces upon us awareness of various perspectives and concerns for their meanings.

Moreover, the broadened political base of the twentieth century and the Third World, with the resultant growth in the significance of public opinion and the power of public discussion, offers ground for the conviction that attention to symbolic processes may pay dividends in human welfare. This is not to say that social and political problems are only verbal, but that our awareness of them is qualified by our ability to interpret purposes and implications. The attempt to clear away verbal chaff in order to get at the facts is essentially a matter of analyzing meanings, or, if one prefers, of analyzing the symbolic processes through which the mind works. The pragmatic study of human affairs indicates that when people aim at political cooperation they might well pay attention to each other's verbal habits, at least to the extent of becoming aware of their common problem-solving deficiencies. Some semanticists have had much to say of the urgency of symbolic analysis for the ends of political cohesion and social intelligence. They may, like Mannheim, aim at a factual description of the relations between thought and action in politics; or, like Ogden and Richards, they may believe that a science of symbolism can furnish an educative corpus for the exposition and treatment of ethical and political ailments; or, like Count Alfred Korzybski, or even P. W. Bridgman in his nonscientific moments, they may feel that semantic training will not only expose but eliminate many of the problems of existence. All this places a normative cast over thought processes that may restrict their utility. The opinion that the study of the nature of symbolism may act as a moral and intellectual curative is fundamental in at least two theories of semantics. Assuming that man's ability to symbolize is his most distinctive characteristic, and that he can become symbol-wise through a program of general education, Richards, Korzybski, and their followers feel that progress can be realized and quickened. It should be noted that this opinion is not shared by all theorizers about meaning.

It was emphasized by at least one semantic theorist whose views on the topic helped to usher in the twentieth century. In 1903, Lady Victoria Welby published an inquiry called *What Is Meaning?* She suggests the establishment of the "science of significs," offered not as a new school of thought but primarily as an educational method. The book is a combination of interesting generalizations on the state of the world, poetic mysticism, and a strong plea for progress in semantic and linguistic analysis. The burden of this message is that the analytical distinction of sense (instinctive perception, signification), meaning (rational thought), and significance (value judgments) offer the possibility of a critique of words for the better interpretation of experience. This may be presumed to be an immediate forebear of the belief that the science of symbolism should be an educative force.

Here, then, are three strands of thought, obviously interwoven, that help to account for modern interest in sign analysis: the importance of symbolism in economic affairs, its significance in politics and ethics, and its place in an educational system that is more public than ever before. A fourth strand, probably basic to all these, is the emergence of an empirical methodology in scientific theory. Many thinkers have turned their attention to the construction of a theory to accomplish the blending of the philosophy of science with the science of philosophy. A priori rationalism and absolute truth are discarded in favor of atomic empiricism and the predictive validity of the laws of probability.

The connection between modern scientific method and a consuming interest in symbolism is patent. The sense data of science are readings, signs, complex wave-forms, computer read-outs, and verbal reports. These must be interpreted according to specific objectives obtained through controlled procedures. "The problem of observation," writes Langer, "is all but eclipsed by the problem of meaning" (1942). Herein is set what she calls the "new key" of philosophy:

> A new philosophical theme has been set forth to a coming age: an epistemological theme, the comprehension of science. The power of symbolism is its cue, as the finality of sense-data was the cue of a former epoch (p. 21).

It is Langer's belief that philosophy, the study of meanings, includes all the rational sciences, and that metaphysics has the same priority in philosophy that physics has among the natural sciences, while logical analysis is the counterpart of empirical observation (1930). In this scheme, the aims of philosophy and science are correlative: to philosophy belongs the task of outlining metaphysical principles and furnishing a logical critique; to science belongs the task of adducing and confirming empirical facts in the laboratory.

The epistemological aspect of this "theme" is quite evident. The analysis of meaning becomes the analysis of knowing, or, as Cunningham puts it, "the acquisition of knowledge is penetration into the significance of reference" (1938). Such an attitude is grounded upon an empirical analysis of the meaning-situation. When any of us are in a critical but uncertain mood, we frequently ask ourselves, "How do we know that?" If the term *knowledge* be generalized as the apprehension, organization, and confirmation of experience, this general thesis about knowing is at one with Langer's idea.

In sum, the nature of the twentieth-century world and the methods of understanding it are such that they direct attention to the problems of meaning, which can only be brought into focus by persistent study of various symbolic activities. Whatever one's attitude toward the idea of progress, one will probably agree that our century has managed to achieve a complexity that has never been known before. In light of the swift linkage between events and their interpretations and their effects, there can be little wonder that special attention is given to a study of words and their ways. This has always been an interesting undertaking, as the literature of the Western World freely demonstrates. It is now an imperative. The modern person is less governed than were some of his forebears by a belief in a fully determinate "block-universe." He has seen the moon; it is no longer a fantasy, a form of folklore. He is apt to insist in a Protagorean vein (Protagoras was one of the philosophical heretics of the fifth century, B.C.) that experience is the sole criterion of knowledge and determinant of truth. Another way to express this may have some appeal: one may believe that only the past offers truth—the future is indeterminate, and governed by the weight of probability. These are the wages of a faith in scientific method. The modern person, for the most part, lives in the here and now. He must order his knowledge and digest it utterly that he may live well. Accordingly, it is necessary to discover a formula for the assimilation of experience in a highly complex society. Even the radical empiricist is willing to take a lesson from Hegel, who taught the utility of systematizing knowledge by rational analysis, a lesson that is clearly reflected in the effort to establish a science of symbolism. In one's study of the meaning-process, one seeks the comprehension of an orderly world.

It may appear to a student of the humanities that some of the aims of modern semantic theory are very old. So they are. Neither the consciousness of the need to study meanings nor the metaphysics of empiricism is new. It is of more than passing interest to observe that many of the most cogent arguments in the presentation of current thinking about meaning were quite forcibly stated in considerable detail in the five centuries labeled B.C. The plan of this book does not permit going deeply into the patterns of ancient thoughts, nor is this really necessary, because they recur in substantively recognizable forms over a period of approximately 2,500 years. Some of these ideas and beliefs are now considered here.

The next section of this book examines some attitudes about meaning in earlier times. First, the ancients, ranging from Democritus, Plato, Protagoras, Aristotle, Epicurus, and Zeno to the schools of Alexandria (Philo Judaeus) and Naples (Philodemus), and some of the early Christian thinking (Augustine) are discussed. Much that is familiar is found in the arguments and counter-arguments of Stoics, Skeptics, Sophists, and their various followers.

After some passing references to the Middle Ages, for the most part in terms of formal schooling, the book next examines some of the concerns of the Post-Renaissance and the development of English Empiricism in the seventeenth, eighteenth, and nineteenth centuries. This involves attention to Bacon, Locke, Hobbes, J. S. Mill, and Bentham. Interesting though much of the material is, a necessarily cursory treatment is offered herein.

The main body of the book contains a fairly detailed critique of the thinking of a considerable variety of twentieth-century theorists within the middle half of the century. One of the troublesome tasks of an undertaking of this sort is the justification of inclusions and exclusions. There is no intention to suggest that an interest in meaning and semiotic is limited to philosophers and methodologists of science. It is taken for granted that the humanistic tradition in rhetoric and poetics, and literature in general, bridges for the arts the years since a theoretical interest in symbolism and meaning arose among the Hellenists. Nor has there been an intention to suggest that an interest in meaning is limited, among philosophers, to empiricists. The history of philosophy points to the contrary. Sign analysis has been the tool both of attack and defense in all manner of dogmatism. Empirical thinking is in the ascendancy today, however, and the empirical tradition seems to account for the greater part of modern concern with theory of signs, whether as philosophical propaedeutic or as social panacea.

A diversity of theories, or concepts, or sets of ideas has been selected to suggest the tone of the past fifty years. They present the subject from an interesting variety of perspectives, all significant and, I believe, instructive. All the writers concerned deal with the relations between meaning and knowing. The first two, G. W. Cunningham and P. W. Bridgman—a professional philosopher and a scientist, respectively—are specifically interested in epistemology. A third discussion centers on the thinking of two psychologists who offer a systematic approach to a science of symbolism and a normative plea for the study of meanings as a foundation for education—Ogden and Richards. Next there is the vigorously systematic and ultranormative "General Semantics" of Korzybski, whose thoughts on "Man-The-Time-Binder" elicited much interest and comment in the early 1930s. Through this period there came into being a set of ideas that exerted a considerable amount of force in middle Europe—the school or circle called "Logical Positivism."

Fifth is a philosopher, C. W. Morris, who presents the outline of a science of sign analysis as a unifier of modern methodology and, next, C. S. Peirce, the source of a metalanguage for the discussion of meanings. Then follows Karl Mannheim's "Sociology of Knowledge," first published in German as *Ideologie und Utopie*. This carries the message of Social Determination, a powerful force in the socioeconomic dynamics of our civilization. A philosopher and logician, Karl Britton, is concerned with the nature of communication. Then there is Gustaf Stern, a semasiologist who follows in the steps of Michel Breal in an effort to answer some of the problems of meaning in psycholinguistic terms. A rather different approach is undertaken by T. C. Pollock. As a teacher of literature, he feels that most modern semantic theories do little justice to the language of literature and its distinctive meanings and uses.

Then follows Langer, with her "Philosophy in a New Key," already referred to. She brings a rather different and profoundly interesting tone to the discussion. The next two presentations, of Vigotsky and Piaget, are juxtaposed because their ideas about thought and language and about language and cognition have so much in common in attitudes and approaches; between them they set up strong foundations for the study of language development in childhood. The chapter on C. S. Peirce and A. G. Bell might be called a natural afterthought. They plainly seemed to fit in very well.

Three of the outstanding specialists in language in this century are grouped together in the next section—Jesperson, Sapir, and de Saussure. Others are grouped with them in the discussion. Finally, there is one of the self-styled curmudgeons of the twentieth century. A great force in jibing at the foibles of humanity and its meaningless ways, and a most considerable scholar of language in use, H. L. Mencken always protested (perhaps too much?), "that he was not a scholar himself, but one who pointed out the quarry for others to bag" (McDavid, 1963). It is fitting that we stop with this most remarkable treatment of "The American Language."

This, it is hoped, presents a loosely-woven picture of the important dimensions of meaning. There is a general summary of some of the impressions with which one may be left. Each of the theorizers, as does the author, shows some bias. Some are precise and definitive, others less incisive. At best, the analysis of language by means of language is a difficult venture. To criticize such analyses only complicates the difficulties. It is hoped that from the combined effort some interesting relations can be demonstrated among language, thought, and experience.

REFERENCES

Cunningham, G. W. "Meaning, Reference and Significance." Philosophical Review (1938) 47: 155–175.

Dewey, J. The Quest for Certainty: A Study of the Relation of Knowledge and Action. London: G. Allen and Unwin Ltd., 1930.

Hook, S. The Encyclopedia of the Social Sciences (1937) 10: 215.

Langer, S. K. The Practice of Philosophy. New York: H. Holt & Co., 1930.

———. Philosophy in a New Key. Cambridge: Harvard University Press, 1942.

MacKaye, J. 1939. The Logic of Language. Hanover: Dartmouth College Publications, 1939.

McDavid, R. I. Jr., ed. H. L. Mencken, The American Language. New York: Alfred Knopf, 1963.

Morris, C. W. 1937. "Logical Positivism, Pragmatism and Scientific Empiricism." Exposes de Philosophie Scientifique (1937) p. 58.

Ritchie, A. D. 1936. The Natural History of the Mind. pp. 225–257. London: Longmans, Green & Co., 1936.

Welby, Hon. Lady Victoria. What is Meaning? Studies in the Development of Significance. New York, London: Macmillan & Co., 1903.

Chapter 1
MEANING IN
THE HISTORY OF IDEAS

THE ANCIENT ONES

The strength of ancient Athens lay in its uniqueness as a city-state, its very practical organization of commerce and culture, and its tremendous commitment to getting things done. There was accomplishment in politics, trade, the arts, and in military might. It flourished in the name of *demos,* the people, the citizens who made their own laws and quite rigidly controlled the functions of a society that lived with a sense of unity. Their gods were many, usually benign, and offered a strong sense of family tradition.

With the force of *demos*, the one-ness of the community, there was the creativity of *logos,* a complex term that meant both mind and thinking, usually expressed through the power of speech, which could explain and persuade toward the common good. Rhetoric in the agora, the meeting place, and poetics in the theater, lent a balance to daily Athenian concerns. Ethical proof, the demonstration of the essential goodness and propriety with which a point of view was argued, was part of the essence of rhetoric. Tragedy, the core of serious drama, was not something strange and terrible, but the expression of the inevitable, of destiny. In man there was good and evil; each life was a balance of the two forces. This was a fatalistic approach to life and living, and catharsis came with the sharing of the hero's destiny. This is a pragmatic, if not venturesome, point of view.

Demos and *logos* came together in a simple, but quite rigid, educational system for the young men of Athens. In charge of this, at least in the time of the "Golden Age," was not Socrates, but Isocrates—an extremely competent superintendent of schools. The maidens were at home learning to run a household and to sustain the family. The latter was a necessity because of young men going off to war, leaving their scions to be raised in the warm arms of a very competent matriarchy. It will be recalled from Homer's crystalline commentary that Penelope was much sought after while Odysseus was wandering in parts unknown, and that her virtue prevailed. Despite the fact that only men could participate in the arguments of the agora, the women were thoroughly well established in managerial activities. Formal expectancy for the welfare of the state resided in the training of the young men for excellence in peace and war, on the athletic field, in the arts, and in science, which was largely centered on mathematics and astronomy. The upbringing of a young man was thoroughly prescribed, and, at least in early times, he was not expected to loaf on the steps of the Parthenon engaged in the vagaries of "what" and "why." The radical thinking of Socrates in an age when truth was simply the commonweal was looked upon with deep suspicion. His insistence was against the nature of things, and his insistence cost him his life.

Those who were non-Greek were "barbarians," and were treated accordingly. When captured in battle (usually undertaken to develop trade routes and keep them open) the prisoners were slaves, and assigned to various noble households. In the general atmosphere of Athens before 500 B.C., there was no space for speculation about the state of man in his world, nor for wondering about life's purposes. These matters were left for barbarians who had nothing better to do. As Boas (1929) makes clear, what we know as the origins of Athenian philosophy came from the colonials of Asia Minor. They were the only ones in touch with men of ideas.

> They were associating with Persians and other Asiatics, with Egyptians, with the primitive people of Italy. All of these people had philosophic meat to exchange for Greek produce (p. 1).

This meant mythology and astronomy from Asia, religion and geometry from Egypt, and some passing suggestions from early Italy. These were gifts that later helped Hellenic culture to flourish. In addition, these influences introduced an early world of meanings, and prompted conjectures about life and living, who made the world, and why.

There was general unrest in the seventh and sixth centuries B.C., both on the Peninsula and in the colonies. The producer (the farmer) and the master of trade (the money man) were in conflict. Again, this is brought into focus by Boas. "It is not difficult to see why the philosophers stood where they did. Their interest in the political turmoil is witnessed by tradition and by their own writings. Almost all of them until Christian times were either participants in it or acute critics of it" (p. 4). In short, the time was ripe for some new thinking, and, because of various circumstances, it first came from the colonials.

The earliest philosopher of the colonial group was Thales of Miletus in Asia Minor. He began a school that lasted for perhaps a century. The tradition was carried on by Anaximander and Anaximenes. Little else is known about the school and its teachers. In general, they were concerned with developing some fundamental laws of nature; no doubt there were some aspects of cracker-box philosophy that endure to the present day.

The reformers came shortly thereafter. Pythagoras offered a "man in the world of opposition"—body and soul. This dual approach to an understanding of man in his world has since furnished material for all manner of analysis and argumentation. Pythagoras also offered the ethical concept of "the golden mean," a harmonious life in perfect balance. Interestingly enough, this was a mathematical doctrine derived from observations of the acoustics of a four-string lyre, and from some simple equations illustrating the relationship between pitch and length of the string. Reputedly he was the originator of a concept of antithesis—good and bad, odd and even, one and many—that became popular in literature and oratory.

Leucippus and Democritus, both of Abdera, developed and taught an atomic theory. In their thinking, atoms whirling in a void come together to compose bodies and worlds, which is a largely mechanical theory of creation by accident. In large part, the thinking of the early philosophers was semantic only in a sense so broad that it was one with philosophy. They were concerned with the origin and nature of the universe.

> The majority of the Pre-Socratic thinkers . . . were keenly interested in the physical sciences and in mathematics. . . . Thales, for example, was a mathematician and astronomer and predicted, we are told, an eclipse of the sun. . . . To Pythagoras tradition attributes various important discoveries in arithmetic, geometry, and acoustics. Empedocles was physician as well as philosopher and Anaxagoras was deeply concerned with physics and astronomy. Furthermore, all these men were largely cosmologists, although Xenophanes and Pythagoras were thinkers more in the field of religion and conduct and the maxims "Know thyself" and "Nothing to excess" of the wise men were familiar precepts (Van Hook, 1923).

Protagoras, also of Abdera, did not agree with the practice of metaphysical inquiries. Why bother? "Man is the measure of all things." Study man and his manners and ways, his practical modes of procedure in law, ethics, and logic. This, the basic philosophy of the Sophists, became a powerful force in the development of Greek thought. It produced an interest in humanism. Another aspect of Sophism paved the way for the later invidious implication of the term. Protagoras was a professional teacher of philosophy, and his followers professionalized (commercialized) their bents, all in the name of "Man is the measure of all things." "This little phrase," writes Boas, "like most influential phrases, has a variety of meanings, and the successors of Protagoras exploited them all to their own profit. They are all eminently interesting, and, what was more important to the professors of philosophy, they all offered ways of making of money" (p. 36).

It is interesting to recall that Pythagoras was exiled, while Anaxagoras, another gadfly of Athens, was imprisoned. Because of his use of dialectic as a teaching technique, Socrates was sometimes mistakenly labeled a follower of Protagoras. He was not a Protagorean, but a teacher (a nonprofessional philosopher who made no money) who pursued the nature of truth in the cultivation of reason, which he felt would lead to each person's Good, according to his lights. Socrates was a humanist and a cynic, the only man in Athens who admitted that he knew nothing.

There followed the Cyrenaics of North Africa, who chose pleasure as an escape from the exigencies of reason, and the Cynics, who reasoned life to death. All worldly goods were forsaken; there were no pleasures. This was man's state of nature. This general approach to life and living continued into early Christianity.

When one considers the importance through these years of Athenian philosophy's Eleatic "forms," the importance of quantitative and qualitative "atoms," and the like, one can scarcely conclude that no attention was paid to symbolism. In fact, much of the early philosophy was concerned with symbolic meanings. These were major descriptors of man's place in the world.

THE PHILOSOPHICAL PEAK

The peak of this long exercise in thinking about existence came with Plato and Aristotle. They lived during the decay of the great Athens after Pericles, and through the supremacy of Macedonia. Plato sought for "form" ("being") in matters of conduct. The dialogues are not conclusive, each to its own topic, but Plato's ideas are usually clear. The "form" is the essence of the person who illustrates it: temperance (Charmides), friendship (Lysis), knowledge (Theaetetus), and so on. When we know the person, we know the essence of the quality. This awareness cannot be achieved by rationalizing. Everything comes from and leads toward the Good through contemplation; the affinity that leads to the Platonic "forms" is Love.

Plato makes an interesting analysis of words in the *Cratylus,* although he does not go far toward recognizing the psychology of language. He is aware of the significance of onomatopoeia as a possible basis for the construction of words, and he expresses his belief in the possibility of verbal usage by convention. There is nothing in the *Cratylus,* however, to suggest a sense of the referential process, or, as Ogden and Richards (1938) prefer to say, Plato "fails to distinguish consistently between symbols and the thought symbolized" (p. 33). In light of the Platonic "theory of Ideas," it is difficult to understand how such a distinction could be brought to mind. Perhaps Plato, the inquirer, could not be satisfied by the Name-souls of Plato, the mystic, and the questions about the nature of names had to be asked. Perhaps, on the other hand, it would not be lese majesty to suggest that Plato (Socrates) was having some fun throughout the dialogue at the expense of some of the current Sophists. Early in the exchange, Socrates responds to Hermogenes:

> There is an ancient saying, that 'hard is the knowledge of the good.' And the knowledge of names is a great part of knowledge. If I had not been poor, I might have heard the fifty-drachma course of the great Prodicus, which is a complete education in grammar and language—these are his own words—and then I should have been at once able to answer your question about the correctness of names. But, indeed, I have only heard the single-drachma course, and therefore, I do not know the truth about such matters (Jowett, 1892).

As is common in the Dialogues, the principal question in the *Cratylus*—Are names natural or conventional instruments?—is left unresolved.

Aristotle answers this question in *De Interpretatione.* Standing at the end of a long line of Athenian philosophers, Aristotle, a naturalist and a classifier, undertook to generalize all knowledge in a systematic fashion. His works were tremendous. He spent his early years in Macedon, then went to Athens for personal reasons of study, but never really entered into the life of the city. He opened his Lyceum and worked hard, with the powerful sponsorship of Alexander the Great. After Alexander's demise, and with the star of Macedon rapidly disappearing in the night sky, the prudent Aristotle practiced his own judicious mean and fled the city.

It was he who perfected the syllogism, the "logic of exposition," and invested the world to come with systematic thinking. It follows that he found he had to pay attention to what we think with. In *De Interpretatione* we find the principle that words are the symbols of thoughts ("mental experience," "mental affections," "notions"); writing symbolizes speech. The linguistic signs (sounds or written symbols) are conventional, "but the mental experiences, which these directly symbolize, are the same for all, as also are these things of which our experiences are the images." The name has conventional significance as a verbal form that varies arbitrarily with various languages; the "notion" that it symbolizes, however, is constant in all men. That is to say, the thought symbolized, the "mind's meaning," arises within the individual in conjunction with his sensual perceptions of objective properties. The mind operates in such a way that words signify thoughts, and thus, indirectly, the things to which these thoughts correspond. This is the traditional account of the psychology of language that obtained until modern times; modern psychology does not accept Aristotle's theory of the sameness of minds and their significations.

Aristotle is specific concerning word meanings. A noun or a verb arrests the flow of ideas "and determines the mind to dwell upon that particular group which is called into meaning" (Grote, 1872), but that is all. Isolated words signify no affirmations, communicate no information, have no truth-values. Only *logos*, connected discourse, can fulfill these functions. Moreover, Aristotle's logic, or analytic, treats only the propositional form of *logos*—that is, "enunciated speech." The other speech forms (the precative and the interrogative) belong to rhetoric or poetics. One concludes that Aristotle is interested, in the *Organon,* only in what Carnap calls "pure syntactics" and "pure semantics"—and in these only as they are limited to a logic of classes. His main topic is deductive reasoning in syllogistic form, designed for the construction of rational science, and differentiated from enthymematic reasoning on contingent propositions. His system is built upon a theory of signs, but he does not think in terms of semiotic; his subject is the means of inference, of arriving at certain judgments by connecting nominal and verbal concepts in causal chains.

So much seems clear. Yet one can go far astray in generalizing the Aristotelian principles of thinking and knowing, because, as Wallace suggests, his theory of knowledge cannot be defined with accuracy.

> Aristotle . . . treats knowledge as a *development* from the impressions of sense, but recognizes that sense, as such, does not give us knowledge, and thus while at one time regarding the formation of general notions as proceeding from the less to the more extended, he at another place conceives knowledge as proceeding from the universal to the particular, the abstract to the concrete (Wallace, 1883).

Aristotle's metaphysics creates a formidable barrier against our exact understanding of his epistemology. Although the *Organon* is essentially devoted to the deductive method, it includes the principles of induction. Perhaps one must conclude that Aristotle is an empiricist by practice, but a rationalist in his scientific methodology.

This point is substantiated, or at least seems to be suggested, by his treatment of the *semeion*. The sign is discussed in only one short chapter of the *Organon, Prior Analytics,* II 27, where it is given a cryptic definition that could be better understood according to a specific theory of knowledge. The sign is "a proposition demonstratively necessary or probable." It appears in discourse as an enthymeme, and its validity varies according to whether it is transposed into a syllogism of the first, second, or third figure; if it is transposed into the first, the sign is an analytic proposition, demonstratively necessary and offering complete proof. In the *Rhetoric,* this is called an "infallible sign." Since few signs presuppose a universal premise, however, the sign typically offers only probable proof. The point at stake, so far as Aristotelian methodology is concerned, can perhaps be better understood if we recall the saying that men talk in enthymemes, but deduce, if they deduce correctly, in syllogisms. It is instructive to note that Aristotle has much more to say of enthymemes, and therefore supposedly of signs, in the *Rhetoric*—the organon of popular reasoning and empirical thinking—than in his treatment of analytic—the delineation of strictly rational principles. Modern scientific methodology makes many changes in Aristotle's formal logic; there is little in his popular rhetorical logic that has been, or needs to be, changed. The Aristotelian sign rarely produces his ideal of proof; its usual domicile is the field of the probable. Accordingly, it has a logical place in empirical thinking.

It is scarcely accurate to insist that experience is given a low place in Aristotelian methodology; the empirical, inductive aspect of knowing is, in his system, of less importance than the rational, deductive scheme of inference, which alone can result in his ideal of science—certain and necessary knowledge. How immaterial thoughts can absorb material things, according to his theory of symbolic representation, is demonstrated by Aristotle's belief in "some community between thought and things" (Wallace, p. 92). How far is credulity strained if this is called a figurative reference to the conditioned reflex and the theory of psychological context?

THE HELLENISTS

The theory of signs assumes a more modern form in the methodology of the Hellenists. DeLacy's studies emphasize the presence of this interest in periods following upon the construction of great philosophical systems. She writes:

> Such a period was the Hellenistic period following upon the great systematic philosophies of Democritus, Plato, and Aristotle. Post-Aristotelian philosophy is distinctly 'modern' in flavor in that Stoics, Epicureans, and Sceptics are concerned primarily with an analysis of meaning and the establishment of a scientific method as the propaeduetic to a philosophic system (1938, p. 390).

There is neither space nor need to review in detail the philosophical warfare of the three schools over a period of several hundred years, but a few generalizations from DeLacy's study serve to characterize the major positions of each of the three.

The Stoics contribute nothing to empirical method, because they are as rationalistic as Aristotle in their search for certainty. They differ from him in that they pay little attention to induction, consider signs able to offer certainty in knowledge, and center their logic upon the hypothetical proposition. Their principal contribution is made to the field of logic, defined as the science of signs.

> It is the science of signs and things signified according to Chrysippus. It includes grammar and language (since words are signs), epistomology, and a theory of perception, also based upon a theory of signs. The medieval division between conceptualists and nominalists is exhibited in the Stoic and Epicurean schools, respectively (DeLacy, 1938, p. 392).

The Stoic theory of perception comes from Sextus Empiricus. The Stoics hold to a "triadic division of the symbolic relation in connection with their analysis of what is true."

> There are three factors joined to each other, the thing signified, the sign, and the object. Of these, the sign is the word, such as 'Dion'; the thing signified is the thing indicated by it, which we grasp in our concept of a co-existent reality, but which the barbarians do not understand although they hear the word; and the object, that which exists outside, as Dion himself. Two of these are material, the word and the object, and one immaterial, the thing signified, or the concept, which is true or false (from Sextus Empiricus).

This is more or less the same explanation of symbolism as that given by Aristotle, except that here the single sign has a truth-value. The Epicureans deny this triadic relation; for them, signs refer directly to objects.

> The Epicureans stress the extensional, as opposed to the Stoic intensional, meaning of words, and maintain that words without extension belong to the realm of opinion and can make no contribution to knowledge. The only propositions which may be known to be true refer directly to objects of experience or are extensions from experience made through the method of analogy (DeLacy, 1938, p. 392).

Both schools differ from the Aristotelian in that they are not concerned with the relation of universal-particular but with that of sign-signified. The important duality is that between the given and the nongiven. "The methodological problem becomes one of establishing a method which will permit the inference of facts about the non-given through observation and reasoning on signs which are given." Both groups recognize the same general array of given and nongiven objects. The given object needs no sign, for it is sensed immediately and involuntarily. There are three types of non-given objects:

1. The class of objects forever obscure (i.e., the number of stars)
2. Those objects obscure at the time, signified by what Sextus calls the "admonitive" sign (i.e., smoke signifies fire)—a relationship "based on the experience of constant conjunction of objects"
3. Things obscure by nature (i.e., atoms and the void), signified by what Sextus calls the "indicative" sign.

It is this third class, of course, that causes logical confusion.

The Stoics define the sign formally as "the proposition in a sound condition which is antecedent and reveals the conclusion." This is the hypothetical proposition of relational logic—"If p, then q." The affirmation of the sign, p, establishes the signified, q, because they are joined by an analytic relation of necessary consequence—they are "woven together." As in the modern logical relation of material implication, the only unsound hypothetical proposition is that in which the first term is true and the second false.

The essential difference of opinion between Stoics and Epicureans comes in their logical account of knowing the objects "obscure by nature." The Stoics reason by a priori necessity. The only criterion of truth for the Epicureans is the senses, and objects "obscure by nature" can be signified only on the ground of analogy with experience, which at all times must underlie scientific construction.

The third group, the Skeptics, as represented by Sextus, takes its stand on a strict phenomenalism. They recognize the "admonitive" sign (defined by DeLacy as "an object which, having been observed along with, or in conjunction with, another object, evidently at some time in the past, leads us to the memory or recollection of the object which accompanied it, now not evidently experienced"), but refuse to admit the validity of the "indicative" sign, which supposedly signifies noumena. The main attack of the Skeptics is directed against the a priori rationalism of the Stoics. DeLacy generalizes the position of Sextus.

> The Stoics are right in so far as they hold that all *a priori* truths are analytic. However, for Sextus such truth is not inference. Inference requires the statement of a new fact not already contained in the premises; in other words, a synthetic relation between premises and conclusion. The Stoic position was that certain synthetic truths can be established *a priori* and thus have the necessity attaching to analytic truths. This is essentially the status of signs for them. The Sceptic argument amounts to the denial of *a priori* synthetic judgments; and to the assertion that the Stoics must choose between *a priori* necessity which accrues only to analytic truths, and *a posteriori* contingency and probability.

Moreover, Sextus attacks the definitions of both sign as proposition and sign analysis as dialectic, because the common man pays no attention to formal logic, yet is quite able to understand signs and things signified on the basis of ordinary experience. The Skeptic's theory, like the Aristotelian sign, is truly empirical, and within the realm of common experience and ordinary discourse. It is obvious that with Hellenistic empiricism there emerges something like modern scientific methodology; it may well be, as DeLacy suggests, that "ultimately scepticism is the preliminary step in establishing a positive empirical science."

To accomplish this establishment it seems perennially necessary to attack dogmatic metaphysical first principles, a task undertaken by Aenesidemus of Cnossus, whose famous ten tropes epitomize the skeptical position. The effect of his attack has been summed up in an axiom that seems to initiate the modern theory that knowledge is obtained by understanding the referential process:

> Knowledge is relative to observer and observed, and the medium between them; without these three items we have no knowledge (Boas, 1929).

If by "medium" we understand "communicative signs," this idea is a counterpart of much modern semantic theory, and of twentieth-century scientific method. Both Aenesidemus and Sextus insist that empirical science can include only the description of phenomena, and the derivation of laws from the repetition of events.

THE CHRISTIANS

Once again, I should prefer to call on professional philosophical opinion to generalize a quite complex picture of the history of thought. With the efforts of the two major Hellenistic schools, founded by Epicurus and Zeno the Stoic, attention was turned to individual morals. Neither school was primarily Athenian, nor were they concerned with Athenian nationalism. Athens was now cosmopolitan, decaying but still alive. Boas emphasizes some of the effect of the historical nature of thought:

> Yet out of this new spirit was to grow something whose appearance was not even hinted at in those days. I am referring to the rise of Christianity. It would have been impossible if Stoicism had not first broken down social and national barriers [probably aided and abetted by Alexander the Great], if Epicureanism had not destroyed belief in polytheism, if Pyrrhonism had not weakened the dominion of reason. But with two hundred years of such preparation behind it, its triumph was not so miraculous as inevitable (p. 81).

A realistic point of view based on an empirical method of dealing with the world emerged with the works of Philo Judaeus in Alexandria, rationalist of the Old Testament; with Aenesidemus, whose Ten Tropes belong in the Pyrrhonic tradition; and with Philodemus, whose Herculanean papyri carried on the Epicurean tradition in the first century—with many deviations and extensions (DeLacy, 1938, p. 409).

"If occidental civilization were not Christian," writes Boas, "it is likely that Christianity as a philosophy—not as a religion—would be called a branch of Neo-Platonism. For throughout its early years that mixture of Pythagorean, Platonic, Aristotelian, and Stoic elements which characterizes the school of Plotinus was equally characteristic of Christianity" (p. 114). Clement and Origen, who went to school with Plotinus, were Christian philosophers—spokesmen for, not fathers of, the Church. They were also Neo-Platonists.

The various works of dogma and doctrine in the early centuries of Christian theology bring little that is fresh to the tapestry. The works of Saint Augustine of Hippo are a possible exception. Writing in the fourth and fifth centuries, he established the doctrine of man, the guilty sinner, whose only guarantee against a future free from guilt was admission to the City of God. Citizenship seemed in the main to include martyrs and saints; the ordinary man did not know how to qualify.

There are a few interesting comments relative to Saint Augustine's recording of language in his major work, *Concerning The City of God Against The Pagans*. In Book XVI, Chapter 3, reference is made to a son of Salah from Shem. This was Heber, after whom the Hebrews were called—Heberaei. "The Hebrew language is the exclusive property of the people of Israel."

Saint Augustine accepts the story of the Creation and the statements of the Old Testament at face value. In Chapter 4 of the same book he continues:

> The narrator goes back to the time when all men had the same language; and then he explains how the diversity of languages arose.

> They settled on a plain in Shinar, and built a city and a tower.

> And the Lord came down to see the city and the tower which the sons of men had built. And the Lord God said, 'Behold, the people are one race, and all of them have one language; and they have begun to build, and from now on they will not fail to achieve anything they may try to do. Come, let us go down and bring confusion in their speech, so that no one may understand what the next man says . . . That is why the name 'Confusion' was given to the city [Babylon]; because it was here that the Lord confused the languages of all the earth. And the Lord God dispersed them from there over the face of all the earth.

Thus we have the Tower of Babel, offensive because it intruded into the sky, God's domain. One more contribution in reference to communication is expressed in Book XIX, Chapter 7, the heading for which, in my translation, is "Human society divided by differences of language." Three levels of society are referred to—the town, the city (state as with Athens), and the world.

> Now the world, being like a confluence of waters, is obviously more full of danger than the other communities by reason of its greater size. To begin with, on this level the diversity of languages separates man from

man . . . For when men cannot communicate their thoughts to each other, simply because of difference of language, all the similarity of their common human nature is of no avail to unite them in fellowship.
This leads to war!

Presumably, the only hope for peace would be the common language of Christian doctrine, as expounded by Saint Augustine.

POST-RENAISSANCE

Occasionally, as one moves rapidly through centuries with attention to language, thought, and experience, time seems to be of little significance. What we have been considering has been spread over a thousand years of thought about man and his world, with much action and interaction between and among constant outpourings of ideas. Through this period there were many more connections than gaps, causing such a rapid recounting of history to seem to be more often a matter of name-dropping, rather than careful attention to the relations we are concerned with. Perhaps, from generation to generation, or century to century, this is the way tapestries come into being.

On the other hand, the Hellenistic approach to logic and epistemology through a theory of signs exerted little enduring influence, and was soon forgotten.

In the sixth century (529) the Emperor Justinian ordered . . . schools closed and forbade the teaching of pagan ideas. But Greek thought never died out and what was lost to the West was carried on vigorously in the East. In Byzantium [Constantinople, Istanbul], in Armenia, in Persia, and in particular in Syria, translations were made of Aristotle and the Neo-Platonists (Boas, 1929, p. 113).

Philosophical expression did not stop in the West, of course, but this was for the most part church dogma. It included the powerful and influential writings of Dominican and Franciscan attitudes, and a very considerable variety of Christian theologians in expositions of Realism.

A different intellectual array was ushered in with the Renaissance. Centered at first largely in Italy, there came about a major revival of the classics. In philosophical terms this was Neo-Platonism, with emphasis on love and beauty. In a relatively short time the resurgence of the old and the building of the new engulfed European thinking and society. Aristotle was rediscovered, and very soon there developed profound concerns with science and mathematics.

Out of the dark years of the Middle Ages there came a new social surge that was active, alive, and full to bursting with energy and spring. Literature changed—the vernacular came into being with Dante, Chaucer, and many others. Dante looked for the perfect world using old themes. Chaucer reported what he saw when people journeyed to Canterbury, "The holy blisful martir for to seke." Village church plays thrived; the people loved the ancient story of the Christchild. Village fairs with song and dance were the custom. Cathedrals were built with devotion and artisanship, the like of which had never been seen. Authority reigned supreme. Troubadours roamed the land, and lovers pined away. In England, the Tudors came to stay, with multiple in-house troubles, but with a firm face set to the world. This was best exemplified in later years by Henry VIII and carried to distinction by Elizabeth I. The great universities came into being, and, in catholic terms, learning and inquiry, long dormant since the time of the Hellenists in Alexandria and the pre-Gothic thinkers of Rome, came to life once again. The times were happy and, in general, orderly. Some kinds of thinking about the ways of the world, and man in it, had never stopped. Then, in the early years of renaissance, it budded and blossomed in countless ways. Some of the thinkers, spurred by the culture of ancient Greece, which had never been allowed to die in the East, once again turned their attention to relations among thinking, sensing, and expressing, and to meanings.

As time went on, folly was renewed along with wisdom, and shortly after Henry VIII came to power, a Scottish cleric by the name of Alexander Barclay undertook to "translate" Sebastian Brandt's extremely popular "Ship of Fools." This was, in fact, Barclay's *Ship of Fools* and clearly shows a rather dour, but no doubt sound, reflection of the times at the beginning of the sixteenth century, the flourishing era of the Post-Renaissance. As Barclay saw the world:

Knowledge of trouth, prudence, and just symplicite
Hath vs clene left; For we set of them no store.
Our Fayth is defyled love, goodnes, and Pyte:
Honest manners nowe are reputed of: no more.
Lawyers are lordes; but Justice is rent and tore.
Or closed lyke a Monster within dores thre.
For without mede: or money no man can hyr se.

Al is disordered: Vertue hath no rewarde.
Alas, compassion; and mercy bothe ar slayne.
Alas, the stony hartys of pepyl ar so harde
That nought can contrayne theyr folyes to refrayne.

Obviously, he goes on, Folly's ships are laden, "but carry not all who should be on board." The influence of Barclay's writing continues well into twentieth-century literature.

An interest in signs was revived with so-called "Oxford Empiricism" in the thirteenth and fourteenth centuries in England. We need not be concerned with the theological ramifications of the Realist-Nominalist controversy; it is enough to notice the direction of the thought. The Realists supported the doctrine of universals, *generalis ante rem*, the doctrine of innate ideas. This was based on Plato's theory of name-souls and on the Aristotelian "essences" (but upon little else of Aristotle). Universal ideas were given reality, a law of authority. The Nominalists, like the Epicureans, held that only particulars were sensible, that universals were mere words, *flatus vocis* (Wilson, 1889). William of Occam, a Franciscan, differed from that position, but he is often referred to as a Nominalist. He offered a view, sometimes called "conceptualism," with some Aristotelian overtones. His basic principle was that, instead of beginning with the universals of authority, we must generalize from observation of the natural order of things, a doctrine expressed three hundred years later by some notable thinkers, including Bacon. His theory of "terminism" stated that "universals are not anything really existing, but are only *termini,* predicables," a fundamental idea in his science of signs. Universals are not real entities, but designatory abstractions.

> We see objects, the essential properties of which constitute the general ideas, and these properties are *in* them "*in re,*" and we form the idea after seeing them, and thus the ideas are *post rem* (Wilson, 1889, p. 105).

The struggle toward scientific methodology complete with testable hypotheses was truly long and difficult.

The next major attack on the dogmatism of *first* principles came with Bacon's theory of inductive method, a set of general principles of investigation that gave great impetus to experimental science. He never did deal with the function of hypotheses in inquiry, but stressed in the *Novum Organum,* common "notions of the mind," and the recognition of the mind's major deficiencies. These are summarized in his concept of the four "idols"—the Tribe, the Cave, the Marketplace, and the Theater. Having been dismissed from very high office in the reign of James I for acknowledged "corruption and neglect," he was in a position to know the intellectual foibles and weaknesses of mankind.

The tradition of semiotic fully emerges in the first ten chapters of Thomas Hobbes's *Leviathan* (1651). His theory need not detain us here, for it is well known and offers nothing, except emphasis, beyond the ideas of Aristotle and Sextus Empiricus. He paid great attention to the definition of terms in his own system, wherein the basis of all knowledge is sensation. Hobbes explained his ideas about sign usage on the basis of faculty psychology, and postulated a rigorous "conditional science" limited to a posteriori propositions and probable conclusions. A normative semiotician, Hobbes gives an account of the origin of language and the abuses of discourse in a fashion that is anything but scientific.

In his *Essay Concerning Human Understanding* (1690), John Locke (1632–1704) became the philosophical spokesman of his time. "He became the philosophical pontiff over whose bridges the world must pass to truth" (Boas, 1929). Relative to the *Essay,* John Stuart Mill referred to him as the "unquestioned founder of the analytic philosophy of mind." Locke devised what is probably the clearest and most systematic analysis of knowledge ever to be conceived.

In Book IV, Chapter 21 of the *Essay,* he generalizes the "three great provinces of the intellectual world," and names them Physica, Practica, and Semeiotica. (I am using an unabridged and unaltered reproduction of the first edition.) Semeiotica "may be called . . . the *doctrine of signs;* the most usual whereof being words, it is aptly enough termed also . . . logic: the business whereof is to consider the nature of signs, the mind makes use of for the understanding of things, or conveying its knowledge to others." He continues:

> For, since the things the mind contemplates are none of them besides itself, present to the understanding, it is necessary that something else, as a sign or representation of the thing it considers, should be present to it: and these are *ideas.* And because the scene of ideas that makes one man's thoughts cannot be laid open to the immediate view of another, nor laid up anywhere but in the memory, a not very sure repository: therefore to communicate our thoughts to one another, as well as record them for our own use, signs of our ideas are also necessary: those which men have found most convenient, and therefore generally make use of, are *articulate sounds.* The consideration, then, of *ideas* and *words* as the great instruments of knowledge, makes no despicable part of their contemplation who would take a view of human knowledge in the whole extent of it. [Herein is the place of the *Essay* itself.] And perhaps if they were distinctly weighed, and duly considered, they would afford us another sort of logic and critic, than what we have been hitherto acquainted with.

In the last sentence of his Introduction, Locke sets up his first objective: How do ideas "come into the mind"? His immediate concern is a clear attack—neither principles nor ideas are innate. Then he demonstrates why he believes this is so. It is clear from the outset that, by any reasonable definition of the terms, he is neither idealist, nor Platonist, nor Neo-Platonist. His is a practical philosophy, intimately related to what currently is often referred to as communicology. Locke is largely concerned not with man-the-thinker, but with man-the-communicator (to others and within himself). A major thesis is the inextricable togetherness of ideas (thought), words (the signifiers), and language (which makes possible the necessary connection between ideas and experience).

Locke's ideas are clarified in Book III, Chapter 2:

> Man, though he have great variety of thoughts, and such from which others as well as himself might receive profit and delight; yet they are all within his own breast, invisible and hidden from others, nor can of themselves be made to appear. The comfort and advantage of society not being to be had without communication of thoughts, it was necessary that man should find out some external sensible signs, whereof those invisible ideas, which his thoughts are made up of, might be made known to others. For this purpose nothing was so fit, either for plenty or quickness, as those articulate sounds, which with so much ease and variety he found himself able to make. Thus we may conceive how *words*, which were by nature so well adapted to that purpose, came to be made use of by man as the signs of their ideas; not by any natural connection that there is between particular articulate sounds and certain ideas, for then there would be but one language amongst all men; but by a voluntary imposition, whereby such a word is made arbitrarily the mark of such an idea.

Toward the end of Book III, Locke addresses the "Abuse of Words" and, finally, "Remedies of the Abuse of Words." The first two remedies make clear his ideas about the activities of the mind: "To use no Word without an Idea annexed to it," and "to have distinct, determinate Ideas annexed to Words, especially in mixed Modes." The latter refers to abstractions, as in the use of *justice* and *law,* which involve the possibility of obscurity. Clearly, this becomes a highly individual matter, as each person's mind is unique—"But whatever be the consequence of any man's using of words differently, either from their general meaning, or the particular sense of the person to whom he addresses them; this is certain, their signification, in his use of them, is limited to his ideas, and they can be signs of nothing else" (Book III, Chapter 2).

It might be interesting to let Locke close this brief summary of his *doctrine of signs* with some of his first statements "of words or language in general" (Book III, Chapter 1).

> God, having designed man for a sociable creature, made him not only with an inclination, and under a necessity to have fellowship with those of his own kind, but furnished him also with language, which was to be the great instrument and common tie of society.

However, articulate sounds would not be enough.

> It was further necessary that he should be able to use these sounds as signs of internal conceptions; and to make them stand as marks for the ideas within his own mind, whereby they might be conveyed from one to another.

Once more, I believe it might be fitting to turn to a professional philosopher for an overview of the state of affairs we have been discussing:

> The care and precision of Locke's analysis, the simplicity of his argument, and the general responsibleness of his point of view made him the leading philosopher of his time. He seemed to have done for the human understanding what Newton had done for the cosmos, robbed it of its mystery and articulated its problems in terms of everyday life. Just as the movements of the planets in Newton were seen to be simply cases of falling bodies, so the operations of the reason in Locke were seen to be simply the combination by the mind of ideas which originated in sensation and reflection (Boas, 1929, p. 207).

With regard to the science of signs, we may generalize the English empirical movement, including the thinkers mentioned here as well as several others, with the comment that there is little evidence of anything but the traditional Aristotelian account of words and their ways, with the exception of Locke. As for the theory of knowledge, English empiricism has been summarized as stressing the individual self, while the social aspects of knowledge and experience—implicit in the Grecian outlook—were disregarded (Morris, 1937). The correction of this state of affairs evidently begins with the work of Comte (1798–1857) in his emphasis on the social character of knowledge, work which is complemented and developed by the American pragmatists from the impetus of Darwinian biology. Notable in the years just before World War II is the rise of the doctrine of "consistent empiricism," and the development of mathematical logic. These interests are discussed at some length as this study of dimensions of meaning proceeds. The next topic of discussion is the "meaning-situation."

REFERENCES

Barclay, A. The Ship of Fools. Edited by T. H. Jamieson. Edinburgh: Advocates' Library, 1877.

Boas, G. The Major Traditions of European Philosophy. New York: Harper, 1929.

DeLacy, E. A. "Meaning and Methodology in Hellenistic Philosophy." Philosophical Review 47 (1938): 390–409.

Grote, G. 1872. Aristotle. Edited by A. Bain and G. C. Robertson. London: J. Murray, p. 157.

Jowett, M. A. The Dialogues of Plato. 2 vols. London: Macmillan, 1892.

Locke, J. 1960 (1959). An Essay Concerning Human Understanding. 2 vols. 1690. Edited by A. C. Fraser. Reprint. New York: Dover, 1959.

Morris, C. W. "Logical Positivism, Pragmatism and Scientific Empiricism." Exposes de Philosophie Scientifique (1937) Paris.

Ogden, C. K. and Richards, I. A. 5th rev. ed. The Meaning of Meaning. New York: Harcourt Brace, 1938.

Ross, W. D. The Works of Aristotle Translated into English. London: Oxford University Press, 1928.

Saint Augustine. Concerning the City of God Against the Pagens. 1467. Translated by Henry Betternson. London: Pelican Books, 1972.

Van Hook, L. Greek Life and Thought. 1923. 2nd rev. ed. New York: Columbia University Press, 1930.

Wallace, E. Outlines of the Philosophy of Aristotle. 3rd rev. ed. London: Cambridge University Press, 1883.

Wilson, W. D. Theories of Knowledge Historically Considered with Special Reference to Skepticism and Belief. Syracuse and Auburn: Walcott and West, 1889.

Chapter 2
THE MEANING SITUATION

G. W. Cunningham

DeLacy once observed that there is a tendency to be concerned with meaning after periods of extensive development or stress. It is perhaps for this reason that interest in various aspects of this topic burgeoned in the two decades after World War I. G. Watts Cunningham, an epistemologist long interested in meaning, made some inquiries during this time that touch upon some of the distinguishing aspects of problems of meaning. His work furnishes a significant point of departure in the field of modern semantics.

Cunningham regards the clear definition of meaning as a fundamental step in philosophical construction, and believes that it will illuminate both the nature of knowledge and the available means of knowing. Accordingly, it is useful to distinguish a dual motivation in his approach to the subject. As a user of language, he regrets the obscurity and lack of stability in the term *meaning,* a term that is basal to most theoretical inquiry. He sets himself the initial task of developing a connotation of the term that is capable of including all denotations. As an epistemologist, he believes that the meaning-situation and the knowing-situation are everywhere closely related, and, although he does not directly develop a theory of knowledge in his three essays on the meaning-situation, he does draw some important epistemological inferences from his findings on the structure of "the meaningful."

The nature of Cunningham's approach to the problem suggests his bias. He believes that there can, and should, be a "proper" definition of meaning. He holds that theoretical construction is in a confused state, primarily because of diverse uses of a concept of meaning. This situation is intolerable; either the concept should be avoided or it should be agreed upon. He believes that a definition of meaning grounded upon a study of typical meaning-situations will expose the "truth" of the concept, and undertakes to set up such a definition. Moreover, his approach to the relation between meaning and knowing appears to be controlled by the conviction that knowledge refers only to discursive reasoning; it is observable that nowhere in his delineation of typical meaning-situations does he seem to make room for the meaningful nature of poetry, painting, or music. Furthermore, he conducts the analysis of the meaning-situation with almost no attention to problems of communication. His bias and his omissions are, of course, significant for an interpretation of his theory; these topics are considered below.

Cunningham's method is rational analysis. Assuming that "the meaningful is a state of affairs," he takes as his working material a set of typical meaning-situations that, in his opinion, are prima facie distinguishable. This is the empirical ground of his study. Analysis of these situations discloses that a meaning-situation is definable as an occurrence composed of several constituent elements: it is a relational process that includes three terms among which the relation holds, and it is the ground of this relationship (Cunningham, 1932). In traditional philosophical terminology, the three terms are *mind, content,* and *object.* In the newer language of semantics, which Cunningham adopts in his last two essays, these terms are, respectively, *perspective, referend,* and *referent.* These three elements are characteristic of any state of affairs commonly said to be meaningful, and Cunningham adopts the pragmatic view that perspective is the most important of the three. A fourth element, the ground of the referential relation, is the *context,* which Cunningham finds to be the logical determinant of the meaning-situation. Whatever truth-claim a reference has resides ultimately in its context. In sum, Cunningham asserts: "This complex whole is a meaning-situation, and is what is properly designated by the word 'meaning' taken as a noun."

This structural definition of meaning, with the interpretations it invokes, commits Cunningham to several theses of interest and of importance to theories of semantics and epistemology. First, meaning is not an entity but a relation, and always a highly complex relation. Second, this relation "involves the activity of the mind" (refer, if you will, to Locke). Because *perspective* is one of the necessary terms of the meaning-situation, meaning is "essentially psychological"—"nothing has meaning unless it is thought about." This is a pragmatic, as well as an idealistic, view. Third, although "reference everywhere involves a psychological complex which is in some way a causal system," it is not a direct causal relation; the relation has the peculiarity of being corrigible—it is projected by the mind, and is therefore in a sense imputed. Here is a modification of the so-called causal theory of conditioned response put forward by Ogden and Richards. To this extent, meaning is relative. Fourth, it is not entirely relative, however, because the referend (content, sign, symbol) is always complex. It not only is related to mind, but also has "a structure and relations independent of the mind," and thus a "contextual relationship" that is actually the logical determinant of the "significance of reference." Herein lies the corrigibility of reference, and on this ground Cunningham differs radically from those semanticists who insist on the purely imputed and purely relative nature of meaning; Humpty Dumpty was ultimately wrong. There is always a contextual, as well as a referential, relationship in a meaning-situation. This context (e.g., a language system, a postulational system, a natural causal order, or a communicative need) exerts a logical compulsion upon the referential relation. Fifth, no reference is meaningless unless it be literally nonsense; it may be insignificant, unimportant, or mistaken, for a critic, but never without significance. This constitutes Cunningham's response to the positivist's assertion that all metaphysical questions are meaningless. Sixth, "the acquisition of knowledge is identical with the progressive exploration of the contextual relationship of what is in reference," that is, with the significance of reference.

Cunningham's analysis, when offered, is discerning and subtle. One has the feeling, however, that he raises more problems than he solves. At many points he is merely assertive, and, primarily concerned as he is with outlining the structure of the meaning-situation, he only suggests some implications that his analysis may have for a theory of knowledge. It would be wise to ask for considerable amplification of many of his inferences. Lacking this, the critic can only hope that he is interpreting correctly. My aim is to present Cunningham's point of view clearly, and limit my critical questions to the topics that he expands and that essential to his position.

The major thesis that there are several distinguishable characteristics of a meaning-situation seems clear cut and complete. There is probably no reasonable theory of meaning that does not recognize some aspect of the three basic terms in Cunningham's analysis. This is to say that there is probably no pertinent disagreement among semanticists as to these structural constituents of meaning. There is considerable disagreement, however, about the interpretation of these constituents, and about their relative importance. The key term of this divergence of opinion is what Cunningham calls the "contextual relationship." He makes this bear the logical weight of meaning with strong and subtle dialectic, but it is evident that his interpretation of the structure of meaning is, as one of his students has pointed out, weighted in favor of "objective," versus "psychological," reference (Williams, 1937). Whatever question may be raised about this logical ground of meaning, the answer pivots on the relation between words and thought, between signs and ideas, or, more particularly, on whatever view one accepts of the relation of logic to psychology. In any event, Cunningham has but little to say about the problems of communication. The implication is that he considers the meaning-situation more fundamental than the communicating-situation. This lack of interest in communication possibly accounts for the weighting reported above. It also suggests that, pragmatic as he is in his analysis of meaning, Cunningham is not sufficiently pragmatic to satisfy the findings of linguistics.

Although this lack of attention to communication constitutes a serious oversight in his interpretation of the structure of the meaning-situation, it does not operate at all against the general outline of the structure. This distinction is not a quibble. We may know the structure of a process in some detail, yet be unable to offer a conclusive description of any single constituent of that structure. This situation seems to exist everywhere. It evidently obtains, for instance, in modern physics, where knowledge consists not of qualities of perceptible entities, but of the relations between submicroscopic constructs. Accordingly, a definition of meaning that undertakes to set up the "proper" connotation of the term might well seem to be structurally sound without offering the means for a definitive interpretation of its constituent parts. The discussion of relations between communication and a theory of meaning is continued below. For the present, it may be useful to examine Cunningham's analysis in more detail, and to note some of his interpretations.

Cunningham assumes that "the meaningful is a state of affairs, that this state of affairs is indicated by common usage of the word *meaning* and its correlates, and that description of this state of affairs is the task which *ab initio* confronts anyone bent on dealing with the problem of meaning" (Cunningham, 1938). His initial inquiry into the subject is made in an essay entitled, "On the Meaning-Situation"

(1932). The five *"prima facie* distinguishable types" of meaning-situations taken as the empirical ground of his analysis are: the perceptual, the conventional, the conceptual, the affective, and the evaluative. Inasmuch as he later reduces these types to four, and suggests, furthermore, that they may be reducible to one, Cunningham seems to attach little significance to them beyond their virtue as analytical springboards. However many types of meaning-situations there may be, the structure of any such situation is constant. This is the contention. For the sake of exhibiting Cunningham's method of description, the original five types are sketched herein. The revised set follows.

The perceptual meaning-situation is perhaps the simplest. It is concerned with the "this-here," and may be *direct* (i.e., a physical or vocal gesture that points—"I mean this."), or *indirect* (i.e., a sign situation that is verbalized as, "'this means that' where both the 'this' and the 'that' are natural things or events.") "'This means' may be said to be the general formula for the type."

The second type is focused in conventions:

And by conventions I understand products of human ingenuity which may on occasion bear meaning. In this type, the 'this' in 'this means' is a convention, not a natural thing or event taken as such; and herein lies the chief difference between this type and the one just described (p. 71).

The conventional meaning-situation has two subordinate categories: the *verbal,* "where the meaning is of some statement whether oral or written or pictographic," and the symbolic, an example of which is a traffic sign along the highway indicating a curve or intersection ahead—a subtype usually composed of "human contrivances" that function as signs and symbols.

As the term suggests, the conceptual meaning-situation is more complicated. Cunningham describes it as "any meaning-situation exemplified in an ideational or inferential structure, such as a scientific system." Here, also, are two subordinate types: the *categorical,* i.e., meaning-situations centering on the body of our knowledge of existence that is considered factual; and *postulational,* including "all of those ideational structures which are founded on more or less arbitrarily chosen initial assumptions—such structures as are exemplified in the systems of pure mathematics, for example, or in any system of logic avowedly built on definitions and postulates." Cunningham notes the implicative nature of postulational meaning-situations, as compared with the categorical.

The affective situation is, as the name implies, one in which "impulsion to action or to gratification of desire plays an important role." The affective situation "is broadly identical with a plan of behavior in the larger sense which includes also satisfaction of interest." It may be *purposive* ("exemplified in overt conduct directed towards the attainment of an end"), or *desiderative,* a simple wish or choice.

The fifth type, the evaluative, is one that involves a process of appraisal. "Here the more obvious subdivisions correspond with the traditional distinction among truth, goodness, and beauty—the ancient trinity of values. Its meanings are, therefore, *logical, ethical,* and aesthetic evaluation; *economic,* in the sense of utility, may be included as well."

Cunningham rules out another possible type, the memory-situation, on the ground that memory is implicit in all situations involving human behavior. The fourth and fifth types might be considered extraneous for the same reason. Purposive behavior and evaluative response seem to be, quite as much as memory, present in all human activities. Since Cunningham holds no brief for this particular classification of types, we may take them for the time being as they are given—empirical meaning-situations.

The next step in the analysis is the observation of two "*prima facie* components" of any meaning-situation—"that which means" and "that which is meant." "That which means" includes *mind* (a general term used with no prejudice to any method of description; Cunningham is satisfied with the characterization of mind as a psychophysiological process) and *content*; "that which is meant" is the *object*. These three terms, it is argued, are fundamental and indispensable in any analysis of the meaning-situation. (It is worth noting that Cunningham explicitly refutes the contention that historical idealism denies the *object*.) If the five typical situations outlined above are said to be meaningful, then "mind, content, and object are all in some important sense ultimate within the meaning-situation; each has its unique office which neither of the others can fill."

For one not inured to traditional philosophical usage, this language may be obcure and misleading. It should be considered that "mind" stands for "that which means," an individual system with a full biography; "object" represents "that which is meant," also a system with a biography. ("System" here means a functionally complex relationship within which and about which one may make significant inferences.) *Mind* may be an idea, a behavioristic description of physiological activity, or the like. *Object* may be an emotion, an attitude, any kind of private or public event, or the like. I believe this terminology labors under the usual difficulties of traditional use and misuse. At first glance, it seems far removed from current behavioral descriptions. Cunningham's concern here is with the structure of the meaning-situation, not with the detailed properties of its terms. Thus, mind and object are two systems operating within a relation.

Content makes the meaning-situation relational. It serves in a dual capacity, and also acts as a mediator between mind and object. It is functionally complex: "in" mind, i.e., as an image or a statement is part of the biography of the person who has the image or makes the statement; and "of" object, i.e., as referring to "that which is meant." This view of content makes imperative the recognition of epistemological dualism.

> And it should be clear (though it is not always so) that this epistemological dualism cannot be avoided by the expedient of denying the "mentality" of the mind and identifying it with the organism biologically conceived. Identify mind with the central nervous system and set it . . . in "nature" as you will, the epistemological dualism remains; organic behavior is not the object and has no element of identity with it. The chasm cannot be bridged in any manner, so long as mind and its objects are held to be distinct entities—so long, that is, as the integrity of the meaning-situation is respected (p. 94).

Here is a dogmatic statement about an argument that many people believe has outlived its significance; the usual discussions of the problem are marred by a confusion of terms and marked by cross purposes. I shall not enter the lists of this philosophical debate. Cunningham suggests, in another place, that its cause rests in the confusion of "two aspects of a meaning-situation and not with two quite disparate relationships" (1938). So long as one concurs in Cunningham's delineation of the meaning-situation, there seems to be no escape from his resolution of questions of monistic-dualistic epistemology.

In sum, Cunningham finds three distinct terms in any situation that is meaningful. Two of them, *mind* and *object,* are distinct systems; the third, *content,* is "in" the mind but refers to the object, and acts as a mediator between these two. The meaning of meaning, therefore, resides in the content as it mediates between mind and object. Cunningham concludes that "the meaning attaches, not to the percipient event or mental state as such, but to it when taken in its ultimate dual reference within the system" (1932). Meaning is a referential relation.

These analytical conclusions constitute, Cunningham believes, an unimpeachable structural description of the formal meaning-situation. A critic may prefer another set of terms, but must agree that Cunningham's analysis is consistent within his terminology. It is an eclectic theory in the sense that it borrows from both sides of the traditional idealist-realist debate over the relative epistemological sanctity of mind and matter, and sets up a systemic reference between these two rival entities. Cunningham refutes both subjective idealism and pure materialism. His conclusion is reminiscent of Bosanquet's judgment after reviewing Alexander's theory: "The double nature of knowledge, as the continuity of mind and reality, is the ultimate truth to insist on" (Bosanquet, 1913). This is a doctrine of uncommon commonsense that brings the meaning-situation and the knowing-situation together in a common structure.

Cunningham's second essay, "Perspective and Context in the Meaning-Situation," detracts nothing from his initial analysis; it is an extension of the earlier theory. This extension specifies two more constituents of the meaning-situation that were more or less implicit in the first investigation. The principal thesis is that abstraction from empirical types of meaning-situations discloses "five distinguishable constituents": "a relation, three terms among which that relation holds, and a ground of the relationship." The terminology is explicit: the relation in the situation is a *reference*; that which refers, or means, is the *content* (the *referend,* in more recent terminology); that referred to is the *referent* (formerly called the object), that for which the reference holds is the *perspective* (formerly called the *mind* that holds the *content*); and that because of which the reference holds is the *context* (the objective system that includes the referent for the perspective). Thus, Cunningham ultimately defines a meaning-situation as "one in which a content refers to a referent for a perspective and because of a context" (1935).

To implement his discussion of perspective and context, he draws attention to three kinds of oversimplification in apprehending the problem of meaning. First, meaning is sometimes equated with the referent, and, because meaning is obviously concerned with some act of the mind, the conclusion may be reached that objects have only a "mental" character; this is a pseudoidealistic view of the nature of the universe. Second, meaning may be considered to be a dyadic relation between content and object (that is, between referend and referent), whereby mind is only a cross-section of events—"nothing more than a nexus among entities." This is a pseudorealistic interpretation of meaning. Third, meaning is often limited to symbolic situations. If this limitation is complete, the conclusion is that sign situations do not convey meaning; if this limitation is partial, one is confronted with the alternative of identifying meaning "either with fact or with a bare relation between symbol and fact." Either identification is unstable. Cunningham considers these three views to be mistaken, mainly because they do an injustice to two constituents of the meaning-situation—perspective and context.

Perspective is defined as the "point of view in respect of which the content 'means' the referent." Point of view seems everywhere to be essential to a situation called meaningful. It entails "a body of beliefs, whether properly to be called knowledge or not"; it is "that part of mind which is relevant to the occurrence of the relation of reference in the special instance; it is what might be called the *occasional mind,* in distinction from mind without qualification." The point here is that on the occasion of any meaning-situation, we do not think of everything we know or believe. This element of perspective in Cunningham's analysis commits him to the view that "the meaning-situation is psychological and . . . nothing has meaning unless it is thought about." It makes little difference to the theory whether the implicit "causal" system of psychology is called by the name of the older *associationism,* or by the newer *conditioned reflex*; the psychology of the referential relation in which content holds for a perspective "is not identical with the causal relation in such a system however described, since it has the peculiar characteristic of being corrigible." If it were perfectly causal, we would make no mistakes. Actually, the referential relation is "projected by the mind and is in that sense an imputed relation" (Cunningham, 1938).

Thus, through the functioning of perspective, meanings are, to a certain extent, relative. "Whatever is a referend refers to that which it is made to refer to, and it is a referend because it is made to refer." That meanings are not wholly relative, in Cunningham's opinion, is an equally important observation that is grounded upon his theory of context.

The context is the ground of the referential relation. For instance, in any situation where the content is an artifact (a red light in a rail-road block, a word, or the like) the context is a set of conventions; the content gains its meaning from the fact that "the conventions are as they are." Again, the contexts may be postulational orders or systems, or the context may be a set of "natural objects" or signs. Accordingly, the context is what Cunningham calls a causal or natural order (1935). Context is always distinct from perspective. As an independent constituent of the meaning-situation, the context is "the *total* whole which is relevant to the verification of an assertion of denial of a relation of reference." It may be impossible to determine this whole in any given instance (a difficulty "which renders verification far from simple and which stands in the way of our making any glib assertions about absolute knowledge"), but, determinable or not, "the context ideally at least is the entire structure or entity which furnishes the logical ground of the relation of reference." Thus, there is a second relation in the meaning-situation, the contextual relationship, that has to do with the part of content that is "of" the object (as opposed to the part "in" the mind). If this were not true, Humpty Dumpty would be entirely right, and meanings would be incorrigible. It is precisely in this contextual relationship, Cunningham insists, that we find the "significance of reference." The fact that every meaning-situation includes this contextual relationship is the sole warrant for the current positivist contention that any meaningful statement must be testable.

Independence of perspective is, however, only one apparent attribute of context. "It may . . . on occasion function within a perspective, and it necessarily does so if it is accurately to be called a context of a meaning-situation—by itself, apart from a perspective, it is strictly speaking not a context at all" (Cunningham, 1938). This conjoined function of perspective and context is, in some respects, the core of Cunningham's theory. He is never entirely happy in describing the precise nature of this conjuncture; he generalizes by remarking that "the perspective is always a disclosure of part at least of the context." He continues:

> Except in sheer illusion, if there be such, there is everywhere an overlapping of perspective and context; in every normal inference, at least, the context functions in the perspective. This functioning of the context in the perspective is made possible by its disclosure there, since the part of the context thus disclosed is *ipso facto* a part of the perspective. In this sense, perspective and context are at one; though, as stated above, they are perhaps never simply identical (p. 44).

This apparent discrepancy between context as independent of, and as conjoined with, perspective causes considerable difficulty in Cunningham's analysis. The difficulty is made more acute by his lack of attention to the problems of communication that relate directly to the problem of meaning. His resolution of the binary function of the context is centered in the content. It is complex. It is a datum, but "a datum *as understood*." The red light in the railroad block is a datum in this sense, and belongs to the context of railroad conventions; as a signal, however, it must be interpreted by the engineer in the on-coming train, and, accordingly, belongs to his perspective. Because the pertinent part of the context in a meaning-situation is always dis-closed in the perspective, it is the given of the context, as interpreted by the perspective, that crystallizes the act of reference. I submit that this operation is possible in human behavior only because we are able to symbolize, and, further, that human symbolic activity underlies the entire structure of a meaning-situation. These observations are expanded below. For the present, it is better to follow Cunningham's theory through to its completion.

The principal point at this state of the argument is that the mean-ing relation derives its sense from the context. In Cunningham's words:

> On the present hypothesis . . . context is at least partly disclosed in perspective and is, so far, consequently at one with it. And from this it follows at once that the relation of reference is also linked with the context. For, since the perspective is one of the terms of the relation and the part of the context disclosed is at one with the perspective, that part of the context at least functions in the determination of the relation. The relation is founded in the context and is therefore under compulsion from it, that is, derives from it a certain "sense" or direction; or what is the same assertion, the referent is at least partly determined by the context (p. 46).

Here is the ground for the semantic assertion of the distinctive importance of context; this assertion appears in various guises in most modern theories of semantics. Cunningham takes more care than most to give it a logical explanation.

This compulsion of the context has so far been treated descrip-tively, that is, as a determinant of the *actual* relation of reference. "But," states Cunningham, "the context exerts compulsion in the further sense that it functions in the determination of what the relation *ought to be,* that is, in the verification of falsification of the statement that the relation holds of the referent." Here the account of context enters the arena of normative logic. Cunningham's main contention is that "context is *eo ipso* a systemic whole." This is admittedly only an assertion, and he does not argue further. Assuming that the assertion is true, it follows that "the part of the context not in the perspective is systematically connected with the part of it which is there." "And with this conclusion we are at liberty to say that the part of the context not disclosed on the occasion may be made to function there as the criterion for verifying or falsifying the relation of reference actually asserted." The part of the context not disclosed can be apprehended by experimental observation or rational analysis. When enough of the context is disclosed "to justify the reference" (that is, "when it is sufficient to determine the referent"), we have certainty and knowledge. When not enough is disclosed, we are either credulous or ignorant. Here is a paraphrase of scientific method: hypotheses are projected, tested, and substantiated, or dismissed.

One more constructive point in Cunningham's theory remains to be stated—the relation between the meaning individual and his critic. "When an observer is, as we say, trying to understand the reference, what he in fact is trying to do is to determine the contextual relationship from the standpoint of the perspective" (Cunningham, 1938). Then, if he finds this relationship acceptable, he accepts the logical ground of the context and calls the reference significant. If he does not find the relationship acceptable, he may reject the reference and call it insignificant:

> It is instructive to note precisely what happens here. The observer sets aside the contextual relationship as specified from the point of view of the perspective and substitutes the specification of it from his own point of view. Thus the old meaning-situation is supplanted by a new one in which the observer's mind becomes the perspective and the reference is grounded in the context as thus determined. This critical procedure is, of course, based on an assumption. The assumption is that the context as specified from the observer's point of view is logically more important than that specified from the perspective functioning in the rejected reference. This assumption is apparently inescapable in criticism, whether of one's own references or of those of another. Thus does preference enter inevitably into critical reasoning, as the pragmatists have rightly urged (p. 171).

At first glance, one might interpret this last statement to mean that the logical compulsion exerted by the context is not so logical after all. There is preference, which can transcend the immediate contextual relationship of a meaning-situation. In other words, there is a choice of logics. It is, supposedly, not an arbitrary choice, because the ground of appeal must be a set of facts in some sense better or more conclusive than those in question. The savage interprets the lightning flash as a reference to some deity, while the more educated perspective (observer) interprets it as a reference to a condition in the clouds; this "educated" preference is grounded in the belief that its reference "more closely exhibits the nature of the flash" than does the other. The critic must always make a choice of significances; he may never say that another reference is without significance. The point here is simply that, since meaning is always a relation, there must always be meaning as long as something is in reference. Meaninglessness can arise, therefore, only as a result of some arbitrary definition of meaning. This interpretation of the meaning-situation seems to effectively dispose of the positivist attack on metaphysics; the positivist may believe that his preference for logical syntax is more the property of philosophy than metaphysical speculation, but that is all he should say. Carnap would not agree with this reading of meaning, of course; he places metaphysics with lyric poetry, and sees both as being meaningless (Carnap, 1935). Langer, among recent writers on meaning, makes a similar disposition. Unlike Carnap, however, she holds that both are meaningful and significant because they are expressed by what she calls "intensive symbolism" and supply us with a kind of knowledge that discursive reasoning can never know (Langer, 1942).

Cunningham's implication is clear: "What at most he [the critic] is at liberty to assert, if his criticism is sound, is that the rejected reference is mistaken or unimportant while his is grounded in fact and is consequently true." This is a seasoned view of criticism that would significantly reduce the number of books on library shelves, if applied. Such a critical procedure, Cunningham believes, relates the analysis of meaning to the pursuit of knowledge. He writes:

> Unless there can be said to be knowledge of the meaningless, that is, something which is not in reference, as has sometimes been maintained, the acquisition of knowledge is identical with the progressive exploration of the contextual relationship of what is in reference. In other words, the acquisition of knowledge is penetration into the significance of reference (1938, p. 172).

Cunningham finally reconsiders the types of meaning-situation in order to clarify the assertion that "every reference has significance." He distinguishes four:

> In the conventional type, what is in reference is some artifact, such as a traffic signal or a dogma, and the contextual relationship is some set of constructed conventions or some historical creed. In the linguistic type, what is in reference is a word or sentence and the contextual relationship is the historically given language-system, or language-systems, in reference. In the postulational type, what is in reference is a symbol or

symbolic expression and the contextual relationship is some set of postulates and definitions and rules of procedure exhibiting a structure which
presumably is in some sense by nature and not by mere convention. And
finally, in the existential type, what is in reference is some supposed
natural object, in contradistinction to an object of artifice as mind-
dependent, and the contextual relationship is some supposed set of facts
with a structure which is by nature in the more common usage of the
word.

Cunningham apparently holds no brief for these types of meaning-
situation; they may or may not be reducible. He asserts that if they
are reducible, the "significance of reference" can be given a factual
statement; if they are not, there must be a different statement of significance for every type of meaning-situation.

The direction of my criticism has already been suggested: Cunningham's analysis is normative; it is weighted in favor of "objective,"
as opposed to "psychological," reference; it does not seem to encompass the meaningful quality of various types of literature, of music and
the fine arts generally; it is developed with almost no recognition of
the importance of communication. Because this last point seems to be
fundamental, the discussion first examines its significance.

Whatever may have been the origins of language, it seems evident
that communication underlies meaning. Meaning is always "of"
something; it is derivative. One must doubt that any concept of meaning can exist that is not derived from man's purposive use of symbols
in active speech. I do not document this statement here; the body of
this essay contains dozens of supporting statements. At the moment,
let us assume it to be self-evident; if this is not satisfactory, one can
appeal to our humanistic tradition. The immediate effect of this
observation, when it is applied to the theory we are considering, is that
it removes at least two of Cunningham's "*prima facie* distinguishable"
meaning-situations, and suggests an entirely different emphasis.

An initial distinction between sign- and symbol-situations ought
to be made. A sunset may send a man home to dinner; a lift of the
eyebrows may express doubt. Whether or not this distinction is maintained often depends upon its utility. Many semanticists generalize the
two under one or the other name, because it is so hard to keep them
apart. Between them they make communication possible, and evidently make possible all human reasoning, representation, demonstration, and expression.

That Cunningham's observation automatically reduces his types
of situations is perhaps not very important; he neither insists on his

final four types, nor does he prefer any particular type. What is important to his theory is that had he begun with sign- and symbol-situations, he probably would have considered some problems of communication and developed a different, or better balanced, emphasis. His typical meaning-situations abstract from the normal events of meaning. They are only prima facie distinguishable. They are empirical, but the experience is frozen. They short-cut the event of meaning, which is always active, changing, purposive, and usually expressive, as well as objectively referential, behavior. Cunningham's lack of attention to communication—of an individual with himself or with another—has led him to emphasize the meaning-situation that exists in scientific discourse, and to minimize or exclude the nature of other kinds of meaning. It has also led him to stress the objective relation of meaning, and to neglect the subjective relation that so obviously identifies meaning with psychological response. It will be recalled that this latter type of meaning was included in the original group of distinguishable meaning-situations under analysis, but did not receive attention in the later grouping. One can only surmise why the content of these groups was changed. My guess is that only the second set of typical meaning-situations would satisfy the requirements of Cunningham's explanation of corrigibility, the contextual relationship, and the significance of reference. These three notions depend upon the fact that the referent is part of a logical system. The emphasis is inevitably thrown upon the meaning relation of objective reference, thus veering away from the relation of psychological reference, or response. I am not contending that a behavioristic description of meaning is the only correct one; I wish only to emphasize the idea that there seem to be many meanings that are not logically objective but are peculiarly in, of, and about the individual. These meanings are included in the scope of Cunningham's structural analysis, but they do not emerge significantly. If I am not beating a straw man, the point can be substantiated within the limits of Cunningham's theory. First, the thesis of corrigibility.

Because our meanings are corrigible, there must be a logical relation between referend and referent; meaning is never wholly imputed. This corrigibility comes in the connection between reference and context, which forms the logical ground of the total relationship. In discussing this point, Cunningham suggests that if one inquires what John Doe means when he makes a statement, three grounds are discoverable: the reference may be its own ground, it may be grounded in the belief of the person concerned, or it may be grounded in fact. Any of these grounds may obtain, but Cunningham insists that, unless corrigibility of reference is surrendered, appeal must be made "to another state of affairs, namely, the contextual relationship of the referential situation within which the reference obtains" (1938, p. 167). That is to say, the court of final appeal is the body of facts that regulates the context—the current stock of knowledge. However, this is a normative notion that could obtain because it is intended (the first ground), or because the reference is based on belief (the second ground). These are psychological grounds. Cunningham agrees that they exist, and that they may, on occasion, be sufficient. However, he insists, if they are put forward to support the reference, there remains the further question *why* the person so believes. This can be answered only by an appeal to the facts, *provided the reference is to remain corrigible.* Therefore, the ultimate context must be grounded in fact *in order to obtain logically.*

This is a kind of circular argument that gains what efficacy it has from the assumption that corrigibility is a necessity in meaning. In our state of ignorance about the exact psychophysiological workings of the mind, the truth seems to be that a great many meanings are not corrigible. People do simply intend; they do believe without factual support that is systematic and publicly recognizable. To insist that intention and "groundless belief" are not end products in many meaning-situations is to remove most of the ethical and political problems of the world. The result is a highly normative, highly specialized definition of meaning, equatable with "strict" knowledge, but unbalanced. This criticism should not be misunderstood: Cunningham recognizes psychological response as meaningful, but, because it seems always to be outside of his theory of contextual relationship, he minimizes its importance. His bias as an epistemologist probably accounts for this attitude toward "psychological reference." It is a significant bias, however. Any definition of meaning that neglects or glosses over the meaningful reference of intention and belief is seriously one-sided.

Two points are involved here: first, the ungenerous treatment of "psychological reference," and second, the contextual validity of "objective reference." I have suggested my criticism of the first, but whether or not "objective reference" must have a logical ground in context remains a question. For scientific discourse the answer is affirmative. Scientific discourse implies a common ground of communication and common habits of communication between the person who means and his critic. The perfect form of scientific discourse is mathematical reasoning. For other kinds of rational analysis, a common technique of communication is equally necessary, and Cunningham seems right in saying that the significance of reference rests upon the logical context. Without a common technique of communication, however, there can scarcely be a logical context. Because of this, one of the major efforts within the biological and social sciences, which are usually non-mathematical in their demonstrations, seems perennially to be the development of just such a common technique. The same is true of ethics and politics, in which the point of importance is perhaps not so much to remember that there must be a logical context, but to master the communicative technique of identifying the context, and of agreeing that a logical system is implicit. On the assumption that ethics and politics, for instance, must be made scientific—and thus knowledge-giving—in their references, it should be noted that, except in mathematical demonstration, perspective, with its accompanying "psychological reference," always impinges upon context, with its "objective reference" to a logical system grounded in fact. Once a clear distinction between fact and opinion is lost, the clean-cut "significance of reference" may also be lost.

I assume here that scientific discourse is actually quite limited within the range of all discourse, and that its communicative technique is gained only at the expense of various tendencies of human behavior—individual wishes, preferences, attitudes, feelings, and the like. In these terms, it appears that Cunningham's interpretation of the relative importance of perspective and context is genuinely ideal, so far as it concerns any kind of meaning except that which interprets mathematical funtions. Corrigibility is not always a feature of the meaning-situation, because meaning is not always relatable to systemic truth. The implication is that Cunningham's use of the "significance of reference" to set up a relation between meaning and knowing is most clearly applicable only when communication is, in some sense, scientific. The only alternative for Cunningham's theory seems to be the conclusion that every man's logical system is his own and that, somehow or other, one logic is made critically available to another that is mysteriously better. Corrigibility is relative to a logical norm that supersedes the individual perspective. There seems to be no such norm that can be applied to "psychological reference," although one may exist in "objective reference."

There is, moreover, still another equally psychological kind of "thinking". It belongs to the "logic" not of representation or demonstration, but of expression. This is the sense of poetry, of music, of painting, of ritual, and of religion. Here a systemic logical ground seems to be entirely cut away. Where is the factual ground for the contextual relationship of a symphony, a lyric poem, or any ritual? The ground of reference is simply the continuum of experience; the art forms are their own references. Yet the truth seems to be that they are meaningful, and that they do give knowledge—an expressive meaning and a knowledge conveyed by what has been called "intensive," as opposed to "discursive," symbolism (Langer, 1942). Whether Cunningham intends his theoretical structure of meaning to apply to this type of knowledge or not, one cannot know. He does not discuss the point. The issue is clearly that, except for certain literary forms, artistic expression is "psychological reference." A publicly available, systemic, logical ground of context is lacking, unless one believes that photography is the highest and "truest" art. That such expressions as art forms are knowledge-giving is perhaps a matter of opinion. In any event, they employ a different communicative technique; some of the theories discussed below pay special attention to the communicative nature of artistic symbolism.

In sum, Cunningham's definition of meaning leaves much to be said. Although his analysis is based on a kind of empirical meaning-situation, he pays little attention to the problems of communication that always seem to underlie the problem of meaning. Because Cunningham interprets the structural constituents of meaning, his is a normative definition, one suggested reason being that it is weighted in favor of "objective reference" to the neglect of "psychological reference." The interpretation comes into better balance with a study of the methods of communication. There is no intention to offer such a study here, but only to suggest its utility. Without exception, the other theories examined in this essay make some attempt to treat the nature of meaning in terms of the communicative problems implicit in sign- and symbol-situations.

Certain points in this discussion have been deliberately pressed, and certain others expanded, in the hope that extended consideration here will clear the air through the rest of this treatment of semantic theories. Although Cunningham contributes little that is new, the ideas he considers seem perennially in need of restatement, and his analysis illuminates many topics important for any discussion of meaning.

The next chapter examines P. W. Bridgman's "operational" theory of meaning, and is directly related to the foregoing discussion. A scientist by training and interest, Bridgman develops a method of narrowing scientific communicative techniques, in order that the logical ground of reference may be kept constantly in view.

REFERENCES

Bosanquet, B. The Distinction Between Mind and Its Objects. England: The University Press, Manchester, 1913.

Carnap, R. Philosophy and Logical Syntax. London: K. Paul, Trench, Trubner & Co., Ltd., 1935.

Cunningham, G. W. "On the Meaning Situation." In Contemporary Idealism In America, edited by C. Barrett. New York: Macmillan, 1932.

―――. "Perspective and Context in the Meaning-Situation." Howison Lecture for 1934. University of California Publication in Philosophy (1935) 16, 2: 29–52.

―――. "Meaning Reference and Significance." Philosophical Review (1938) 47: 155–175.

Langer, S. K. Philosophy in a New Key. Cambridge: Harvard University Press, 1942.

Williams, M. H. "A Study of Meaning." Ph.D. dissertation, Cornell University, 1937.

Chapter 3
OPERATIONISM
P. W. Bridgman

Within the past several decades, the term *operationism* has become very much a part of the scientific idiom. It represents a specifically linguistic approach to scientific methodology, and emphasizes what seems to be an urgent requirement of experimental research—the practice, or habit, whereby "science shall employ only such initial statements and predictions as lead to definite handling operations" (Bloomfield, 1939). Operationism is a semantic term with a special use. In Cunningham's lexicon, it refers to the attempt to make as rigid as possible the contextual relationship in a scientific meaning-situation; it designates the limits beyond which the interpretation of research findings cannot go at any given time.

P. W. Bridgman first stated the operational theory of meaning in his *Logic of Modern Physics* (1927). Since then he has written several articles and books on various aspects of the idea. His first statement was received with hearty acclaim, although most reviewers admired it only for its significance in physical theory. In more recent years, Bridgman's notion of operational meaning has had various interpretations. His initially clear statement of the relation between terminology and experimental technique has entered the muddy realm of "isms," and operationism has been praised and damned, adopted and rejected—for various complex reasons—by a host of philosophers and scientists. It is not my purpose to enter into the implications of this stream of eulogy and vituperation any further than is necessary to place operationism as a semantic theory. What the philosophical and scientific specialists choose to do with Bridgman's principle is their own affair. They have been voluble, and the skein of words appears to be endless. The fundamental idea of operational meaning is simple, and its criticism should not be needlessly complicated.

As Bridgman himself has pointed out, he does not use the term operationism in his statements. Whether he does or not is perhaps beside the point, because the term is now, for better or worse, publicly attached to his name. It is worth noting, however, as at least one commentator does, that operational meaning is actually not a theory (Bentley, 1938). It is simply a habit, a pragmatic point of view. It is what the phrase *operational meaning* most directly suggests: the assignment of meaning according to the operations performed. As the operations—actual or possible—vary, so meaning varies. As Bridgman testifies, this idea is not so much theory as it is useful practice based upon the activities of a scientist in his laboratory. The corollary is equally simple: for the purpose of the physicist's work, a concept (term) that cannot readily be translated into handling activities is useless, and does not lead to knowledge. Operational meaning is, in other words, the application of a rigorous scientific habit whereby the theorist makes a practice of distinguishing between what he actually knows and what he might like to know.

This is essentially a simple idea, and if there were not ample evidence of complex and often distorted interpretations of it, there would be little point in extending a discussion of Bridgman's principle. An article in *Psychological Review* suggests a not unusual confusion. The author summarizes the varied uses to which operationism is being applied in psychology, and notes that the term is currently stretched to include some extremely varied psychological activities (Crissman, 1939). He suggests that *operationism* is an inadequate substitute for *meaning* (not defined), because it "fails clearly to discriminate the *pointing* from the thing *pointed to*." Later, he inquires: "Of *what* do we possess knowledge; to *what* do our operations refer?" Finding no concrete answer among the psychologic apologists under consideration, he concludes that, although operationism is timely in its insistence upon empirical methods, it is neither a novel theory of meaning nor clear "as respects its meaning and implications."

This may be operationism in some aspects of psychology, but it is not Bridgman's idea. Part of the trouble may lie in the fact that much psychological experimentation is concerned with the description of mental properties, instead of the material space-time events of theoretical physics. Nevertheless, Bridgman's principle is unquestionably not an inclusive theory of meaning; it is a description of one kind of meaning that is useful in the laboratory. Operational meaning does not do away with formal definition. It is another kind—what has been called definition by demonstration.

Bridgman's description of the operational meaning of concepts—particularly the notorious comment made in his *Logic of Modern Physics*—is quite as ingenuous as a parent's method of teaching a two-year-old the meaning of *doll* by holding up the object while the word is uttered. Bridgman considers what the physicist must keep in mind even when he works with so simple a concept as length, and he assumes the physicist's usual requirement—that the description of physical events are to be made as exact as possible. He may be measuring anything from yard goods to stellar distance; the concept of length, as it is applied in the laboratory of the physical theorist, is by no means the same for these two operations of measurement. Bridgman concluded:

> The concept of length is therefore fixed when the operations by which length is measured are fixed: that is, the concept of length involves as much as and nothing more than a set of operations by which length is determined. In general, we mean by any concept nothing more than a set of operations: *the concept is synonymous with the corresponding set of operations* (Bridgman, 1927, p. 5).

This statement is followed by another of equal significance, often quoted but frequently forgotten: "The true meaning of a term is to be found by observing what a man does with it, not by what he says about it."

Together, these two statements form the core of Bridgman's principle. It goes almost without saying that this is not a full-blown theory of meaning conceived to explain the psychophysiological events that make up thinking. Nor are "mental" operations excluded (Bridgman, 1938). Bridgman simply offers a practical means to satisfy the physicist's need to depend upon what he actually does and actually sees in his laboratory. He plainly stated:

> Observation shows that ambiguity is latent in any operation defined in terms of its properties, because of the inherent experimental error with which properties can be established . . . Hence arises the demand that the concepts or terms used in the description of experience be framed in terms of operations which can be unequivocally performed. We have here no esoteric theory of the ultimate nature of concepts, nor a philosophical championing of the primacy of the 'operation.' We have merely a pragmatic matter, namely that we have observed after much experience that if we want to do certain kinds of things with our concepts, our concepts had better be constructed in certain ways (1938, p. 119).

This is definition by demonstration. Length is relative to experimental conditions. The answer to the question, "Of what do we possess knowledge; to what do our operations refer?", is that we have knowledge of the limits of our activities because our operations refer to the terms we employ. The use of operational meaning, therefore, is neither new nor radical, but, like so much else of the old and familiar, it is apt to be overlooked. There seems to be nothing subtle about Bridgman's principle. It is a safety valve to check the dangers of misinterpretation and overstatement. It is a rigid control over the conditions of communication that obtain in strictly empirical science. If it is agreed that a "typical act of science might consist of the following steps: observation, report of observations, statement of hypotheses, calculation, prediction, testing of predictions by further observation" (Bloomfield, 1939), then it follows that the first and last steps—the scientist's handling activities—include the necessary physical operations upon which the theorist must depend for his description of physical events. These operations, and these alone, constitute the raw material of his data. He also employs, other operations, of course, because "man acting" is also "man thinking". However, unless his other activities lead to handling operations, the physical theorist is without data. Accordingly, says Bridgman, the theorist's terms are meaningless, which is to say that they cannot be transferred into handling activities. Here is a rather special use of *meaning* and *meaningless*, and perhaps one of the reasons for the confusion about operationism is this narrow use of terms. At least the usage is not so recondite as much interpretation has made it appear.

It may be wise to emphasize that, to the best of my knowledge, neither Bridgman nor anyone else has said that concepts are *only* handling operations. This interpretation could be made of the statement quoted from *The Logic of Modern Physics,* but it would be a distortion of the context. The point is that concepts, to be scientifically useful, must *lead* to handling activities, physical operations, the arrangement and reading of instruments in the laboratory—in other words, to sign-situations. This observation is made in one of the early commentaries on Bridgman's thesis, when C. A. Benjamin suggests that operational meaning does not replace formal definition. Rather, it is "a description of the processes involved in determining its [the formal definition's] measure, i.e. its quantitative correlate . . . Force is, operationally, a description of the technique of attaching and reading a spring balance" (1927). The physicist no doubt employs countless other concepts in his mathematical manipulations.

The reasons for Bridgman's emphasis are not obscure, if one remembers that physical theory as a field of knowledge depends upon laboratory activity for its demonstrations. The sense-data of modern physics are pointer-readings, and the physicist, if he is truly empirical, must limit his context to these readings, and avoid letting his terms stand for substantial properties of the object under consideration. Bridgman believes that if definitions of laboratory concepts in terms of properties are avoided, "we need run no danger of having to revise our attitude toward nature." The theorist must make his descriptions as consonant as is humanly possible with the nature of what it is he describes:

> For if experience is always described in terms of experience, there must always be correspondence between experience and our description of it, and we need never be embarrassed, as we were in attempting to find in nature the prototype of Newton's absolute time. Furthermore, if we remember that the operations to which a physical concept is equivalent are actual physical operations, the concepts can be defined only in the range of actual experiment, and are undefined and meaningless in regions as yet untouched by experiment (Bridgman, 1927, pp. 6–7.

Bridgman is here responding to the influence of Relativity, and believes that new kinds of experience bring new facts "of an entirely different character from those of our former experience."

The effect of applying operational concepts is to emphasize the relative character of knowledge, which closely fits Cunningham's thesis that knowledge is penetration into the "significance of reference." Bridgman extends this principle and qualifies it, at least so far as it obtains in physical experimentation. "Whether a given property is absolute or not can be determined only by experiment, landing us in the paradoxical position that the absolute is absolute only relative to experiment" (Benjamin, 1927). This observation, in turn, is a redaction of the principle of indeterminacy, which is "founded on the fact that we cannot observe the course of nature without disturbing it" (Sullivan, 1933, p. 105). These ideas do not constitute "a novel theory of meaning," it is true, but evidently some of those who employ research techniques need to have them brought to mind afresh.

Aside from emphasizing the relativity of knowledge, Bridgman applies his principle of operational meaning to describe the nature of physical problems. In *The Logic of Modern Physics,* he develops operational definitions of the physical concepts of space, time, causality, identity, velocity, force and mass, energy, thermodynamics, electricity, light, rotational motion, and quanta. I have neither the interest nor the critical equipment to examine his analyses, and to pursue them in detail would serve no purpose here. The relation of his conclusions to his operational theory is, however, quite clear. As the physicist passes from the domain in which a concept is originally defined, he cannot carry out the operations involved in its definition. He needs a new set of terms. Lacking the operational technique to convey a new set, he must admit that he has gone past experimental limitations, and that he is left with a haze in which he has lost his way. This is one of the fundamental ideas involved in operational meaning—as the experimenter approaches experimental limits, he exhausts his empirical context. The significance of his terms, thus of his ideas, slips away from him. In this state of affairs he has no data, and had better not think that he has knowledge (Benjamin, p. 664). The haze is not always admitted, however, and it is possible—easy, says Bridgman—"to invent expressions or to ask questions that are meaningless," that is, insignificant for the experimenter (Bridgman, 1927, p. 28). The test must be operational—terms must lead to handling activities. Otherwise, the theorizer is lost in a verbal skein. "If a specific question has meaning, it must be possible to find operations by which an answer may be given to it."

In sum, the principle of operational meaning is, strictly speaking, not a definition of meaning in general, but only of the relations between an experimenter's physical terms and the operations that they designate. This is a special kind of meaning that is extremely valuable to the physical theorist. Whether it is useful to other sciences—psychology, for instance—is not so clear. Perhaps operationism can only be useful in laboratory operations, where the objects are physical events. It is not a new principle; Dewey suggests that C. S. Peirce's essay, "How To Make Our Ideas Clear," is the source of Bridgman's notion (Dewey, 1930). Whether or not he anticipated Bridgman's use of the idea of operational meaning, Peirce was in the van of many twentieth-century ideas, and offers a capable summary of operationism in his statement that the meaning of a proposition is a "general description of all the experimental phenomena which the assertion of the proposition virtually predicts." This is the original creed of pragmatism. Operational meaning is one aspect of what Langer calls "selective symbolization," and it supports her judgment that "the great work of science is to find out those ways of conceiving an object which shall be most appropriate to certain purposes" (Langer, 1930, p. 142).

To close the discussion at this point would preserve its unity. There remains, however, one aspect of "Bridgmanism" to be considered. Both in *The Logic of Modern Physics* and *The Nature of Physical Theory,* Bridgman undertakes to become a critic of biosocial activity; in a later book, *The Intelligent Individual in Society,* he speaks as a sociologist. In Chapter 3 of *The Nature of Physical Theory,* he undertakes, almost casually, to distinguish between experience, thought, and language. Various critics have found this attempt considerably less than satisfactory; there is no need to present the criticism here. The trouble seems to lie in the fact that Bridgman proceeds with his analysis without stating his assumptions and without a creditable method; the result is mere verbalism—and inconsistent verbalism, at that (see Bridgman, 1936, p. 24).

Of more immediate interest is a series of remarks that Bridgman makes in Section I of *The Logic of Modern Physics*—remarks that, so far as I know, have not before been especially noted. He writes:

To adopt the operational point of view involves much more than a mere restriction of the sense in which we understand 'concept' but means a far-reaching change in all our habits of thought, in that we shall no longer permit ourselves to use as tools in our thinking concepts of which we cannot give an adequate account in terms of operations. In some respects thinking becomes simpler, because certain old generalizations and idealizations become incapable of use; for instance, many of the speculations of the early natural philosophers become simply unreadable. In other respects, however, thinking becomes much more difficult, because the operational implications of a concept are often very involved. For example, it is most difficult to grasp adequately all that is contained in the apparently simple concept of 'time', and requires the continual correction of mental tendencies which we have long unquestioningly accepted.

Operational thinking will at first prove to be an unsocial virtue; one will find oneself perpetually unable to understand the simplest conversation of one's friends, and will make oneself universally unpopular by demanding the meaning of apparently the simplest terms of every argument. Possibly after every one has schooled himself to this better way, there will remain a permanent unsocial tendency, because doubtless much of our present conversation will then become unnecessary. The socially optimistic may venture to hope, however, that the ultimate effect will be to release one's energies for more stimulating and interesting interchange of ideas.

Not only will operational thinking reform the social art of conversation, but all our social relations will be liable to reform. Let any one examine in operational terms any popular present-day discussion of religious or moral questions to realize the magnitude of the reformation awaiting us. Wherever we temporize or compromise in applying our theories of conduct to practical life we may suspect a failure of operational thinking (pp. 31–32).

This is reminiscent of the "define-your-terms" school of semantics, and Bridgman is quite right about the normal accretionary social stigma. Operational meaning in scientific methodology is unquestionably a normative canon of thinking; there seems to be a decided value in this kind of hyperempiricism for the situation in which the physical theorist finds himself. Applied as Bridgman suggests here, however, it becomes almost "abnormative." This is utopia, and perhaps not such a pleasant one. Where is the pragmatism upon which Bridgman raised the principle of operational meaning? Where is the sociologist of knowledge who, in another context, asserted that "it is evident that the nature of our thinking mechanism inevitably colors any picture that we can form of nature, and we shall have to recognize that unavoidable characteristics of ours are imposed in this way"? Granted that all logic is in some sense normative, and that the principle of operationism is demonstrably sound and useful to the physical theorist, it seems neither sound nor useful to apply normative logic to the broad sweep of human nature. One can never successfully replace the whole with the part. Operationism is mainly concerned with what C. W. Morris calls the semantic dimension of meaning, the relation between words and facts (see below, Chapter 7). However, to recommend it for social activities in general is to forget that there is a pragmatic motivation in all human relations—a "drive" that is by no means usually scientific. The human race does not live in a physical laboratory, nor is there much evidence to suggest that its vagaries can be translated into experimental operations (Bridgman, 1938). The empirical scientist finds it to his advantage to define his fundamental terms with the utmost rigor; the average man learns his meanings from his social perspective.

It seems that Bridgman oversteps the bounds of reason only when he neglects the proper setting of his operational point of view. As an activity of the physical theorist, operational meaning well stresses the relativity of scientific knowledge; it implicates a strict empiricism that is irreplaceable in experimental research. Nobody can doubt that operationism is very much a part of the stream of twentieth-century ideas. Boas, for instance, characterizes "our new ways of thinking" as a replacement of the older rationalism by voluntarism, and observes that the "voluntarist tests the meaning of his terms not by logical consistency, but by operational efficacy" (Boas, 1930, p. 186). For better or worse, conscious operationism is a major force behind the extensive modern interest in a science of symbols. Whereas the rationalist has usually found direction for his use of symbols within a pattern of logical consistency, the voluntarist, thinking always in terms of interest and purpose, seeks knowledge in variant meanings, and finds it only natural that "science grow old and truth decay."

One of the earliest and most provocative modern attempts to develop a science of symbols consonant with this modern way of knowing is found in *The Meaning of Meaning,* by C. K. Ogden and I. A. Richards. These theorists are committed to an approach to epistemological problems by way of a psychological analysis of the communicative principles that underlie our use of words and our habits of thinking. With their work, which is the next consideration, modern semantics blooms as a systematic study of the nature of symbolism.

REFERENCES

Benjamin, A. C. "Review of the Logic of Modern Physics." Journal of Philosophy (1927) 24: 663–665.

Bentley, A. F. "Physicists and Fairies." Philosophy of Science (1938) 5: 132–165.

Bloomfield, L. "Linguistic Aspects of Science." In International Encyclopedia of Unified Science, edited by O. Neurath. I, 4. Chicago: University of Chicago Press, 1939.

Boas, G. Major Traditions of European Philosophy. New York: Harper, 1929.

Bridgman, P. W. The Logic of Modern Physics. New York: The Macmillan Co., 1927.

———. The Nature of Physical Theory. Princeton: Princeton University Press, 1936.

———. "Operational analysis." Philosophy of Science (1938) 5: 114–131.

Crissman, P. "The Operational Definition of Concepts." Psychiatric Review (1939) 46: 309–317.

Dewey, J. The Quest for Certainty. London: G. Allen and Unwin Ltd., 1930.

Langer, S. K. The Practice of Philosophy. New York: H. Holt & Co., 1930.

Sullivan, J. W. N. The Limitations of Science. New York: Viking Press, 1933.

Chapter 4
THE SCIENCE
OF SYMBOLISM
Ogden and Richards

C. K. Ogden and I. A. Richards are two modern pioneers in the study of symbolism and communication. Their first collaboration was *The Meaning of Meaning* (1923); they have since published more than two dozen books and many articles concerned with various problems of the relations of language to thought. Their interests have led them to work on a theory of signs, which is the basis of what they call the "science of symbolism." (Thirty-odd years ago, this term was translated into the more popular *semantics,* and this was the term employed later by Richards, H. R. Walpole, Stuart Chase, S. I. Hayakawa, I. J. Lee, and others. It is still current.) In addition, Ogden and Richards extended themselves to discourse on the nuclear idea of meaning itself, on theories of interpretation, definition, translation, and on the development of Basic English as a universal language.

Their theories have stimulated a considerable body of polemic literature—the obvious outcome of the scope of their views and their style. They rarely hesitate to trespass, and their flippant dogmatism has won them both converts and antagonists. From the onset, Ogden and Richards have been notable for their psychological approach to the problem of meaning. This fact may help to account for the wide interest early accorded their theories, particularly among educationists, inasmuch as modern ideas in psychology have motivated many restatements, revisions, and extensions of thinking about thought as a matter of course. In the years after the emergence of their first book, Ogden has busied himself especially with Basic English, a subject that is allied with, but outside of, the scope of this essay. For this reason much of the later material examined here is concerned with Richards alone.

Although neither of these men ever made an outright commitment to a traditional school of philosophy—a negative status that has aroused suspicion among some critics—many of their ideas can be associated with the tradition of empiricism in England. (John Crowe Ransom, for instance, refers to Richards as "a thinker who may be defined, I imagine, as another case of the psychologist who proposes to pursue his thinking without a philosophy" 1939, p. 411.) In general terms, they adopt the current nominalist attitude against the magic of words. The work of the Orthological Institute of London, of which Ogden and Richards are the moving spirits, is in part the task of tracing the development of the science of symbolism; it is obvious that these authors find their intellectual genealogy in the linguistic theories of Bacon, Hobbes, Locke, Berkeley, Hume, and Bentham. The journal of the Orthological Institute is an annual called *Psyche.* In Volume XIV (1934), Ogden published an account of noteworthy English philosophical attempts to overcome word-magic. He traced and interpreted the analysis of symbolism, covering Bacon's "idols," the work of Hobbes and Locke, Berkeley's theory of signs, and Hume—who was judged to have no more than "a superficial appreciation of the symbolic function."

Ogden's and Richard's theory of semantics is complex and enveloping, because it attempts to weave the fabric of man's understanding. It is normative theory; the principal aim is to furnish a means to improve communication and, through this, civilization. This goal determines the direction of their analysis of the relation between language and thought, and their choice of topics. They find that many of the ills of the world are traceable to the magic of words. Accordingly, they concentrate upon an account of interpretation, the uses of language, definition, and meaning. They offer this account as the foundation of a science of symbolism, which becomes the organon of education. Their theory of knowledge is agnostic—only the "how" of reference can be known, never the "what." This relative nature of knowledge is, of course, a common denominator of much modern thought. They find that neither philosopher nor scientist has heretofore been able to sustain an explanation of meaning or of knowing, because all preceding accounts have failed to develop a theory of sign-situations—that is, of communication—to explain satisfactorily the triadic relation of reference that underlies all meaning and all knowing.

It is fairly easy to be critical of these authors' accomplishments. Judged by their claims, their work falls far short of their goal.

However, semantics, as they describe it, is a young science, and they come early in the chronology of modern semantic theories. Semantics has already changed considerably from their ideal, and it may eventually become quite unrecognizable from their early point of view. Meanwhile, several shortcomings are discernible. Their "causal" account of interpretation, an early application of the theory of conditioned response, leaves unanswered a host of questions—linguistic, sociological, and philosophical. Their statement of the uses of language sets up a dichotomy that is indefensible as a description of linguistic behavior. Their analysis of meaning is dogmatic and uninclusive. They fall into the trap, not unusual in semantic circles, of confusing verbal with material problems; it seems legitimate to doubt that the major ailments of the human race are only verbal. Ogden and Richards evidently overestimate the pragmatic aspects of verbal situations and underestimate the pragmatic aspects of the states of affairs that underlie them. They have made a cartographical contribution to the study of symbolism, but their science is vitiated by their normative zeal.

There is reason to believe that their pioneer work on a science of symbolism as an educative instrument is focused principally in their theory of the two uses of language. It is here, they suggest, that the remedy for word-magic must lie. It is with the implications of this dichotomy that the criticism in this chapter is most concerned. Their work on the theory of signs, on definition, and on the meaning of meaning is included by way of explication of this major division.

This is not to say that Ogden and Richards are interested only in the uses of language. *The Meaning of Meaning* was written with a variety of purposes in mind, all of which relate to the study of symbolism. We are told in the preface that the book came into being "out of an attempt to deal directly with difficulties raised by the influence of Language upon Thought." The authors remark that their science of symbolism offers a "new avenue of approach to traditional problems hitherto regarded as reserved for the philosopher and the metaphysician." They call attention to four contributions that they feel they make to the psychology of language. First, they give an "account of *interpretation* in causal terms by which the treatment of language as a system of signs becomes capable of results, among which may be noticed the beginning of a division between what cannot be intelligibly talked of and what can." Second, they offer "a division of the functions of language into two groups, the symbolic and the emotive." They believe that "many notorious controversies in the sciences . . . derive from confusion between these functions, the same words being used at once to make statements and to excite attitudes." With this conservative observation, they note that the inescapable result of this confusion is the presence of "fictitious differences," and make the point that the only analgesia is a clear understanding of the different uses of language. Third, the authors present "a dissection and ventilation of 'meaning' the centre of obscurantism both in the theory of knowledge and in all discussion." Fourth, they describe a "freely mobilizable technique of definition" that should serve to solve the difficulties of verbal questions. A knowledge of definition serves automatically either as a reagent or a cathartic. These four accomplishments constitute a large order of business for one book. The authors set out to run through the agenda with a breezy confidence that has led Max Eastman to refer to the "precocious quality" of *The Meaning of Meaning.*

SOME BASIC ASSUMPTIONS

One must pay close attention to the definitions of the central terms employed by Ogden and Richards, because it is in these definitions that their assumptions are exposed. They write:

> Symbolism is the study of the part played in human affairs by language and symbols of all kinds, and especially of their influence on Thought. It singles out for special inquiry the ways in which symbols help us and hinder us in reflecting on things.
>   Symbols direct and organize, record and communicate. In stating what they direct and organize, record and communicate we have to distinguish as always between Thoughts and Things. It is Thought (or, as we shall usually say, *reference*) which is directed and organized, and it is also Thought which is recorded and communicated (p. 9).

This statement equates reference with thought. Furthermore, the traditional distinction between thought and thing is the critical point in symbolism. Throughout the book, Ogden and Richards return to this Hobbesian warning: "Words, as every one now knows, 'mean' nothing by themselves, although the belief that they did . . . was once equally universal." The authors find the word *thing* "unsuitable for the analysis here undertaken," and employ the term *referent* to stand for the object to which reference is made. Thought, then, becomes cognition, and *reference,* in the authors' terminology, abstracts cognition from the total mental process that is traditionally defined to include conation as well as cognition. In his *Principles of Literary*

Criticism (1926), Richards says that thought "in the strict sense varies only with evidence" (p. 88). "What is essential in thought is its direction or reference to things" (p. 125). "So far as an impulse owes its character to its stimulus (or to such effects of past accompanying or connected stimuli as are revived) so far is it a *reference,* to use the term which we introduced . . . to stand for the property of mental events which we substitute for thought or cognition" (p. 262). In sum, reference means cognition; referent is a "technical term to stand for whatever we may be thinking of or referring to." These definitions make it possible to talk about the referential use of language "which for all reflective, intellectual use of language should be paramount" (1923, p. 10).

Yet words have functions other than the referential. These "may be grouped together as emotive." These functions "can best be examined when the framework of the problem of strict statement and intellectual communication has been set up." Ogden and Richards urge that the reader must not think that the "importance of the emotive aspects of language is . . . thereby minimized," because "anyone chiefly concerned with popular or primitive speech might well be led to reverse this order of approach." Ogden and Richards call the influence of language resulting from an emotive use of words "nonsymbolic." "But for the analysis of the senses of 'meaning' with which we are here chiefly concerned, it is desirable to begin with the relations of thought, words and things as they are found in cases of reflective speech uncomplicated by emotional, diplomatic, or other disturbances."

These are important dicta, because many qualifications are implicit in this classification. The assumptions made by Ogden and Richards are genuinely fundamental and extremely limiting. Their definitions and approaches in *The Meaning of Meaning,* a book basic to all their theories of the use of words, apply only to a stringent, scientific use of language—the stripped protocols of laboratory findings, reports of sense-data, and the like. The rhetoric of persuasion, poetry, prose-fiction, and drama is automatically classified as nonintellectual. These classes include no important elements of cognition and are, by implication, meaningless. (Later we shall observe that, in *The Principles of Literary Criticism,* Richards holds not that the emotive use of language makes no use of reference, but that its aim "goes beyond, is deeper than reference.")

This is not the point at which to question these exclusions from intellectual processes; these are considered in detail below. The object here is to call attention to the inclusions made by Ogden and Richards. It appears that the title *The Meaning of Meaning* is somewhat misleading. Although they do offer a definition of meaning, this definition is only a tautology, a repetition of the terms of their basic assumptions. They assume that words refer to objects *or* express the feeling of their users, and that meaning resides only in the former of these capacities. This criticism suggests that the uses of this classification of referential and emotive words are seriously limited, and, possibly, not so sound as certain other approaches to the problems of language and thought. The inevitable conclusion is that a science of symbolism based on such assumptions and definitions fails to describe accurately the facts of sign usage.

T. C. Pollock makes this limitation clear in his book on *The Nature of Literature* (1942, Chapter 8). Pollock is chiefly concerned with the uses of language in literature. He notes that the dual classification made by Ogden and Richards weights their theory in favor of the scientific use of language. That is to say, if the referential use of language in literature—obviously expressive of emotions and attitudes—must be not so meaningful and, at best, is secondary in importance. Pollock develops the thesis that throughout *The Meaning of Meaning* the authors give strategic answers to the question of the relation of thought to language.

It may be argued that Ogden and Richards have a right to try to control their readers' thoughts; it would be impossible, otherwise, for them to develop a convincing theory. All theoretical definitions must be ad hoc by the very nature of a theory, and are, consequently, strategic. Authors may, within reason, apply whatever definitions they see fit to carry out their purposes. These points are well taken. Yet, unless both definitions and the resulting theory are genuinely serviceable, and true to the facts as we know them, they are open to question. Furthermore, inasmuch as Ogden and Richards are outspoken in their claim to have answered the prevailing difficulties of relating thought to language, they are doubly open to exacting criticism.

LANGUAGE AND THOUGHT

The comment was made above that this descriptive science of symbolism is vitiated by the authors' normative zeal. *The Meaning of Meaning* is also a prolonged attempt to remove emotional responses from cognitive habits, a bit of psychological prestidigitation that is exceedingly difficult to perform. The inescapable result of classifying language into referential (meaningful) and emotive (meaningless) uses is that truth and knowledge must reside in the one, while the product of the other can be nothing but fancy and dreams. Man-the-knower is somehow separable from man-the-feeler, not for the purposes of analysis, but as descriptive reality. On the face of it, this kind of dogma appears to be the fruit of a cranky mind. That Richards has had to struggle with these implications is evident in his later championing of the poetic use of words, a topic discussed below. There is no doubt that *The Meaning of Meaning* is heavily weighted in favor of some kind of scientific reference, and that the science of symbolism gets off to a bad start. A few generalizations may serve to point the issue.

The science of symbolism is the study of the influence of language upon thought. "There are three factors involved when any statement is made, or interpreted; mental processes, the symbol, and a referent—something which is thought 'of'" (p. 243). The theoretical problem is the determination of relationship among these three terms. The ultimate point of the study of symbolism, however, is the answer to a practical problem:

> The *practical* problem, since we must use words in discussion and argument, is—
> *How far is our discussion itself distorted by habitual attitudes towards words, and lingering assumptions due to theories no longer openly held but still allowed to guide our practice?*
> The chief of these assumptions derives from the magical theory of the name as part of the thing, the theory of an inherent connection between symbols and referents. This legacy leads in practice to the search for *the* meaning of words. The eradication of this habit can only be achieved by a study of Signs in general, leading up to a referential theory of Definition by which the phantom problems resulting from such superstitions may be avoided. When these have been disposed of, all subjects become more accessible and more interesting (pp. 243–244).

The science of symbolism is primarily a study of the referential use of words, a conclusion reached by putting theory and practice together. Emotive expression is ruled out of the analysis of meaning. One may infer that the "magical theory of the name as part of the thing" is, in the main, traceable to the confusion of emotive with referential uses of words. They must be kept apart. Herein lies the prevailing normative quality of the teachings of Ogden and Richards. They join the ranks of those who would save mankind from its verbal frailties by pedagogical dogma, based, it is true, upon some of the findings of modern psychology. The problem in interpreting this theory is to keep the psychological findings separate from the ad hoc definitions, lest the one suffer unfairly from the companionship of the other.

Some confusion is apt to arise very early in *The Meaning of Meaning*:

> Between a thought and a symbol causal relations hold. When we speak, the symbolism we employ is caused partly by the reference we are making and partly by social and psychological factors—the purpose for which we are making the reference, the proposed effect of our symbols on the other persons, and our own attitude. When we hear what is said, the symbols both cause us to perform an act of reference, and to assume an attitude which will, according to circumstances, be more or less similar to the act and the attitude of the speaker (p. 10).

This is reminiscent of Cunningham's admission of the pragmatic element in the "logical compulsion of the context." It seems that the symbolic use of words is not purely objective; part of the causation of reference is brought about by "social and psychological factors." Furthermore, attitudes creep into the referential use of words, and unless these attitudes are somehow essentially cognitive and can be divorced from emotions (to which they are usually at least partially attributable), it seems that the chasm between the two uses of words is neither deep nor wide. Yet this may be only a logic-chopper's criticism. Ogden and Richards reiterate that the distinction is difficult to make, but that, at the same time, it must be made. The classification is a normative device that must perforce generalize on the total effect of a use of words. The authors supply the necessary formula.

The best test of whether our use of words is essentially "symbolic or emotive is the question—'Is this true or false in the ordinary strict scientific sense?' If this question is relevant then the use is symbolic, if it is clearly irrelevant then we have an emotive utterance." If this "ordinary strict scientific sense" means that there must be sense-data that are the referents of the symbols, then this dictum lends a thorough-going positivist note to the theory. What is involved in this strict, symbolic use of words?

TRIANGLE OF REFERENCE

The major formula that furnishes the crux of a necessary theory of signs is the "Triangle of Reference." Hugh G. Walpole, whose book on semantics (1941) was published with Richards's blessing, makes an interesting comment:

This Triangle of Reference is the one detail in this book which needs to be remembered outright, by force if necessary. If the reader lost his book he could build up again for himself the subject matter of semantics, on the basis of the Triangle of Reference (p. 82).

For the record, the "Triangle," in its original form, is reproduced here as Figure 1.

Ogden and Richards explain the meaning of this diagram as follows:

> Between the Thought and the Referent there is . . . a relation . . . more or less direct (as when we think about or attend to a coloured surface we see), or indirect (as when we 'think of' or 'refer to' Napoleon), in which case there may be a very long chain of sign-situations intervening between the act and its referent: word—historian—contemporary record—eye-witness—referent (Napoleon).
>
> Between the symbol and the referent there is no relevant relation other than the indirect one, which consists in its being used by someone to stand for a referent. Symbol and Referent, that is to say, are not connected directly (and when, for grammatical reason, we imply such a rela-

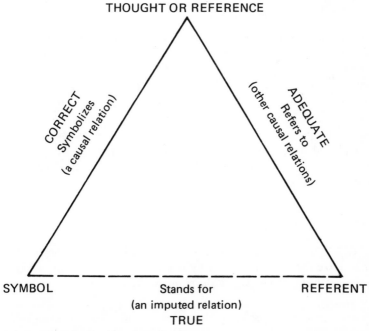

Figure 1.   The Triangle of Reference.

tion, it will merely be an imputed, as opposed to a real, relation) but only indirectly round the two sides of the triangle (pp. 11–12).

There is nothing startling here. It is simply a graphic exposition of mediated knowledge. At best, it serves to hammer home the lesson that words are not the things to which they refer, which is the dogmatic keystone of modern semantics. The trouble is that men forget this truth, and the authors labor in *The Meaning of Meaning* to make this forgetting impossible (thereby agreeing with Dr. Johnson that "men more frequently require to be reminded than informed"). If only the magic of words could be exorcised, man's ability to symbolize could do him no disservice. The problem relates to communication. It is difficult to know precisely what a person means when he talks:

> We need some technique to keep the parties to an argument in contact and to clear up misunderstandings—or,·in other words, a Theory of Definition. Such a technique can only be provided by a theory of knowing, or of reference, which will avoid, as current theories do not, the attribution to the knower of powers which it may be pleasant for him to suppose himself to possess, but which are not open to the only kind of investigation hitherto profitably pursued, the kind generally known as scientific investigation (p. 15).

Here is the positivist position in a nutshell. Similar statements are found in the writings of Korzybski and his followers. The proper use of referential language (equatable with Korzybski's insistence upon "denotative utterance") based upon a "scientific" relation of words to things, will provide a means of definition the like of which the nonscientific world has never known. It should, if constantly and consciously employed, erase the discrepancies of meaning that have haunted and held down humanity since the beginning of symbolization. The theory furnishes a striking instance of the modern idea of progress.

DEFINITION OF MEANING

Granted that an understanding of the "Triangle of Reference" helps to cauterize the wounds caused by word-magic, what theory of knowing does it sustain? The key is the sign-situation:

> Throughout almost all our life we are treating things as signs. All experience, using the word in the widest possible sense, is either enjoyed or interpreted (i.e., treated as a sign) or both, and very little of it escapes some degree of interpretation. An account of the process of Interpreta-

tion is thus the key to the understanding of the Sign-situation, and therefore the beginning of wisdom.

Morgan's celebrated instance of the chicken and the cinnabar caterpillar is pressed into service:

> This simple case is typical of all interpretation, the peculiarity of interpretation being that when a context has affected us in the past the recurrence of merely a part of the context will cause us to react in the way in which we reacted before. A sign is always a stimulus similar to some part of an original stimulus and sufficient to call up the engram formed by that stimulus.
>
> An engram is the residual trace of an adaptation made by the organism to a stimulus. The mental process due to the calling up of an engram is a similar adaptation: so far as it is cognitive, what it is adapted to is its referent, and is what the sign which excites it stands for or signifies (p. 53).

This is what Ogden and Richards call their "causal" theory of interpretation. Anticipating critical rejoinder, however, they expand this account:

> The suggestion that to say 'I am thinking of A' is the same thing as to say 'My thought is being caused by A,' will shock every right-minded person; and yet when for 'caused' we substitute an expanded account, this strange suggestion will be found to be the solution.

The enlarged explanation is called the "contextual" theory of interpretation:

> If we recognize . . . as the basis of this account the fact that experience has the character of recurrence, that is, comes to us in more or less uniform contexts, we have in this all that is required for the theory of signs and all that the old theory of causes was entitled to maintain.

"Psychological context" is further extended as "a recurrent set of mental events peculiarly related to one another so as to recur, as regards their main features, with partial uniformity." If, for instance, we are acquainted with the properties of a box of matches (that is, have experienced them as recurrent entities), when we take out a match and strike it on the box, our "psychological context" is such that we expect the match to light. We have been led to expect this result from our experience with boxes of matches.

One might suggest that this figure of a box of matches is oversimplified. Is the reference false if the match is wet, or if the striking surface is worn, or if the match is clumsily handled, or if the flame sputters and goes out before it can be applied? The pitfalls of oversimplicity in a psychological explanation of interpretation are many and varied. The answer given by Ogden and Richards is that an external, as well as a psychological, context is operative. "If there be an event which completes the external context in question, the reference is true and the event is its referent. If there be no such event, the reference is false, and the expectation is disappointed" (p. 62). In this case there is a modification for the future of the "psychological context." This is a good statement of the process called verification, or, more recently in positivist circles, confirmation.

The generalization of the meaning of meaning is made from this theory of signs:

> All thinking, all reference . . . is adaptation due to psychological contexts which link together elements in external contexts. However 'universal' or however 'abstract' our adaptation, the general account of what is happening is the same. In this fashion we arrive at a clear and definite sense of 'meaning'. According to this the meaning of A is that to which the mental process interpreting A is adapted. This is the most important sense in which words have meaning (p. 200).

In its main features, this account of meaning is an early interpretation of the theory of the conditioned reflex, and offers a general description of some of the psychological features of symbolism that make communication possible. However, it says very little because, as the authors suggest, psychology will have to be devoted almost exclusive to a study of all possible contexts before this process of adaptation can be understood. Moreover, if the current psychophysiological methods of experimentation are used in the study of these contexts, it is extremely doubtful that either "thought" or "causation" will remain in the findings.

There is some doubt about these terms even as they now stand in this theory of signs. Several critics have found this analysis of interpretation unsatisfactory as a definition of meaning. C. M. White has subjected it to an exhaustive logical analysis, and concludes that there are some vital discrepancies (White, 1933, pp. 2–73). The trouble arises in the theoretically typical explanation of sign-situations in perception. White finds that the ambiguity as to whether the initial phases of sensory perception—for example, retinal modifications in "seeing"—are given or are interpreted, leaves undetermined the answer as to when interpretation begins. White's dialectic is not pursued here, but I recommend it for those who have a special interest in critical detail on the topic. White's general conclusion is the pertinent point in this discussion: there are two different theories of meaning. One, the "causal," seems to make the referent not a concept or an idea but an objective entity, outside the skin of the perceiver; the result is that the second apex of the "Triangle of Reference" (thought) is practically omitted. The other, the "contextual" account, on the contrary, concentrates so fully upon psychological responses that the third apex (referent) is seriously slighted.

H. M. Williams, following White's analysis, arrives at the same conclusion, and makes the additional observation that Ogden and Richards mix their definitions of meaning mainly because they confuse two kinds of meaning-situation—psychological reference and objective reference (Williams, 1937, pp. 74–78). It is helpful to keep in mind that neither White nor Williams is especially interested in communication; their points of view are marked by a concentration on meaning-situations, much like Cunningham's.

Nonetheless, their criticism is well taken. The "causal" explanation of sign-situations can be classified as associationism or as conditioned reflex; the choice turns upon whether one begins by considering engram or symbol. Neither of these approaches, however, explains how a perspective learns to use a symbol to stand for an object. The "contextual" explanation, on the other hand, offers further difficulties: here an external object is required in order to complete the reference, and one is led to believe that only denotative of a word is useful, or in some sense "true." This is the doctrine of positivism, in which the biography of the perspective is subordinated to a material context. Consequently, the intentional, purposive quality of communication is, by definition, beside the point. Finally, neither of these explanations makes any allowance for sign-situations, which are anything but verbal. In sum, the theory of interpretation offered by Ogden and Richards is not only confusing in its alternative possibilities, but is uninclusive.

Perhaps they wish the definition of meaning as "mental adaptation" to stand as their final word. This is nothing more than an interpretation of the theory of conditioned response. It may serve as a rough description of man's ability to communicate, but it throws little light upon the psychophysiological workings of the mind. Relatively little is known of the process of adaptation; Pavlov makes no claims to have explained it. (Both Vygotsky and Luria, whose work is later discussed in this book, undertake to extend some Pavlovian principles.) Moreover, there is a reasonable doubt that any psychology that deals exclusively with individual mental content can every account for meaning, a relational function that is essentially social, intersubjective, in origin. It is one matter to generalize individual habits and tendencies; it is quite a different matter to find a valid causal relation, within the individual, of symbolic habits that come about only by the participation of the individual in a group. As Bloomfield puts it:

> The solution of the problem of meaning will doubtless lie in the psychologist's study of substitute stimuli; under what conditions does the child, when learning to speak, first say *apple* in the absence of an apple? But here again the study will be largely social, for we may suspect that to a large extent the function of substitute stimuli is determined by social tradition (Bloomfield, 1927, p. 216).

Bloomfield's criticism is that the "Triangle of Reference," including as it does the second apex of "Thought," solves "with magic ease" the problem of *displaced speech*. He follows the behavioristic view that any theory of meaning that takes refuge in this apical term is unacceptable; "concepts" or "mental images" have no place in a scientific explanation of the use of words when the object to which they refer is not present, or when they refer to relations (that is "causality," "although," and the like). Bloomfield here represents the critical trend of early modern linguistic science.

The implication of this criticism is that Ogden and Richards do not satisfy their own denotative requirements in explaining their theory of interpretation. So far as the "Triangle of Reference" is concerned, there is no external, objective, publicly discriminable event for "thought" that can serve as a verifiable referent. *The Meaning of Meaning* pays no attention to the positivist's bugaboo, the intersubjectivity of reference. By the study of substitute stimuli, an explanation in causal terms may someday be forthcoming from social psychology.

If one puts these various criticisms together, only one inference is possible. So far as it furnishes a logical basis for a theory of meaning, the theory of interpretation in *The Meaning of Meaning* holds with the hare and runs with the hounds. It is internally hazy and externally tentative; the meaning of meaning as psychophysiological adaptation has not been forthcoming from the study of conditioned response. There is no doubt that important conclusions on the nature of substitute stimuli have been reached, nor that something is known of the physiology of the conditioned reflex, but experimenters have as yet made no claim to have discovered the essence of psychological adaptation. As one commentator has said, the conditioned response "even in its simplest form . . . is a very complex organismic phenomenon which is not to be interpreted as a penny-in-the-slot mechanical reaction" (Pollock, 1942, p. 29). It is unfortunate that throughout *The Meaning of Meaning* the authors oversimplify and lean upon the hope that psychological findings will eventually support their dogma. (Perhaps a fresher approach is being made in current thinking in terms of psycholinguistics, but this is far from the expectancies of 1923 regarding the conditioned response.)

CANONS OF SYMBOLISM

The causal theory of adaptation unquestionably has its uses, however. On the assumption that all meaningful communication is symbolic reference, with a clearly discernible objective (or external) context that furnishes the criterion of truth, Ogden and Richards develop a normative set of "canons of symbolism" that are sound rules for scientific discourse (Chapter 5). Perhaps the most important of these is the "Canon of Definition": "Symbols which can be substituted one for another symbolize the same reference." The chapter on definition is, in a way, the culmination of the thesis of *The Meaning of Meaning* (Chapter 6). It need not detain us long, for the suggested method of definition is implicit in the theory we have been considering.

Words are not things. When we define, we define words, not things. A true reference is completed by a psychological context that furnishes a link between a speaker and an external context (the objective referent). "A symbol refers to what it has actually been used to refer to." (This is the fourth canon.) Therefore, all that is necessary for definition is to find the referent. This is easy. "Find first . . . a set of referents which is certainly common to all concerned, about which agreement can be secured, and locate the required referent through its connection with these" (p. 113). In other words, begin with a publicly discriminable object. Then, since there are only a few relational categories with which men think, select the proper category (or combination of categories) that will relate the unknown referent to the known object. Granted that individual purposes and biographies differ radically, any referent can be brought to light so long as the starting point and the route of definition are known. "At what point our definitions are thorough enough must be left for the occasion to decide." This is truly a simple account of definition. It has been said before; it will be said again. In the meantime, disputes wax, conversations wane, there are at least two sides to every argument, some differences of opinion are not basically symbolic but evaluative, and men must be about the business of the world, which is not utopia. Ogden and Richards offer only another "operational" theory of definition.

A ONE-EYED VIEW

How do these theories of interpretation and definition—the causal, the demonstrative—relate to the distinction between referential and emotive uses of language? One would expect not only that these uses can be kept apart, but that the experimental findings on the conditioned response would support the dichotomy. Actually, neither of these expectations is realized. There are two questions involved here: how can emotions and attitudes be kept out of referential language, and how can reference be eliminated from expressive language? Ogden and Richards rule that the meaningful response must be that which is adapted to a context in some way public, external to the nervous system of the subject. Meaning, then, cannot reside in intention, for intention has much to do with affective-volitional processes. The authors discuss this point at some length, and specifically repudiate the intentional nature of meaning (pp. 191–196). Yet more recent work with the conditioned response indicates that affective-volitional processes are important in the causal chain upon which Ogden and Richards base their theory of interpretation.

G. H. S. Razran, reporting experiments with adults, finds that humans are less subject to unconditioning than are animals, that recollection may be more stimulating than an external context, and that "the attitude of the adult greatly affects conditioning" (Razran, 1935). It would seem that the causal chain of the psychological context is not simply conditioned response to external stimuli, but, as Korzybski puts it, condition*al* response—conditional upon the biographies of speaker and listener, and upon every feature of the communicative situation. Although little is known about the operation of substitute stimuli, enough is known of it to infer that it is by no means limited to a direct cognitive interpretation of objective data. This is recognized in *The Meaning of Meaning,* but it is consistently played down in favor of a theoretical divorce between cognition and affective-volitional response. Ogden and Richards treat with oversimplicity what they cannot dispose of by ad hoc definitions.

The former method obtains in their discussion of "Symbol Situations":

> A symbol as we have defined it symbolizes an act of reference; that is to say, among its causes in the speaker, *together no doubt with desires to*

record and communicate, and with attitudes assumed towards hearers,
are acts of referring. Thus a symbol becomes when uttered, in virtue of
being so caused, a sign to a hearer of an act of reference (p. 205, italics
mine).

This is confusing terminology; the extended definition of a symbol
scarcely serves to clarify its implications. If a typical act of reference
includes desires and attitudes—and Ogden and Richards never argue
against this inclusion—wherein comes the distinction "in principle"
between the one use of words that is clearly referential and the other
use that is only the projection of attitudes and desires? One is forced
to conclude that the authors' object is to define meaning as objective
reference, and thus reduce meaningful communication to operationism. If it is protested that they mean their distinction to apply only
generally, so be it. In that case, the classification becomes a mere
device, somewhat useful for initial purposes of analysis. Ogden and
Richards are not willing to evaluate their work so modestly, however;
they claim to have invented the organon of education. They insist
throughout their book that the conscious division between referential
and emotive uses of words must be absolute, that it is a scientific
abstraction from psychological findings. The truth is that psychology
does not support them; experimental work has made it plain that
attitudes and desires (internal psychological states) actually control or
negate external reference in many instances.

   This produces a curious state of affairs. There is much in *The
Meaning of Meaning* that is pertinent and searchingly thought out,
even though the ground has been covered many times by thinkers on
the nature of symbolism. One wonders why the authors feel it
necessary to insist upon their bifurcation of verbal usage. Perhaps, as
Pollock and others have suggested, the answer is that at the time they
were developing the theory for this first book, the writers had one eye
solidly fixed on the protocols of physical science and the other tightly
closed; their view led them to a positivist expression of the value of
training in the scientist's use of language. Fortunately or unfortunately, only a meager percentage of mankind is scientific in daily
habits of communication, or is ever likely to be. Many of the normative semanticists like to quote history, usually in despair, but do not
seem to believe it.

   Clearly the criticism here has thus far been directed mainly
against the exclusions from the symbolic, meaningful use of words—
not the inclusions. Ogden and Richards weight their theory at the
outset in favor of scientific statement. For the time being, let us

assume that their accounts of interpretation, definition, and meaning are satisfactory as explanations of scientific discourse, and turn our attention to their theory of the emotive use of words. The most pertinent question becomes whether reference is unimportant in purposive expression.

"What is certain," write the authors, "is that there is a common and important use of words which is different from the scientific or, as we shall call it, the strict symbolic use of words." This is the statement that bears the burden of argument in much of *The Meaning of Meaning,* and, as I interpret their theory, it stands or falls with this dichotomy. The division is made explicit:

> Under the symbolic function are included both the symbolization of reference and its communication to the listener, i.e., the causing in the listener of a similar reference. Under the emotive function are included both the expression of emotions, attitudes, moods, intentions, etc., in the speaker, and their communication, i.e., their evocation in the listener (p. 149).

However, Ogden and Richards no sooner say this than they find it necessary to insert a most important qualification:

> It is true that some element of reference probably enters, for all civilized adults at least, into almost all use of words, and it is always possible to import a reference, if it be only a reference to things in general. The two functions under consideration usually occur together but none the less they are in principle distinct (p. 150).

One has the feeling that one is being fed a monstrous fiction with this turn of words, for the statement begs the entire question of communication. "In principle" can only mean "by definition." By definition, the causal theory of interpretation and the demonstrative theory of definition support the initial assumption that only objective reference conveys meaning. Granted this assumption, the dichotomy between the uses of words is not an empirical analysis at all, but a normative, educational device that is evolved by fiat. The thesis that only referential language has meaning is simply tautological. Ogden and Richards do not proceed by a scientific method of setting up hypotheses to be tested by empirical data. What should be hypotheses turn out to be fundamental value judgments.

LANGUAGE IN LITERATURE

It cannot be that *The Meaning of Meaning* was written only to substantiate the point that scientific language is scientific. What about the use of language in literature? According to the rulings made on symbolic reference, literature cannot be significantly meaningful; the poetic or fictional use of words is too much concerned with "emotions, attitudes, moods, intentions, etc."

Pollock is pointed in his criticism of this emotive classification and its implications for literature:

> Some critics have found Richards' theory of literature something less than adequate, and I share this conclusion. But in view of the limiting assumptions with which his theory of the "emotive" use of language begins, it may well be considered a tribute to his understanding of literature that he has done as much with this classification as he has done (p. 150).

After discussing the limitation of the emotive use to the expression or excitation of feelings and attitudes, Pollock continues:

> Accepting such an assumption, the classification of the "emotive" use of language cannot logically include in any important way "reflective" or "intellectual" communication. Nor can it include the communication of "experience" in any inclusive sense: for "experience" in any inclusive sense contains in a more than subsidiary way reflective and intellectual activity, the Thought with a capital T, which according to this theory is the essential function of the "symbolic" use of language to communicate (p. 151).

As Pollock notes, Richards defines a poem in Chapter 30 of *The Principles of Literary Criticism* with no reference whatever to emotions or to emotive language; he refers only to "experience," a term he does not define. The obvious inference is that by "experience" Richards means "arousing attitudes," a quite limited sense of the word.

Perhaps a means of determining how reference might be excluded from literature can be found in Richards's discussion of emotions and attitudes. He asserts that he uses the term *emotion* in "what may perhaps be regarded now as the standard usage in psychology":

> Two main features characterize every emotional experience. One of these is a diffused reaction in the organs of the body brought about through the sympathetic systems. The other is a tendency to action of some definite kind of group of kinds . . . As a result of all these changes a tide of sensations of internal bodily origin comes into consciousness. It is generally agreed that these sensations make up at least the main part of the peculiar consciousness of an emotion (1938, p. 101).

Do they also make up the main part of the literary experience of poetry and drama? Evidently this is what Richards means, because he specifically differentiates and rules out the possibility of "aesthetic emotion."

Richards defines attitudes as "imaginal and incipient activities or tendencies to action." He says that they are not overt and that "the classification and analysis of attitudes is not yet far advanced." He writes:

> So far as a feeling or an emotion does refer to anything, it refers in the way described, through its origin. Feelings, in fact, are commonly signs, and the differences between those who 'see' things by intuition, or 'feel' them, and those who reason them out, is commonly only a difference between users of signs and users of symbols.
>
> Emotions are primarily signs of attitudes and owe their great prominence in the theory of art to this. For it is the attitudes evoked which are the all-important parts of any experience.

Emotions are signs of attitudes that, in turn, are covert tendencies to action. These are private responses, whereas the intellectual use of words depends upon adaptation to objective entities. One wonders how these observations help to substantiate the supposed fact that reference is not important in the evocation of attitudes. There must be some attribute of the mind that makes it possible for a referent to remain external while attitudes go their ways within the organism. J. C. Ransom has analyzed this phase of Richards's theory with care.

Ransom is particularly interested in examining how Richards can dispense with cognition in poetry. He writes:

> I venture to offer a little diagram of my own [Figure 2] to illustrate Richards' peculiar understanding of the immediate value of a poetic

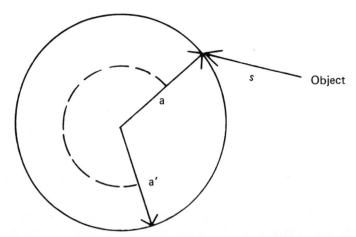

Figure 2.   Ransom diagrams Richards's theory in terms of attitude (*a*) and stimulus (*s*). The circle symbolically separates the objective from the private mental world.

experience in what it will do for an attitude. The circle represents the boundary that encloses the private mental (and bodily) world from the objective world. The arrow *a* represents an attitude, or organized conative impulse which looks outward, as if to invade the external world at the periphery and make use of it. . .

The stimulus is *s*, the cognition that we take of an object to which we are exposed (1941, pp. 27–28).

The cognition is only the *stimulus* of the emotions and attitudes, which, because of their minute and essentially mysterious character, Ransom appropriately calls "infra-psychological" entities. Referring to these entities, he continues:

Their independence of it [cognition], once they have started, is indicated in the diagram in that the cognition which comes from the object in the external world appears to be stopped at the boundary, where we will assume that it stays just long enough to pass its stimulus over the barrier; whereupon the attitude which has been stimulated starts upon business of its own, and moves about within the periphery till finally it takes up the position *a*, where it poses ready for stimulus from some other object. But the laws of the motion of the attitude within the periphery remain unknown to us (p. 29).

Ransom adds that this "reading of Richards could be documented rather copiously."

There can be little dispute with this interpretation of Richards's aesthetic as it appears in *The Principles of Literary Criticism*. He insists that poetry is the evocation of attitudes—an important but unintellectual activity. In a little book called *Science and Poetry* (1926), however, he describes poetic experience in different terms that seem to modify his earlier ideas. His thesis is that poetry alone can help people interpret the world and save them from chaos and confusion. That this represents a violent shift from Richards's views heretofore discussed is beside the point. Here the poetic experience is given a kind of chronological exposition. First occur "the sound of the words 'in the mind's ear' and the feel of the words imaginarily spoken." Then follow images "of the things for which the words stand"; these images are variable and are not present in everybody.

Thence onward the agitation which is the experience divides in a major and a minor branch, though the two streams have innumerable connections and influence one another intimately. Indeed, it is only as an expositor's artifice that we may speak of them as two streams (p. 18).

The minor branch is the intellectual stream. The major branch, the active or emotional stream, "is made up of the play of our interests."

The intellectual stream is easy to follow; it is less important and is only a means to direct and excite the active stream. "It is made up of thoughts, which are not static little entities that bob up into consciousness, and down again out of it, but fluent happenings, events, which refer or point to the things that thoughts are 'of'" (p. 19). "Our thoughts are pointers and it is the other, the active stream which deals with the things which thoughts point to." The active stream is directed toward our "organization of interests." Richards summarizes:

> This is the main plan of the poetic experience. Signs on the retina, taken up by sets of needs . . . thence an elaborate agitation and reorganization, one branch of which is *thoughts* of what the words mean, the other an emotional response leading to the development of *attitudes*, preparations, that is, for actions which may or may not take place; the two branches being in intimate connection (Richards, 1926, p. 20).

There is still a trace here of the infra-psychological convolutions diagrammed by Ransom, but, to the immediate point, Richards has succeeded in marrying the two uses of language better than any critical dialectic. Unless he is performing unprecedented tricks of diction, he is saying that cognition and conation play intimate roles in poetry, and, however much he may be anti-intellectual in his aesthetic, he manages to allow reference a meaningful place in poetry.

It is not the purpose of this study to search far into the thickets of aesthetic criticism; at most it is to examine the phases of Richards's aesthetic principles that throw particular light on his treatment of meaning. There is some information to be gained, however, from the views of other critics who have found his theory of the aesthetic use of language "something less than adequate."

Max Eastman is gracious about the contributions made by Richards, but believes that his psychology is wrongly based. Eastman interprets *The Meaning of Meaning* as a "logic for scientists" that would allow them to strip their use of words down to simple denotation. "But in order to do this they [Ogden and Richards] had to ignore the great part played by attitudes in the very constitution of 'things'. They had to imagine a distinction between the intellectual and the active phases of man's nature far sharper than does, or can possibly, exist" (1931, p. 207). Eastman suggests that "all of Mr. Richards' books may be described as brilliant effort to smuggle back into poetry its own essence which he has excluded by an initial error." He catches up Richards's explanation of the effect of meter in poetry. By definition, Richards classifies poetry as the evocation of attitudes. His comments on meter are generalized in the idea that meter induces something like a hypnoidal state in the reader that serves to heighten his emotional responses (1938, Chapter 17). Eastman finds this explanation out of accord with the facts of hypnosis and of metrical verse. Hypnosis induces not "emotionally," but an utter willingness to believe. This imposition upon the subject corresponds with the poet's technique, and accounts for the importance of meter in poetry. The poets "are not interested in evoking attitudes but in conveying experience;" this is best achieved when the "subject" is "in a receptive state."

A plausible generalization of the theory in *The Meaning of Meaning, The Principles of Literary Criticism,* and *Science and Poetry,* is that science is interpreted as pointing at things, with attitudes and emotional impulses held in abeyance, while poetry is interpreted as action toward things as a result of man's capacity to organize his impulses into strong attitudes, and thus "feel" the world of reality and the nature of things. Science is "knowingful," cognitive; poetry is "feelingful," conative. Richards's critics do not regret his obvious devotion to literature; they simply do not agree with his streamlined hypotheses. Eastman, for instance, takes strong exception to this theory:

> He is wrong in his conception of science as merely referring to things and *not interpreting them with a view to action.* And so he is wrong in his conception of poetry as essentially *not* referring to things but merely *interpreting them with a view to action.* He has got the whole thing exactly upside down, and nothing but a revolution can mend him (p. 312).

I suspect that Eastman could argue with Richards far into the night on this particular matter. It is hazardous at best to state in a phrase what either science or poetry does. Richards leaves himself open to such an attack, and in fact he invites it by his dogmatism and his tendency to "argue" by fiat. D. G. James, Ransom, Pollock, and Wilbur M. Urban—to name only a few—attack him on this same ground: the volitional character of much of the work of science.

On this aspect of Richards's theory, James writes:

> Building up his views on the misleading distinction between language used for reference and language used emotively, he has failed to realize the imaginative character of scientific construction. And therefore he has failed to see that the 'world-picture of science' is an imaginative construction, evolved with a view to the formulation of generalizations of strictest fact (1937, p. 70).

Ransom makes much the same point, and Pollock expands the description of the physical sciences.

This topic is worth pursuing for an understanding of the relations between cognitive and conative activities of the mind and thus of language in communication. Ogden and Richards never discuss fully the volitional implications of the pointer-readings of the physical sciences. The singularly meaningful referent looms so large in their theory of scientific discourse that they give the impression of failing, somehow, to do justice to the creative aspect of the scientific mind. It is generally agreed that much of scientific meaning is made exact by demonstration. The handling activities of the laboratory furnish the necessary referents in a clear-cut fashion. "Things" are at hand, and they contain properties determined by definition from pointer-readings. Yet in the theoretical activities of the physical sciences there appears to be ample room for the use of the imagination in apprehending highly abstract relationships that are far removed from "objects," "things," or external referents. This use is particularly important when a scientist is concerned with shaping hypotheses that will, in turn, mold his "world-picture" and thus direct his future exposition of demonstrable facts. When Einstein was at work on his concept of simultaneity, his mental processes assuredly included something more than the awareness of objects. A. S. Eddington drives home with amusing clarity the idea that the physical scientist is not at all concerned with "reality" (1930). The only "object" in the laboratory is an instrument for measuring events in time and space. Aside from the meanderings of the mentally incapacitated, the mathematical world of physical formulae is the only "unreal" world that we "know," and we "know" this world only because we build the instruments and define their readings in quantified terms.

Of course, Ogden and Richards are aware of all this. What they do not emphasize is the fact that the physical scientists make use of their pointer-readings (the referents of sense-data) to construct an imaginary "world-picture" unlike anything that the senses can apprehend. This is an act of the imagination in which conation is at least as important as cognition. True, as James makes clear in his criticism of Richards, the scientist is not interested in "resting, so to speak, in the imagination." He presses on "to the discovery of demonstrable fact." James takes considerable care in stating his understanding of scientific discourse, and offers a correction of some of Richards's positivist notions. James is interested in Coleridge's idea of the imagination as a creative prehension of the world. Quoting Russell, he observes that, strictly speaking, the physical sciences can record only sense-data, but goes on to remark that, inasmuch as the physical sciences are concerned with "demonstrable facts," the experimenters have to talk about various "objects" as though they exist (e.g., the atom, electron, proton). There is nothing essentially obscure about this. The scientific hypothesis is an imaginative construction. Whether or not the scientist thinks he is talking about "reality" when he refers to an atomic system is unimportant; "it remains true that he has gone beyond what 'sensations' have been given him by his experiments, and has grasped them imaginatively within an imagined whole" (James, p. 31). The use of hypothesis is implicit in experimental science, as it is in all creative thinking, and there is reason to believe that metaphysics has furnished considerable inspiration to the laboratories of physics and chemistry. (Ogden and Richards inveigh against metaphysics with typical positivism.) "The imagination, then, is an integral part of our experience," writes James. He concludes:

> It is the necessary condition of all perception, and is present in the simplest apprehension of the world; for it is that which in all experience, of whatever kind, gathers the limited and fragmentary data which are given to the senses into unity. It gives order to the data by transcending and unifying them into imagined wholes, which as such have no place in scientific knowledge; for scientific knowledge, proceeding by observation and experiment, has to do . . . only with sense-data (James, 1937, p. 33).

If one agrees with the general direction of this analysis, one must agree with Eastman that science is not only reference, and poetry is not only interpretation. One must also agree that Eastman's inversion of Richards's doctrine is equally at fault.

The center of confusion in this diversity of opinion seems to be the term *imagination*. In Chapter 32 of *The Principles of Literary Criticism*, Richards discusses the imagination, and offers several definitions of the term. He indicates that his fifth definition has to do with science:

> Next we have that kind of relevant connection of things ordinarily thought of as disparate which is exemplified in scientific imagination. This is an ordering of experience in definite ways and for a definite end or purpose, not necessarily deliberate and conscious, but limited to a given field of phenomena. The *technical* triumphs of the arts are instances of this kind of imagination. As with all ordering, value considerations are very likely to be implied, but the value may be limited or conditional.

Richards appears to believe there are many different senses of the same "thing," the imagination. That useful to science is simply a "kind of relevant connection of things ordinarily thought of as disparate." Here is a loose use of words, helpful, no doubt, to Richards's specific purpose in the chapter, but scarcely definitive. Perhaps electronic theory is only a "kind of relevant connection of things." These "things" are somewhat more obscure than the objects "ordinarily thought of," and the "thinking of them" appears to be a rather complex and highly inferential undertaking, governed by the imagination and conducted "with a view to action." Richards is apt to sidestep a question by definition, and he does it here. Somehow, the psychological theory in *The Principles of Literary Criticism* manages to cause the reader to concentrate upon the emotional-volitional phases of the mind, while the cognitive element is reserved for scientific statement. The trouble with dichotomizing is that sooner or later it gets one into difficulties, and Richards is in difficulty from the opening pages of the first of his books. The distinction of two uses of language may be serviceable as a crude analytical device, but when Richards makes it the thesis of a magisterial disquisition on the problem of meaning, he overshoots the mark. It is somewhat easier to uphold so far as scientific discourse is concerned, but in poetry it becomes incongruous. Richards's psychological explanation breaks down when he is faced with the need to describe the movements of an attitude independent of an object. Emotions by themselves are psychological fictions.

LANGUAGE

The difficulty of following Ogden and Richards is augmented by the confusion in their diction between the "uses" and the "functions" of language. These two terms are frequently interchanged, although in Chapter 10 of *The Meaning of Meaning,* on "Symbol Situations," the authors attempt to distinguish between them. Perhaps it is pertinent to comment that their dicta on the two uses of language is normative, while their derivation of the functions is descriptive. They make a distinction this way:

> Returning now to complexities in references and in their symbols, the attempt to trace correspondence leads to the adoptions of two distinct sets of considerations as guiding principles. With one of these, with the study of reference, we have here been throughout concerned. Symbolic form varies with variation of reference. But there are other causes for its variation . . . Besides symbolizing a reference, our words are also signs of emotions, attitudes, moods, the temper, interest or set of mind in which the references occur. They are signs in this fashion because they are

grouped with these attitudes and interests in certain looser and tighter contexts. Thus, in speaking a sentence we are giving rise to, as in hearing it we are confronted by, at least two sign-situations. One is interpreted from symbols to reference and so to referent; the other is interpreted from verbal signs to the attitude, mood, interest, purpose, desire, and so forth of the speaker, and thence to the situation, circumstances and conditions in which the utterance is made (p. 223).

This analysis appears to be reasonable; it could be interpreted to mean that the authors find cognitive and conative elements present in every speech situation. Of course, they do not mean that. Are words actually "signs" of emotions? One might suspect that a genuine emotional sign is a sigh, a grunt, or a groan. Such a sign is classified with our other nondistinctive speech activities—gestures, facial expressions, and intonations—or with what could be called secondary phonemes. One might suspect, furthermore, that the descriptive difficulty begins when Ogden and Richards refer to "two sign-situations." Why is there not only one, the composite speech situation, that includes the experience of the hearer in a total configuration? To deduce two situations is to make a violent abstraction from most speech processes, with the possible exception of the "strictly scientific." The authors continue their reference to two situations:

> The first of these is a symbol situation as this has been described above, the second is merely a verbal sign-situation like the sign-situations involved in all ordinary perception, weather predictions, etc. *Confusion between the two must be avoided, though they are often hard to distinguish.* Thus we may interpret from a symbol to a reference, and then take this reference as a sign of an attitude in the speaker, either the same or not the same as that to which we should interpret directly from his utterance as a verbal sign.
>   The ordering of verbal sign-situations is a large subject in which various branches may be distinguished. The following seem, together with strict symbolization, which it will be convenient to number as (1), to cover the main functions of language as a means of communication (pp. 223–224, italics mine).

Ogden and Richards then enumerate and describe briefly the other four functions. If we adopt their scheme of numbering the "symbolic" or "referential" function a (1), the list is as follows (pp. 224–227):

1. Symbolization of reference: that is, the symbol causes a thought of a referent
2. The expression of attitude to listener
3. The expression of attitude to referent

4. The promotion of effects intended: the speaker's intention to evoke action from the hearer (probably the fundamental function of communication)
5. Support of reference: ease the thought of the referent.

These five functions "appear to be exhaustive." However, there is a most important caveat: "Each of these non-symbolic functions may employ words either in a symbolic capacity, to attain the required end through the references produced in the listener, or in a non-symbolic capacity when the end is gained through the direct effect of the words." The two "uses" here become capacities, and the circle is complete. The authors' interpretation of the functions of language has some farreaching implications:

> If the reader will experiment with almost any sentence he will find that the divergence which it shows from a purely symbolic notation governed solely by the nature of the reference which it symbolizes, will be due to disturbing factors from one or more of the above four groups. Further, what appears to be the same difference will sometimes be due to one factor, at other times to another. In other words, the plasticity of speech material under symbolic conditions is less than the plasticity of human attitudes, ends and endeavours, i.e., of the affective-volitional system; and therefore the same modifications in language are required for quite different reasons and may be due to quite different causes. Hence the importance of considering the sentence in the paragraph, the paragraph in the chapter, and the chapter in the volume, if our interpretations are not to be misleading, and our analysis arbitrary (p. 226).

This is the usual warning to interpret from verbal context. Yet there is clear recognition that one's affective-volitional system is divorceable from one's cognitive system. The corollary must be that we feel because we are human, but our set of linguistic symbols should, properly, not be disturbed by our human frailties, desires, wants, and intentions.

The analysis of the five functions of language offered by Ogden and Richards is penetrating. Unfortunately, four-fifths of it is meaningless by definition; it must not be forgotten that only the first function, the "symbolic," directs thought to a referent and conveys meaning. Obviously, the two analysts are caught in a tangle of fictions when they make their step from the five functions to the two uses. Aside from the pointer-readings of science, and without excepting scientific statements that are not directly operational, all speech situations are constructed from all or most of these five functions. The functions are descriptive of the way speech works—through induction.

The two uses are fictions in which the verbal alchemy of the authors has led them to hypostatize four of the functions.

Some might think it unfair to have concentrated attention thus far upon the earlier works of Ogden and Richards; I am not aware, however, that either has disowned this early theory of the science of symbolism. Yet Richards is far less dogmatic in some of his later works. As a matter of fact, in *Practical Criticism* (1929), he uses a set of classifications that is quite inconsistent with those that have been under consideration. An important part of the critical apparatus of Richards's later theory is his transposition of the functions of language into Sense, Feeling, Tone, and Intention (pp. 179–188). Far from limiting meaning to Sense, which corresponds with the earlier "symbolic function," he here extends it to all four features of a communicative situation. "The all-important fact for the study of literature—or any other mode of communication—is that there are several kinds of meaning." Unless Richards has contravened two of his own "Canons of Symbolism," this statement is directly opposed to much of *The Meaning of Meaning.* One can only suspect that when writing the early book with Ogden he felt constrained to weight his theory in favor of scientific statement, and that he has been trying ever since to turn it in favor of, or at least meet halfway, the exigencies of literary statement and common speech.

He goes on to say in *Practical Criticism*:

> Whether we know and intend it or not, we are all jugglers when we converse, keeping the billard-balls in the air while we balance the cue on our nose. Whether we are active, as in speech or writing, or passive, as readers or listeners, the Total Meaning we are engaged with is, almost always, a blend, a combination of several contributory meanings of different types. Language—and pre-eminently language as it is used in poetry—has not one but several tasks to perform simultaneously, and we shall misconceive most of the difficulties of criticism unless we understand this point and take note of the difference between these functions. For our purpose here a division into four types of functions, four kinds of meaning, will suffice (Richards, 1929).

We set out to run down a lion, track him to his lair, and find a fox! Meaning is no longer the congitive specialization of reference; it is "total," complex. Ogden and Richards were severely critical of the philosophers whose perambulations with meaning they analyzed in their early work. (In Chapter 8 of *The Meaning of Meaning* the authors are ironical, at times bitter, in their treatment of the vagaries of "The Meaning of Philosophers".) Richards evidently determined later that his nice, "scientific definition of meaning would not do for nonscientific communication"—a none too startling discovery. Richards spent years after the initial work on the verbal analysis of poetry—his favorite pastime, and a pedagogical recreation at which he excels. Were he to have limited himself to the analysis of the "meaningless," "emotive" use of words that his early theory calls for, he could not have easily indulged his critical finesse. Richards, the critic, has severely modified the ideas of the earlier Richards, the dogmatist.

My peregrinations with Richards's theory of meaning are brought to a close with the theses of *Interpretation in Teaching*. It is his next to last book, and he makes some comments that should not be omitted from the record:

> Statements and the expression of attitudes are, of course, by no means so separate from one another as these writers [the members of his class whose protocols he is considering] (and scores of others with whom I could back them) seem to assume. Their close interconnections—which are usually blurred by such favourite terms as 'inspiration', 'spirit' and 'emotive' of which the last is the worst—I can illustrate (p. 160).

He does illustrate, quite adequately. At the end of *Interpretation in Teaching,* Richards expresses the hope that someday "the sometimes crude antithesis between Emotive and Scientific utterance" will be "translated into happier terms" (p. 393). *Requiescat in pace.* At long last author and critics are in agreement.

The revolution in Richards's thinking, predicted as a necessary one by Max Eastman, is not difficult to trace. He has always been interested in "context," and wrote and lectured extensively on the "interinanimation" of meanings. He pursues this subject in his *Philosophy of Rhetoric* (1936, the printed version of a series of six lectures delivered at Bryn Mawr), and inveighs against the "Doctrine of Good Usage." What has happened is that the "symbolic," "referential," "scientific," and "meaningful" use of words has been engulfed by the early theory of the "psychological context." Emphasis on the individual's adaptation to the symbol-situation necessitates a sense of meaning not limited to the "strictly scientific." It was noted that in *Practical Criticism* four of the functions of language become four categories of meaning, all interactive. It is only a short step to the "interinanimation of words," and for several years Richards talks mainly of "interpretation." This term is used in the early "causal" theory of signs, but, whereas *interpretation* (1923) is a causal-demonstrative theory, *interpretation* (1938) has more of the elements of humanism.

Enough has been said of meaning and context in *The Meaning of Meaning*. *The Principles of Literary Criticism* is concerned with the emotive use of words, and thus, in 1924, with an essentially meaningless use; *context* here retains its earlier significance. A thought is "'of' the missing part of the sign, or more strictly 'of' anything which would complete the sign as a cause" (p. 127). In *The Philosophy of Rhetoric*, a context is defined as "a name for a whole cluster of events that recur together" (p. 34); this is simply a nontechnical version of the conditioned response. Meaning is "delegated efficacy," and "what a word means is the missing parts of the contexts from which it draws its delegated efficacy." In Chapter 3, Richards develops the point of the "mutual dependence of words," and in the following chapter upholds the thesis that "a word by itself is meaningless." Meaning is the "delegated efficacy" of signs "by which they bring together into new unities the abstracts, or aspects, which are the missing parts of their various contexts." A word "is normally a substitute for (or means) not one discrete past impression but a combination of general aspects." The general import of this is that Richards has stopped anatomizing meaning and has concentrated his attention on how words work; or, to put it another way, he has come around to the view that, strictly speaking, a word does not have *a* meaning—it means.

This idea is given prominence in *Interpretation in Teaching:*

> If we recognized frankly that *how* any word whatsoever is used is a matter of choice, of invitation and consent, not of regimentation, conformity and compulsion, should we not *then* better understand how artificial are the imagined discrete senses of our words, how dependent they are on the meaning we give to the sentence. The more optative our view of definition, the more humane Logic becomes. On this view we can do as we please and the more we take any sentence as an invitation or request, to be considered on it merits, to be suffered or repelled—the more we civilize communications (p. 393).

Richards has mellowed. His view of science, too, has changed somewhat.

> So, all through the scale, the modes of utterance vary. Our meanings, not only in content but in modality, are in flux. Until recently, however, it would have been supposed that at least the indicative mood stood put! . . . Nowadays, very evidently in Science, the indicative rests on an optative basis and is indicative (over widening fields) only within operative consistencies. 'Let us think so, and go on still further thinking so, while we see what happens, that is what we have to compare today, have we not? with 'It is so.'

The generalization on meaning is summed up in one of Richards's later utterances to the effect that we "understand no word except in and through its interactions with other words." He states this idea fully.

A word, a question or its answer, does all that we do, since we do all that in the word. Words are alive as our other acts are alive—though apart from the minds which use them they are nothing but agitations of the air or stains on paper.

A word then by this sort of definition is a permanent set of possibilities of understanding, much as John Stuart Mill's table was a permanent possibility of sensation. And as the sensations the table yields depend on the angle you look from, the other things you see it with, the air, your glasses, your eyes and the light . . . so how a word is understood depends on the other words you heard it with, and the other frames you have heard it in, on the whole setting present and past in which it has developed as a part of your mind. But the interactions of words with one another and with other things are far more complex than can be paralleled from the case of the table—complex enough as those are. Indeed they are not paralleled anywhere except by such things as pictures, music or the expressions of faces which are other modes of language. Language, as understood, is the mind itself at work and these interactions of words are interdependencies of our own being (1942).

This is a broad view of meaning-in-action that is by no means new or unique. Perhaps it cannot too often be repeated.

OVERVIEW

In summarizing the cycle of Richards's theory of meaning, it may help to clear the air to refer once again to the statement in *The Meaning of Meaning* of the "practical problem" of the science of symbolism:

How far is our discussion itself distorted by habitual attitudes towards words, and lingering assumptions due to theories no longer openly held but still allowed to guide our practice? (p. 243)

Ogden and Richards wrote that "the chief of these assumptions derives from the magical theory of the name as part of the thing, the theory of an inherent connection between symbols and referents" (pp. 243–244). Their early answer to the avoidance of word-magic is a concentration upon the referential use of words, a concept of linguistic usage weighted in favor of scientific statement, that hardly meets the facts of the ordinary, daily use of language.

"How far is our discussion itself distorted?" This is a question-begging start in an investigation of a general theory of meaning, mainly because of the loaded character of the word *distorted*. The fact that Ogden and Richards begin here makes the normative quality of their theory in *The Meaning of Meaning*, and, to an equal extent, in Richards's *The Principles of Literary Criticism*, inevitable. The theorists take it for granted that discussion is distorted, thereby applying a set of values. This is useful provided their source is known. The source of values in this early book appears to be a special reading of the significance of the "scientific attitude," with its severe habit of objective statement. At this stage in their theory, Ogden and Richards do not look behind the referential statements of science to discover their volitional source, and thus give only a half-truth about the "scientific attitude." The foundations of the science of symbolism actually rest upon the general linguistic question: how do meanings come into being? The authors answer this question normatively and thus, too simply—"find the referent." They set out to improve some traditional empirical attitudes toward meaning, and create their ad hoc definitions of symbolism, reference, thought, and, inferentially, of meaning itself.

In their initial work Ogden and Richards miss the real point of investigation. They base their science upon the question of the confusion between words and things—a confusion with a long history, the problems of which philosophers have pondered since the *Cratylus*. They might better have based their science upon the investigation of the confusion between verbal and material issues, or, as James MacKaye puts it, upon a delineation of "definitive" and "material" propositions (pp. 39–40). The keenest, as well as the dullest, of minds are open to this confusion. As Ogden and Richards themselves point out, "Just as we say that the gardener mows the lawn when we know that it is the lawnmower which actually does the cutting, so, though we know the direct relations of symbols is with thought, we also say that symbols record events and communicate facts" (p. 9). We know that men do the recording and the communicating. We know, too, that a man's experience is a flowing continuum of events, attitudes, impressions, emotional responses, cognitions, conations, and the like—experience is social. There is much more to it than a simple operation of reference. The authors' failing is typical of the work of many earnest students; they must study their data according to the limits of their own definitions and terminology. Their definitions are not useful for every purpose. They frequently overreach themselves by making abstractions from total experience. The study of communication has fairly well established the fact that meaning is the total situation of speaker and hearer, and that anything further said about it is purely inferential, and will remain so until science can fully explain and describe every connection made in the mind. *The Meaning of Meaning* is far off the track of the facts that relate to the total situation of speaker and hearer.

Had Ogden and Richards put more emphasis upon the social aspects of meaning, they might have added many pertinent facts to their concept of reference. J. R. Kantor remarks, however, that they "seem to overlook entirely the influence upon thought of cultural institutions of all sorts . . . It is really here rather than in the individual causal connection of ideas or language and things that words have acquired their symbolic and referential character (1924, pp. 216–217). This is the serious omission to which C. W. Morris alludes when he writes, in *The Foundations of the Theory of Signs,* that many investigators of meaning have confused or slighted the various "dimensions of semiotic," one of which is the word-thing relationship. Ogden and Richards pay little attention to what Morris calls "pragmatics"—the facts about the users of a language that underlie its entire structure. (Nor has Richards ever emphasized its importance.) The theory of the sociology of knowledge, summerized below, focuses attention sharply upon this phase of language, and promises some useful information. With the inductive approach of "pragmatics" and the sociology of knowledge, the evil influence of words becomes a relatively minor issue, a by-product—simply a set of facts to be noted and put with many other facts concerning verbal intercourse. The lack of consideration of the history of language, of the way people learn words and actually employ them, is the outstanding weakness of many modern theories of semantics. It is evident in the writings of Ogden and Richards.

It is true that in later years Richards appears to have modified his earlier position. Yet, as late as 1940, in the introduction to Walpole's *Semantics,* he says in effect that semantics would guard us against misunderstanding the "great words." He has not yet been able to adopt a scientific attitude towards investigating the use of words; he continues to be less concerned with discovering facts than with stressing values. So it is that Richards, with many other semanticists, shows more devotion to formative than to informative education in verbal usage. True, he repeatedly says he wants the facts of the inadequate use of language brought to light, and, in *Interpretation in Teaching,* claims that the primary need of our students is "practice in examining misinterpretation." However, the overall context of his writings is the predilection that the world will be a better place as a result of this semantic training. His is not quite the technological ideal envisioned by Korzybski, but it is closely related.

So much for one basic theory of the use of words. It has been made sufficiently clear, I hope, that Richards later employed this theory only indirectly, if at all. He became more interested in the problems of literary interpretation, and in working out devices for the classroom whereby a much revised version of the ancient Trivium is given the principal place in the curriculum. In this system, as of old, Rhetoric is the organon, but Rhetoric for Richards "should be a study of misunderstanding and its remedies." He writes regretfully of "our hourly losses in communication." He attacks the traditional masters of rhetoric—Whately is a particular mark—on the ground that they do not explain how words work in discourse (Chapter 1). Rhetoric, the study of misinterpretation, needs help, however, from grammar, which is "for *our* purposes, nothing but the study of the cooperation of words with one another in their contexts." The rhetorical "exercise in comparisons" directs the student's attention to the metaphorical basis of communication, and, as he learns to discover the grammatical "co-operation of words with one another," he enters the realm of logic that "for our purposes, is just a more thorough inquiry" about the translations of figures of speech into relatively nonfigurative language. Richards's logic—the protracted analysis of the implications of a statement—is fairly closely connected with that of the Cambridge School. He is eager to teach his students a kind of logic that is readily available to the man in the street.

It is beyond the scope of this study to examine these ideas. In passing, however, one may observe that Richards's attack on the traditional rhetoricians is, as most of his attacks are, more dogmatic than accurate. Perhaps it is a matter of emphasis. The ancient rhetoricians and most of the "moderns," from Bacon on, consider rhetoric and the use of language in terms quite as functional as Richards's. Above all, unlike Richards, most of them were much concerned with "pragmatics," with the technique of discourse as it related to the ethics and politics of speakers and hearers. The best of them understood quite well "the influence upon thought of cultural institutions of all sorts," and concentrated upon the use of this understanding to teach those less well informed.

The development of Richards's theory of discourse is an interesting study. Insofar as his work has focused the attention of the twentieth century upon problems and values that have ever needed attention, he has made a decidedly worthwhile contribution. A comparison of his theory of the late 1930s with that of the early 1920s indicates a healthy growth, and one may well agree with one of his discerning comments:

Language, with its inexhaustible duplications (which here are duplicities), ceaselessly presents to us the old as though it were new, familiar ideas in novel disguises, understood distinctions as fresh opportunities for confusion, already assimilated combinations as unforeseeable conjunctions (1938, p. 4).

There are semanticists who do not believe this, who frame their theories upon a divorce from the ideas of the past. Count Alfred Korzybski is such a theorist. Predicated as it is upon tenets of radical positivism, his system of General Semantics is offered as a new science. In many ways Korzybski's analyses of world events and world problems are at one with the views implicit in *The Meaning of Meaning*. General Semantics has enjoyed sufficient stature, however, to be treated as an independent system. It is still one of the most influential of modern theories of meaning.

REFERENCES

Bloomfield, L. "On Recent Work in General Semantics. Modern Philology (1927) 25: 211–230.
———. Language. New York: Henry Holt, 1933.
Eastman, M. The Literary Mind. New York: Scribner's, 1931.
Eddington, A. S. The Nature of the Physical World. New York: Macmillan, 1930.
James, D. G. Scepticism and Poetry: An Essay on the Poetic Imagination. London: Allen and Unwin, 1937.
Kantor, J. R. "Review of the Meaning of Meaning." Journal of Philosophy, (1924) 31: 212–219.
MacKaye, J. The Logic of Language. Hanover: Dartmouth College Publications, 1939.
Ogden, C. K. and Richards, I. A. The Meaning of Meaning. 5th rev. ed. New York: Harcourt Brace, 1938.
Pollock, T. C. The Nature of Literature: Its Relation to Science, Language and Human Experience. Princeton: Princeton University Press, 1942.
Ransom, J. C. 1939. Yale Review, XXVIII.
———. The New Criticism. Norfolk: New Directions, 1941.
Razran, G. H. S. "Conditioned Responses: An Experimental Study and a Theoretical Analysis." Archives of Psychology. Columbia University. New York.
Richards, I. A. Science and Poetry. (K. Paul, Trench, Trubner) New York: W. W. Norton, 1926.
———. The Principles of Literary Criticism. New York: Harcourt Brace Jovanovich, 1926.

――――. Practical Criticism. (K. Paul, Trench, Trubner) New York: Harcourt Brace Jovanovich, 1929.

――――. The Philosophy of Rhetoric. New York: Oxford University Press, 1936.

――――. Interpretation in Teaching. (Harcourt Brace Jovanovich) London: Routledge & Kegan Paul, Ltd., 1938.

――――. "The Interactions of Words." In The Language of Poetry, edited by A. Tate Princeton: Princeton University Press, 1942.

White, C. W. "Meaning and Instrumentalism." Ph.D. dissertation, University of Cornell, 1933.

Williams, M. H. "A Study of Meaning." Ph.D. dissertation, Cornell University, 1937.

Chapter 5
GENERAL SEMANTICS
Alfred Korzybski

Late in 1933, an arresting title was added to the sagging shelf of modern works on meaning—Count Alfred Korzybski's *Science and Sanity, An Introduction to Non-Aristotelian Systems and General Semantics.* This is the bible of the then newest, most radical, and possibly most striking of available semantic doctrines. Under the banner of General Semantics, as this system is called, Korzybski enlisted a cosmopolitan assortment of people ranging from established members of town and gown to perennial malcontents and protestants. In the forty-odd years since the initial celebration, things have quieted down. Without doubt World War II had something to do with that. In the meantime, some of the good in the effort remains. Other claims and statements have been foregone. This chapter examines the more important ones.

MAN THE TIME-BINDER

Even before the publication of *Science and Sanity,* Korzybski was not entirely unknown among the speculators on man and his destiny. He made some impression, at least upon a small group of people, with his *Manhood of Humanity* (1921); in succeeding years he lectured and wrote occasional articles on various aspects of his central interest— man as the *time-binder.* These earlier writings and lectures form the foundation upon which the principles of General Semantics are built.

The Manhood of Humanity (1921) presents the mild thesis that man, because he can know the past through his highly developed use of symbolism, is different from other mammals and therefore must be thought of differently. Animals are only space-binding. They have a crude freedom of movement, but no more—each generation must learn anew. Man, however, is time-binding. He inherits a storehouse of human experience that gives him the opportunity to develop order, to acquire knowledge for his own survival. Man, among all living organisms, can progress. Unfortunately, asserts Korzybski, man does not take advantage of his symbolic powers. Failing to recognize that the structure of his language is an inheritance from prescientific times, he fails to recognize the world structure demonstrated by modern science. His potentialities for survival and sanity are vitiated. His language, and therefore his thinking, includes mythical constructions and the word-magic of yore. He continues to tolerate a world of wars, internal strife, misunderstanding, false values, and inefficiency. His antiquated linguistic habits falsify the facts of the modern world. He forfeits his time-binding capacity; "he copies animals." Not until man learns to reconstruct his linguistic habits according to the scientifically revealed structure of the world can he expect to found a sane, safe, balanced, progressive, and enduring community. *Science and Sanity* undertakes to introduce the process of rehabilitation.

Here, then, is not simply a modest appraisal of humanity, but a "science of man." Like Ogden and Richards, Korzybski finds that the seat of man's troubles is the blind use of word-magic. Unlike them, however, he does not stop with the proposal of a science of symbolism—he must have more scope. Man himself—not a few of man's habits, important though they may be—is the subject of this new science. This is a fairly extensive undertaking with some messianic overtones. It is unified by the belief that man's behavior depends, directly or indirectly, upon his semantic habits.

Korzybski long enjoyed a measure of popularity, and became accustomed to a retinue. Inspired by his insights, his followers in the depressed years after World War I formed organizations called Time-Binding Clubs. Their replacements flocked to the First American Congress for General Semantics in 1935, and to the second in 1941. This magnetism was probably not a feature of the man, but of the ideas to which he was devoted. It is worth mentioning here only to emphasize what is no doubt obvious: there is a strong tendency among those who are familiar with Korzybski's work either to accept him as a prophet or to dismiss him as a zealot. Both attitudes have been clearly expressed in various forms of opinion.

A few more biographical details might help to suggest Korzybski's point of view. He was trained as an engineer and was with the Russian army in World War I. Struck by the fact that an engineer's predictions, calculated in mathematical relations, usually resulted in a sound, useful, technological structure, he pondered over mankind's failure in general to predict accurately enough to build enduring, beneficial institutions. Mathematics seemed to him to represent man's greatest thinking achievement. Ordinary language, through which man institutionalizes, lacks what mathematics has—a relational structure that fits the facts of the world. *The Manhood of Humanity* was the outcome of this train of thought. For the next twelve years Korzybski studied mathematics (its foundations and history), general science, physics, physico-mathematics, logic, psychology, physiology, anthropology, psychiatry, linguistics, colloidal chemistry, neurology, and some other related fields of knowledge. Materials from all the nooks and crannies of this inquiry were assayed in the composition of *Science and Sanity,* and were offered to point the way "not to panaceas, but to suggestions toward an expedient, constructive, and unified scientific program whereby future disasters may be avoided or lessened" (p. 561).

Here is a magnificent conception—a science of man, truly a "first philosophy." The present essay does not probe deeply into multifarious problems raised in Korzybski's work. He has had many congenial interpreters whose opinions have been consulted for this presentation, but none, so far as I am aware, have attempted a genuine appraisal. (Three useful synopses were written by men who later attached themselves to the Institute of General Semantics, Chicago. These are J. C. Trainor, social psychologist; D. G. Campbell, psychiatrist; and C. J. Keyser, mathematician. Also helpful is H. Baugh, editor of *General Semantics,* a report of the First American Congress on the topic.)

A glance through *Science and Sanity* should serve as an incentive to welcome some interpretative aid. Composed of three books comprising ten parts, 41 chapters, and three supplements, it is a ponderous tome, badly organized, confused and confusing in diction and cross-reference. The reader might well be impressed with the fact that *Science and Sanity* is only an introduction to General Semantics. Short of another book like it, there can be no complete treatment of Korzybski's interests. I shall be satisfied to have sketched an outline of his principles.

THE SYSTEM OF GENERAL SEMANTICS

Science and Sanity offers a system of metaphysics, epistemology, scientific method, and language to end the pursuits of all future speculations. Korzybski's primary concern is to build a system of symbolism enabling human evaluations to be better adapted to the survival of the race. His interpretation of time-binding is a version of the idea of progress. His perspective is based upon a radical scientific acceptance of the universe. Neither philosopher nor scientist, he is public relations counsel for a universal technology. Korzybski does not claim novelty. There is probably not a single new idea in his system. That General Semantics is like, and yet transcends, other world views of a technological utopia is, doubtless, a feature of the times and of the author's persistent spirit.

Keyser offers a succinct summation of Korzybski's concepts:

> The general science of *human semantics* must have for its subject-matter the entire range and body of significant reactions or responses of the human organism to the countless kinds of stimuli, internal or external, verbal or non-verbal, that play upon it at any stage of its life from the first to the last. It is, in a word, the science of significant behavior (1938, p. 30).

A partial list of Korzybski's theses, postulates, and assertions furnishes some clues to this subject-matter. Among the working ideas of the system are (Chapter 1, 7, Supplement 3):

1. The world is composed of absolute individuals.
2. There are no objects in isolation.
3. Knowledge is reducible to, and therefore must be founded upon, several undefined terms—order, relation, structure, difference and function. Of these, the first three are the most important, structure being the fundamental "state" of knowledge.
4. The world is a dynamic process of events, to be comprehended only by means of the five undefined terms.
5. The acceptance as axiomatic of the findings of experimental science of a given date leads to
   a. The non-identification of words with things.
   b. The multi-valued logic of probability.
   c. Non-elementalism in language, that is, the avoidance of splitting organismic relationships, instead of elementalism "as exemplified by the assumed sharp division of 'senses' *and* 'mind', 'percept' *and* 'concept', 'emotions' *and* 'intellect'."
   d. A theory of definition based upon undefined terms and the use of extensional instead of intensional methods.
   e. The absolute individuality of events on the nonverbal object levels of apprehension (macroscopic, microscopic or submicroscopic).

6. The behavior of the human organism as a whole.
7. A theory of meaning based upon non-identification, extensional definition, the absence of universality, and the conditionality of all conclusions; its most essential feature is consciousness of abstracting.

This list is incomplete, but it is probably sufficient.

Korzybski's rejections are no less significant. He opposes the use of: subject-predicate, two-valued logic; the *is* of identity (so often confused with the predictive copula); elementalism; the theory of definition that disregards undefined terms; three-dimensional propositions; intensional aspects of meaning; the "additive" definition of man as an animal. He generalizes these ideas, among others, as "postulates" of the "Aristotelian system," and finds implicit in their use the word-magic that clutters up language and thought (same references).

A close account of these various theses of *Science and Sanity* is difficult to assemble. In broad terms, a description of Korzybski's perspective runs something like this. The survival of humanity depends upon the best use of its potential intelligence. The aim of humanity is sanity. Sanity is gained only from regular, ceaseless adjustments between people and their total environment. Correct adjustments are impossible, however, unless a person—considered always as an absolute individual acting as a total organism—conforms to his natural neurological structure, the description of which is possible only by science. Thus, the pursuit of sanity depends upon the services of science, because it is only science that has for its purpose the apprehension of the structure of the world in all orders and relations—structure, indeed, being the sole content of knowledge. The main tool of science is, of course, language, which to be scientifically effective, in terms of experimental accuracy and therefore of sanity, must be similar to the structure of the world. That is to say, it is only mathematics, the linguistic medium of experimental physical science, that at any given date is a structurally perfect language. Deeply imbedded in all natural languages are vestiges of primitive concepts, beliefs, convictions, misapprehensions, and superstitions. Their structure makes it impossible to use the known facts of the world; natural languages are illusive. It is notable that all recent advancements in the natural sciences and in mathematics have been achieved only through (in operational terms) a revision of the language of science, that places less emphasis on natural languages with their ingrained primitivisms. In sum, the goal of sanity is achievable only if language is so transformed and reconstructed as to throw out its primitive mythologies and metaphysics. Only mathematics has done this, and mathematics stands as man's greatest time-binding accomplishment; only here have man's symbolic potentialities conformed to his natural neurological structure.

The central problem of man's lack of sanity, the problem met and answered in General Semantics, is that:

> Our everyday forms of verbalization represent an extraneural storehouse of human experience which survives the death of individual nervous systems which have in their turn drawn upon it and contributed to it. Obviously, however, this storehouse of structural assumptions, language, does not represent, in the main, current structural abstractions . . . but rather the primitive archaic, macroscopic, prescientific sense abstractions such as those made by contemporary primitive peoples. This is a language of 'animalism' because of its lack of awareness that sensations, objects and symbols are nervous constructs of different *orders of abstraction,* projected on the outside world. Primitive and infantile people are forced, by the structural assumptions of such a linguistic, time-binding mechanism to live, as it were, in a demonological world consisting of objectified sense-abstractions, emotions, thoughts and symbols (words) (Campbell, 1937, p. 802).

There are a good many assumptions implicit in this statement of the problem and the answer in General Semantics. Obviously, Korzybski's perspective finds a major sanction in neurology. Without the belief that modern neurology has both a consistent method and a sound content, the fundamental thesis that man has a natural neurological structure, and therefore a knowable semantic structure, is simply indefensible. The critic is free to question whether neurology has advanced quite so far. Like Ogden and Richards in their early writing, Korzybski assumes that the sciences having to do with brain and mind are comparable with the natural sciences in methods, structure, and conclusions. When one regards the psychiatric study of "unnatural" behavior, upon which much of Korzybski's work is based, one is left even more dubious of methods and objectives. I believe it was Dr. Henry Head, an eminent British authority on neurological disorders, who warned that the negative findings from case studies of mental disability must never be translated into positive principles. The reason for this warning is fairly evident: there exists only a *legal* definition of sanity. So far as the mental sciences are concerned, *sanity* is a verbal football, or, at best, the fundamental, undefined term of much clinical activity.

Nowhere in *Science and Sanity* does Korzybski offer a comprehensive definition of sanity, either extensional or intensional.

Yet it may be that the whole book should be considered as a definition of this term. In the section entitled "Notes and References," one finds "general sanity" called "the elimination of delusional worlds" (p. 763). As Richards suggests, all definitions are ad hoc. Assuming that Korzybski's book is a definition of sanity, it is both ad hoc and circular. His reasoning appears to have this form: a man is sane if his linguistic habits correspond by definition with the structure of the world, this structure, in turn, is known only by the science of most recent date, because the language of science must correspond with the neurological structure of the scientists, who are, accordingly, sane. If one is struck by the naiveté of this kind of reasoning, so be it. So far as I can determine, this "definition" of sanity rests at the core of Korzybski's perspective; it is the rationale of his fundamental thesis of mathematicism.

This has not been a digression, because Campbell's statement of the problem to be answered centers around the idea that there is an "extra-neural storehouse of human experience" that is incompatible with the mathematical demonstrations of science. The fallacy of this statement seems to lie in the Scholastic quality of Campbell's thinking. The Scholasts set up the array of knowledge as a scala perfectionis, the top rung of which was theology. General Semantics, too, presupposes a perfect ladder, topped not by theology but by science. Somehow, natural languages have plodded their delusioned way, ever static, diffusing a primitive logic based on word-magic. Mathematics, the language of science, is seemingly unadditive. It burst upon the twentieth century like Athena from Zeus' brain, man's perfect creation. In truth, the fundamental principles of General Semantics are like the doctrines of theology held in the Middle Ages—perhaps appropriate for their time but stultifying for the "modern" mind (Myers, 1942). This topic is developed below. For the time being, some of Korzybski's theses need more detailed treatment.

Wendell Johnson offers a useful tabulation of the particular objectives of General Semantics in a monograph used as an outline for a course in language and speech hygiene (1939, pp. 37–38).

1. To make clear that the cause of many human disorders, of much discord and "unsanity" lie in man's "unnatural" ideas about, and misuses of, meanings in language.
2. To abolish the following symptoms of these disorders:
    a. Identifications between words and objects—("I hate him; he's a Red!").

    b. Allness—("Everybody knows it is true!" "Of course apples are good to eat!").

    c. Hypertonicity.

    d. Undelayed reactions—jumping to conclusions.

3. To stress the primary need for consciousness of abstracting, so that

    a. Necessary re-evaluations of linguistic usage may be made.

    b. Adequate methods of evaluating language can be used consistently.

4. To urge that man make his sanity possible by following the principles of

    a. Extensional definition and orientation, that is, by denotation instead of connotation.

    b. Uncertainty—"allness" probably does not exist in fact and so should not be "used" in words.

    c. Optimal tonicity.

    d. Conditionality, the "if" of conclusions, as scientific "conclusions" are tentative.

5. In summation, man must employ the general scientific method in relating his language and the events of the world: observation with suspended judgment in a calm manner with readiness to alter ideas and reactions; observation of direct experience, then description, then inferences, then observation and direct experience again to check inferences, etc., as a continuous process.

If these are the objectives of General Semantics, and they seem to be, one can have little quarrel with Korzybski's vision. In fact, one can never quarrel with the objectives of utopia—one can only believe or doubt that they are attainable. How does Korzybski propose to attain them?

Science and Sanity presents an outline of the science of man, "necessitating," writes Korzybski, "a modern, scientific, *functional, non-elementalistic, sharp definition* of man," to the effect that "man differs from animals in the capacity of each human generation to begin where the former generation left off" (pp. 538–539). In dealing with ourselves and the world around us, we must take into account the structural fact that everything in this world is strictly interrelated with everything else, and so we must make efforts to discard primitive *el* [elementalistic] terms which imply structurally a nonexisting isolation (p. 108). Man can never be sane until he gets his language out of the slough of ancient linguistic structure and primitive metaphysics.

The initial attack is directed against the nonscientific language of the world. This language, together with the "Aristotelian" thinking in which it is used, differs

> entirely in structure from the well-known and established 1933 structure of the world, ourselves and our nervous systems included. Such antiquated map-language, by necessity, must lead us to semantic disasters, as it imposes and reflects its unnatural structure on the structure of our doctrines and institutions. Obviously, under such linguistic conditions, a science of man was impossible; differing in structure from our nervous system, such a language must also disorganize the functioning of the latter and lead us away from sanity (p. 59).

This statement is the basis for Campbell's explanation given above. Somehow our natural language, which is evidently a product of our nervous systems, is unnatural to those nervous systems. "Natural" assumes a terrific burden of significance in these Korzybskian polemics.

Although his principle of "non-identification" seems too simple to serve as the fulcrum with which he raises his thesis of time-binding —an idea reminiscent of Erskine's insistence on "our moral obligation to be intelligent"—this is precisely the effect of Korzybski's thinking. "Say whatever you choose about the object, and whatever you might say is not it" (p. 35). On the basis of this negative, "un-Aristotelian" truism, the system of General Semantics is constructed. The healthful operation of man's time-binding abilities essentially depends upon his realization of the truth of word-fact relationships. The basic observation about objects is that they are not objects at all but events, describable only as processes, never as static entities. This doctrine might be called physical monism: any commonsense distinction between mind and object, individual and environment, internal and external, is nonsense, or at best reflects primitive, elemental word-magic. Ordinary perceptions of a table are crude, inaccurate; there is no worthwhile "perception" of a table except that of science, which "sees" not an entity but an event. The importance of ordinary objects like food, or air, or a chair, is found in the physicochemical effects that result from eating, from breathing, and from resting on a chair, and so "... these hidden characteristics, revealed only by science, appear much more important than the gross characteristics manufactured by our nervous systems which we recognize as an object" (p. 479). (The question how men managed to eat, breathe, and sit before the enunciation of quantum mechanics, is, of course, merely a superstitious inquiry.) These two concepts, the non-identification of words with things and the eventual nature of process, are the major-domos of the house of General Semantics. Korzybski protests that his denial of identity is not new. However, identification persistently seeps into thinking, an Eleatic forebear of our "Aristotelian" system. "Identification" is the first law of thought in traditional logic, and so long as it remains, man shall possess habits of thinking that are inimical to the known facts of the modern structure of the world; thus man can never use language properly and become fully sane.

"Proper" use of language depends upon correct apprehension of the content of knowledge. There can be nothing that is unknowable; the concept of knowledge that includes something beyond what is knowable is untenable. The paradox is resolved if one realizes that the only possible content of knowledge is structure—which is interaction in terms of order, relations, function, and difference, among events (pp. 101–110). This seems to follow from the assumption of the absolute uniqueness of events. Here we find the modus operandi of Korzybski's system:

> As words *are not* the objects they represent, *structure, and structure alone,* becomes the only link which connects our verbal processes with the empirical data. To achieve adjustment and sanity and the conditions which follow from them, we must study structural characteristics of this world *first,* and, then only, build languages of similar structure, instead of habitually ascribing to the world the primitive structure of our language. All our doctrines, institutions . . . depend on verbal arguments. If these arguments are conducted in a language of wrong and unnatural structure, our doctrines and institutions must reflect that linguistic structure and so become unnatural, and inevitably lead to disasters (p. 59).

On this hypothesis, the last spike of mathematicism is driven home. Korzybski makes his point with typical ingenuousness:

> That languages, as such, all have some structure or other is a new and, perhaps, unexpected notion. Moreover, every language having a structure, by the very nature of language, reflects in its own structure that of the world as assumed by those who evolved the language. In other words, we read unconsciously into the world the structure of the language we use. The guessing and ascribing of a fanciful, mostly primitive-assumed, structure to the world is precisely what 'philosophy' and 'metaphysics' do. The empirical search for world-structure and the building of new languages (theories) of necessary, or similar, structure, is, on the contrary, what science does. Any one who will reflect upon these structural peculiarities of language cannot miss the semantic point that the scientific method uses the only correct language-method. It develops in the *natural order,* while metaphysics of every description uses the reversed, and ultimately a pathological, order (pp. 59–60).

One might be led to suppose from this reasoning that a physical scientist has no use for natural language. Korzybski gives the impression that his scientist goes through life mumbling complex formulas. He probably does not mean this, but it follows from his unequivocal views about mathematics as a language different in structure from natural language.

Perhaps enough has been presented to make Korzybski's perspective fully evident. Two propositions are involved, one of fact and one of value, one or both of which may be affirmed or denied. As to the first, relating to the history of mathematics, there is probably little question. In discussing the service of mathematics to the Greeks and its utility to science ever since, Dewey has pointed out that scientists in ancient days needed a symbolic medium of pure form. Without such an unworldly system for calculating, they could not attain perfect correlations in their findings (1930, p. 254). Mathematics has been so used by science ever since. As to the second proposition, relating to the transcendency of mathematics, there is no matter for argument; one can only assert from what, in Cunningham's terms, is to him a more encompassing perspective. Korzybski's absolute faith in the priority of mathematics can be understood, but, as with any faith, it cannot be refuted; it is an act of will. On the face of it, Korzybski's view seems no different from that of the Pythagorean mystics who were devoted to a religion of numbers. Myers puts it:

> The Pythagorean theory . . . maintains that only objects reduced to mathematical proportions have real significance. Numbers are essences, and numerical relations are the only trustworthy relations. The objects of other perspectives are ore as yet unpurified; in them essences are hidden by the sensuous cloak of error (Myers, 1942, pp. 15–34).

Not a scientist himself, Korzybski apparently labors under two misapprehensions—one as to the nature of language, the other as to the nature of a scientific event. He has discovered that any language has a structure, but he has evidently not yet learned that mathematics and symbolic logic are only special uses of natural language. Initially and finally, both must be related to some "ordinary" language if they are to be comprehended. Leonard Bloomfield discusses the structure and relations of our various languages in a monograph with which Pythagoreans should acquaint themselves. He writes in his summary:

> Specialized uses of language involve no great alterations of structure; the specialization consists rather in the way that language is applied. Thus, the study of literature requires that we investigate the institutions and traditions of the community and the psychology (physiology, social

status, biography) of the creative individual. In connection with science, language is specialized in the direction of forms which successfully communicate handling responses and lend themselves to elaborate reshaping (calculation). To invent and employ these forms to carry on mathematics. The critique and theory of scientific speech is the task of logic (Bloomfield, 1939, p. 55).

Scientific language is not limited to the mathematics of physical theory, nor is it structurally different from a natural language. Several sciences, linguistics among them, make very little use of numbers. Korzybski's mathematicism hypostatizes a useful kind of language that works exclusively with substitute signs, and that supersedes the whole of which it is only an economic part.

This, however, is only half the story. The most obvious flaw in Korzybski's statement on the epistemological priority of physical science is its circularity. Only science can know the truth of events, because the scientist uses language, or develops language, that is especially designed to apprehend the truth of events; this language is mathematics, therefore only mathematics can demonstrate the facts of the world. What is the nature of these events, these scientific facts that are the realities of existence? Korzybski's repeated assertion that only science discovers and interprets the facts of the world is at stake here.

Reference is made above to Dewey's observation on the unreality (that is, the purely formal nature) of mathematics. On the theory of mathematical demonstrations of world structure, Max Planck offers some supporting evidence (1934, pp. 350–351). This eminent physicist discusses his redefinition of the term *event*, and uses it, on a deterministic basis, to enable him to predict:

> It is not to one single actual measurement, always containing causal and unessential elements, that the theoretical physicist gives the name of event. He reserves this name to an imagined process, going on in another world: we will call it the "physical world-picture," which is substituted for the actual one given by our senses and by measuring instruments acting as a kind of refined sense. The physical world-picture is a mental construction, arbitrary to a certain extent; an idealization, created for the purpose of escaping from the uncertainty which inheres in every individual measurement, and of becoming able to establish sharply defined conceptual relations.
>
> In physics, therefore, all measurable quantities—lengths, intervals of time, masses, charges, and the rest—have a double meaning, according as to whether we consider them as given directly by measurement or as transferred into the physical world-picture. In the first meaning such quantities can only be defined inaccurately, and can therefore never be

represented by precise numbers. But in the physical world-picture they stand for definite mathematical symbols, which can be operated with according to strict rules.

Rosser, writing about multi-valued logics, suggests this same empirical state of affairs:

> The physicist introduces wave functions and all sorts of complications in order to achieve compatibility between a mathematics with sharp edges and a physics without sharp edges. The situation cries for a mathematics without sharp edges, and a three-valued logic happens to produce a mathematics without sharp edges (1941, p. 212).

It is apparent from comments such as these that the events of theoretical physics are several inferential steps away from the empirical state of affairs. However, these mathematically created events partake, structurally or otherwise, of a status of reality that is in some sense more perfect than the reality of the affective occurrences of the poetic imagination? It would seem that the minds of physicist and poet have much in common: each creates (infers) an eventual structure of nature from his own perspective, and according to differing levels of perception. There are quite as many affective responses in the physicist as in the poet. Indeed, a case has been made for the proposition that the poet is several levels closer to life than the physicist. The physicist must use extrasensory media; the poet uses more "natural" means of apprehending the event. I do not argue that case here; I wish only to make a point that Korzybski has evidently not yet thought out. Poet and physicist alike follow their "natural neurological structures." Long known to poets and philosophers, this is a truth not always appreciated by scientific enthusiasts. Yet it was Einstein himself who likened Planck's lifelong search for the ordered harmony of nature to the "emotional condition . . . of the religious devotee or the lover," dictated by "no principle or programme" but arising "from an immediate personal need" (Sullivan, 1934, p. 265). Here is more evidence of a more fundamental truth, emphasized by Henri Bergson: there may be many perspectives of the same object, each of which observes the nature of things at a different angle. Korzybski's devotion to the perspective of physics is understandable, but it is nonetheless only *one* perspective of what philosophy calls the metaphysical object. One might accept Korzybski's tenet that the content of knowledge is structure, if structure is interpreted here to mean system; one cannot accept his particular view of the nature of system as anything more than one aspect of a manifold facade—

In nature's infinite book of secrecy
A little I can read.

As mathematics demonstrates science, so poetry demonstrates life.
With the establishment of these two arguments—that mathematics is not significantly different in structure from natural language, and that the physical process-event is a derivation from an ideal world picture and thus only one of many possible perspectives—Korzybski's particular bias is brought to light. His scientism is not an empirical study of man and his ways, but a utopian projection. Knowledge is not science: science is the process of systematizing knowledge. Mathematics is useful to the physical sciences, but it is no more the highest linguistic development of man's "natural neurological order" than is poetry. Any natural language has structure, order, and relations; if mathematics did not have a structure similar to that of the daily language of its users, it could not be used to demonstrate science. True, mathematics is primarily denotative, whereas a natural language is both denotative and connotative, but this semantic characteristic of mathematics in no way changes its structure (Korzybski's claim to the contrary notwithstanding). Korzybski assumes that linguistic structure is a semantic phenomenon—that is, obtains only in word-fact relationships. Actually, it is the syntactic element of language that legislates its order, and so controls its structure. The exclusively denotative quality appears in mathematics in its purely formal language, without any semantic element aside from that ascribed by the calculator. All languages are arbitrary and conventional. Any question of differences among them can relate only to the nature of the conventions adopted, and to the uses for which the languages are designed. To assume the priority of the physical object as event-process automatically limits the scope of General Semantics. It becomes not the science of man, but the study of man-the-scientist. This is an interesting study, but only a part of the whole. The experience of the world seems to be much more extensive than any single method of describing it.

WORKING PRINCIPLES

With the caveat, then, that *Science and Sanity* is considerably more limited in perspective than it purports to be, one may examine some of its working principles.

The primary linguistic significance of General Semantics rests in the claim that it operates with a theory of meaning that is scientific.

Korzybski is no believer in Richards's theory that symbolic reference and emotive expression can be divorced. His view of the meaning-process is based upon three fundamental tenets: 1) the nature of matter as a process, 2) the non-identification of words with objects, and 3) the healthful operation "as-a-whole" of the human nervous system. It should be kept in mind that Korzybski believes in the neurological description of behavior. Here, in the treatment of meaning, the postulates of non-elementalism and of non-identification are put to use.

> The explanation is quite simple. We start with the negative A premise that words are *not* the unspeakable objective level, such as the actual objects outside of our skin *and* our personal feelings inside our skin. It follows that the only link between the objective and the verbal world is exclusively structural, necessitating the conclusion that the only content of all 'knowledge' is structural. Now structure can be considered as a complex of relations, and ultimately as multi-dimensional order (1933, p. 20).

From this view, Korzybski argues, "all language can be considered as names either for un-speakable entities on the objective level, be it things or feelings, or as *names for relations.*" Objects may be treated as "relations between the sub-microscopic events and the human nervous system." They represent abstractions "of low order produced by our nervous system as the result of the sub-microscopic events acting as stimuli upon the nervous system." Words are "still higher abstractions from objects," and since *A* cannot know what *B* abstracts unless *B* tells *A*, the meaning of a word is its definition. However, definitions ultimately go back to a set of terms not further definable, the meanings of which "we 'know' somehow, but cannot tell." This is the "un-speakable" level.

> This 'knowledge' is supplied by the lower nerve centres; it represents affective first order effects, and is interwoven and interlocked with other affective states, such as those called 'wishes', 'intentions', 'evaluation', and many others. It should be noticed that these first order effects have an objective character, as they are un-speakable—are not words (1933).

A meaning, then, has no "general content."

> We can only speak legitimately of 'meanings' in the plural. Perhaps, we can speak of the meanings of meanings, although I suspect the latter would represent the un-speakable first order effect, the affective, personal raw material, out of which our ordinary meanings are built (1933).

One wonders how Korzybski, or any neurologist, *knows* that these "first order effects" are all nonverbal. Evaluation, for instance, or intention, seems to imply much more than endocrinological change. If they are not all nonverbal, the reduction of meaning to undefined *terms* seems to be a play on words. Where do these wordless words come from? From what do they derive their being? The neurological approach to the problem of meaning has its limits, and they become immediately apparent. The answer may be found not in an analysis of the individual nervous system, but in the realization that people learn their language, even their undefined terms, within the bounds of a biosocial community, and that every language is normative to a certain extent. It is true that each person enjoys individual connotations that are unique, but, with all its imperfections, the act of communication does take place. What takes place is not a mystic fusion of affective nervous states, but the transference of stimulus and response between two nervous systems by the medium of a series of signs. This use of signs is a conventional activity, not subjective but intersubjective from the earliest moments of sign-learning in the infant. The fallacy in Korzybski's account of meaning is the lack of consideration of the social nature of language. His analysis of meaning is serviceable for the understanding of any one nervous system, but not of two, and at least two are concerned in any communicative situation such as he describes. Here we leave the realm of neurology for that of social psychology.

Korzybski agrees with Cunningham that meaning and knowing are intimately related. Men are commonly aware that standard definitions of words convey different meanings to different people. Past experiences vary considerably. So do one's evaluations (affective states) that are induced by verbal terms. These evaluations of the terms constitute knowing. However, because words *are not* objects or events, "structure, and so relations, becomes the only possible content of 'knowledge' and of meanings." This statement is expanded:

> Because relations can be defined as multi-dimensional order, both of which terms are *non-el* [non-elemental], applying to 'senses' and 'mind', after *naming* the unspeakable entities, all experience can be described in terms of relations or multi-dimensional order. The meanings of meanings, in a given case, in a given individual at a given moment . . . represent composite, affective psychological configurations of all relations pertaining to the case, coloured by past experiences, state of health, mood of the moment, and other contingencies (1933, p. 23).

This is precisely what the student of language means when he says that all meanings are individual connotations; Korzybski's explanation does not add much to our knowledge of how meanings come into being. He is interested mainly in the fallacy of unreal descriptive dichotomy:

> If we consistently apply the organism-as-a-whole principle to any psycho-logical analysis, we must conjointly contemplate at least both aspects, the 'emotional' and the 'intellectual', and so deliberately ascribe 'emotional' factors to any 'intellectual' manifestation, and 'intellectual' factors to any 'emotional' occurrance (1933).

The result of eliminating this dichotomy is that "not only the structure of the world is such that it is made up of absolute individuals, but that meanings in general, and the meanings of meanings in particular . . . also share, in common with ordinary objects, the absolute individuality of the objective level."

The steps of this familiar generalization, as Korzybski traces them, seem convincing. It is the common ground of many semanticists; meanings are imputed. Yet one wonders if Korzybski does not go too far in the expression of the individuality of meanings. We do manage to talk, and people respond appropriately. The answer is normative. Korzybski takes it for granted that we live our lives on objective levels, not on verbal levels—the latter are only auxiliary. The verbal levels fulfill their function properly

> only if these verbal processes are translated back into first order effects. Thus, through verbal intercourse, in the main, scientists discover useful first order abstractions (objective), and by verbal discourse again, *culture* is built; but this only when the verbal processes affect the un-speakable psycho-logical manifestations, such as our feelings, 'emotions' (1933).

This idea seems pat enough—so pat, indeed, that it oversimplifies and approaches nonsense. The assumption is that objective levels and verbal levels are different. Yet on every hand it seems impossible to keep them apart. This is apparent in Korzybski's explanation of "semantic reaction."

From the foregoing account one concludes that the clue to a happy, sane society lies in the individual's ability to analyze his "unspeakable psychological manifestations." The mechanism for this analysis is physiological and simple. It involves conscious description of the details of affective states. This is nothing more, of course, than introspection, but the method constitutes, in Korzybski's opinion, a positive rejection of everything connected with the elementalism of faculty-psychology. Any analysis that involves such terms as body *and* mind, thinking *and* feeling, time *and* space, is incorrect and fundamentally unsound, because it overlooks the uniqueness of organismic responses. A more realistic method is at hand:

The working tool of psychophysiology is found in the *semantic reaction.* This can be described as the psycho-logical reaction of a given individual to words and language and other symbols and events *in connection with their meanings,* and the psycho-logical reactions, which *become meanings and relational configurations* the moment the given individual begins to analyze them or somebody else does that for him. It is of great importance to realize that the term 'semantic' is *non-elementalistic,* as it involves conjointly the 'emotional' as well as the 'intellectual' factors (1933).

This recondite expression of the importance of context emphasizes the point that contexts have psychological *and* logical references and implications. The added term "semantic reaction" simply labels the demand that the individual do for himself what the psychotherapist does for his patient—bring his unconscious states into consciousness by description, and thus discover meanings of which he is not usually aware. The General Semanticist, then, acts as a psychiatrist: "The condition for a successful treatment seems to be that the processes should be managed in a non-elementalistic way" (p. 25). Here, in a nutshell, is the reason why many psychiatrists have flocked to the banner of General Semantics. A rudimentary knowledge of linguistics offers the possibility that a medical-social art can become an empirical science.

There is obviously nothing new in this rather uncongenial treatment of linguistic habits. It is simply a heightened behaviorism that depends upon the theory of conditioned response for its sanction, and possesses the usual limitation that, as yet, very little is known of the process. Korzybski no more accounts for *displaced speech,* than do Ogden and Richards. He emphasizes the point that conditioned behavior is conditio*nal* upon a great many factors (pp. 326–340). The point is well taken, and Korzybski does not fail to stress what others have noted, that man is not quite like an animal. Beyond this, the explanation of meaning does little more than pound home the lesson that the human organism operates as a whole. It can do little else. Despite his evident devotion to rigorous empiricism, Korzybski does not treat the events through which the relationship of meaning is set up between a word and an object that is not present (displaced speech). In serveral chapters on linguistics he fails to mention the manner in which the "unspeakable" affective states become referents for words. He says only that psychological states become meanings—that is, semantic reactions—when they are analyzed. What is the explanation of the process that makes this analysis possible? To say that meanings "represent composite, affective psychological configurations of all relations pertaining to the case" is merely to wave a verbal wand. Korzybski's answer will not pass a linguist's test as a satisfactory account of the nature of meaning. As Bloomfield remarks: "In order to give a scientifically accurate definition of meaning for every form of a language, we should have to have a scientifically accurate knowledge of everything in the speaker's world" (1933, p. 139). Because he is not a linguist, Korzybski is perhaps satisfied with less than this by way of empirical data.

It is obvious that General Semantics is not a science of man in any descriptive sense of recording and interpreting empirical data; it is a normative system especially concerned with educative procedures. As Korzybski explains, it "is not a medical science, but represents a necessary bridge between exact sciences, medical sciences (psychology included), home and existing school . . . education, and daily life and daily orientations" (1938, p. 1). It is designed to underlie an empirical theory of human evaluations and orientations, and is based upon a study of the human neurological mechanism. In summary:

> It discovers direct neurological methods for the *stimulation* of the activities of the human cerebral cortex and the direct introduction of beneficial neurological 'inhibition', etc., which restore nervous balance to the over-stimulated human nervous systems. It discovers also that most human difficulties are due to intensional orientations and languages, and the solution of many of them can be brought about by *extensional* orientations and languages, which is accomplished simply and automatically by a few linguistic *extensional* devices (1938).

That is to say, General Semantics is not a science at all. It is an educational theory, with the same objectives as dozens of others— Couéism is one example. It is concerned with safeguarding the world by rehabilitating its human occupants.

A few stimulative devices carry the burden of this retraining. The clue to method can be found in a comparison between extension and intension, a feature of General Semantics that has been thoroughly explored and exploited by O. L. Reiser (1940, p. 37). Intensional orientations, Korzybski and Reiser declare, involve nominal or verbal definition emphasizing connotations, usually based upon nonempirical ideas, without considering facts; this is definition by postulation. Extensional orientations employ "real" definitions that emphasize denotations, and are based upon empirical science; this is definition by inspection. Facts are observed, then described, and inferences are then made from the descriptions. Intensional, or nominal, definition, says Reiser, is "peculiarly appropriate to the subject-predicate mode of thinking." Thus, in a purely intensional logic, terms are defined by the connotations of the words used. "Employed exclusively, this leads to *definition by postulation,* and the purely verbal (symbolic) discipline of a non-empirical science, such as formal logic." This type of thinking would be acceptable "provided we operated exclusively on the level of concepts, and did not insist upon referring our 'thoughts' to the world of 'things', or the perceptual world of 'concrete objects'. It is because we must use 'thoughts' in our orientations that we get into difficulties. Words and symbols must *denote* as well as *connote.*" There are several confusions here, but for the time being let us observe Korzybski's extensional recommendations, devices to enable people to relate their discourse to the facts of the world and to reason calmly.

The most important mechanism is the Structural Differential, an *anthropometer,* which is to be kept at hand and consulted at all times; it is employed as a therapeutic device to insure non-identification of word with object, and to emphasize the process of abstracting in language. The other devices are the liberal employment of: 1) indexes—cow_1, cow_2, cow_3—to denote the absolute individuality of persons and events; 2) dates—$science_{1828}$, $science_{1933}$, $science_{1943}$—to suggest the space-time relations of inferences from world-facts (knowledge); 3) etc.—without which we should have to keep on writing indexes and dates forever; 4) hyphens—to avoid the "elementalistic" splitting of concepts that cannot in fact be separated, as in *space-time,* and to create new "non-elementalistic" combinations out of the old limiting categories, as with *psycho-logics*; 5) quotation marks—to indicate that we are aware of the confinement and inappropriateness of our old language—"emotions," "ideals," "mental," and the like. Johnson adds two devices to those suggested by Korzybski: plurals—to emphasize further the individual differences between any two of anything relating to men, as in "cause*s* of stuttering*s*" instead of "stuttering;" and underlining—to stress key words and centered phrases. Johnson, interpreting Korzybski, suggests that these devices "need not be used overtly at all times." While one is training oneself in extensional orientation, one should employ them explicitly much of the time until one gets the habit of using them. "Ordinarily, however, they are to be used implicitly" (Johnson, 1939, pp. 44–45). Korzybski discusses these devices throughout the book. (See particularly pp. 13–16, and Chapter 2 on "Terminology and Meanings.")

Educational vigor and linguistic necessity are at great odds here. One shudders to think about the number of "et ceteras" necessary for a statement referring to the fact that cows are different from horses,

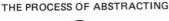

THE PROCESS OF ABSTRACTING

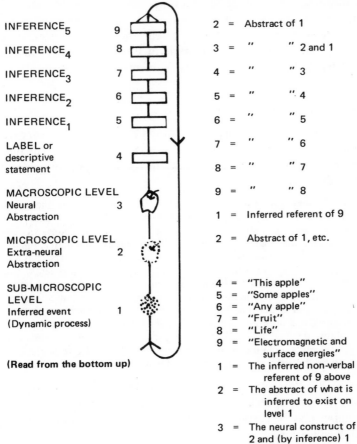

INFERENCE₅	9	2 =	Abstract of 1	
INFERENCE₄	8	3 =	"	" 2 and 1
INFERENCE₃	7	4 =	"	" 3
INFERENCE₂	6	5 =	"	". 4
INFERENCE₁	5	6 =	"	" 5
LABEL or descriptive statement	4	7 =	"	" 6
		8 =	"	" 7
MACROSCOPIC LEVEL Neural Abstraction	3	9 =	"	" 8
		1 =	Inferred referent of 9	
MICROSCOPIC LEVEL Extra-neural Abstraction	2	2 =	Abstract of 1, etc.	

SUB-MICROSCOPIC LEVEL
Inferred event   1
(Dynamic process)

4 = "This apple"
5 = "Some apples"
6 = "Any apple"
7 = "Fruit"
8 = "Life"
9 = "Electromagnetic and surface energies"

(Read from the bottom up)

1 = The inferred non-verbal referent of 9 above
2 = The abstract of what is inferred to exist on level 1
3 = The neural construct of 2 and (by inference) 1

Figure 3. "This diagram represents a modification of Korzybski's Structural Differential. . . . *Both the macroscopic and microscopic levels represent sense data* . . . both the macroscopic and microscopic *sense data* are to be sharply differentiated from the sub-microscopic *inferential data*." [From General Semantics Monograph I (Language and Speech Hygiene), Chicago, 1939, p. 14.]

or that cows have horns, or that horses do not have horns. The General Semanticist is congenitally unable to believe that other people besides himself are occasionally interested in thoughts about what a class of objects has in common. Linguists make the observation that a highly analytical language like English is readily available for nice expression; they note that the very essence of language is its abstract quality (Jesperson, 1924, pp. 63–64). "Cow$_1$, cow$_2$, cow$_3$ . . ." reduces the meanings of language to an evanescence that could only stultify communication. As a training device for an understanding of language, it is probably analogous to learning higher mathematics by counting one's fingers. A clean style in English is clearly not one of Korzybski's objectives, nor accomplishments.

EDUCATION AND TRAINING

Whether or not *Science and Sanity* offers any fresh insight on psycholinguistic problems, what about its status as an educational theory? Korzybski seems to have no difficulty in visualizing his system as "the way of the world." He writes:

> The researches of the present writer have shown that the problems involved are very complicated and cannot be solved except by a *joint study* of mathematics, mathematical foundations, history of mathematics, 'logic', 'psychology', anthropology, psychiatry, linguistics, epistemology, physics and its history, colloidal chemistry, physiology, and neurology; this study resulting in the discovery of a general semantic mechanism underlying human behavior, many new interrelations and formulations, culminating in a A-system. This semantic mechanism appears as a general psychophysiological mechanism based on four-dimensional order, present and abused in all of us, the primitive man, the infant, the 'mentally' ill, and the genius not excluded. It gives us an extremely simple means of training our s.r. [semantic responses], which can be applied even in elementary education (Korzybski, 1933, p. 750).

Chapter 29, "On Non-Aristotelian Training," is devoted to a rapid survey of various techniques whereby beneficial training in General Semantics may be carried on in the classroom, even at the elementary level of education.

The use of the Structural Differential, already referred to, constitutes the core of educational procedures. It offers a graphic means of remembering to differentiate between orders of abstraction and between the "unspeakable" object-levels and the verbal levels of reference (see Figure 3). The educational process is variable as to details and methods of instruction. "We must select the data according to the age of the children or the knowledge of the grown-ups. Everything said should be demonstrated empirically from a structural point of view" (p. 473). The first educative step is the breakdown of the concept of "allness," that appears to be a heritage from the primitive roots of language. Because the foundation of all orders of abstraction in language is the scientific, submicroscopic, inferential level of process (which is itself an objective abstraction), conclusive universality is untenable. As we use words of a high-order abstraction, words that are far removed from the level of process-event to which they actually refer, we tend to think we know all about something, forgetting that the higher the order of abstraction, the more details are left out. "Allness" at best can never be true; at worst, it is likely to confuse our thinking, and perhaps lead to serious errors of assertion and judgment. Amen!

Another phase of the educative process is practice in non-identification. Because the object-event-levels are "un-speakable," and because all language is abstraction of some order from these levels, there can be no complete sameness in the relations between event and language. It follows that abstraction must be carefully explained; an important part of the curriculum is the necessary training in the "consciousness of abstracting." In fact, Korzybski claims that in his system *consciousness,* heretofore without a satisfactory definition, becomes "consciousness of abstracting" (p. 413). This in turn may be defined as "*awareness* that in our process of abstracting we have *left out* characteristics," or as "*remembering* the 'is-not'," where "some characteristics have been *left out*" (see Chapter 26). Because the submicroscopic, inferential, process-level is the lowest order of abstraction we know, all other orders above it (see Figure 3) are "higher orders of abstraction," that is, leave out more characteristics of the event. Therefore, if we identify or confuse words with objects and feelings, or memories and ideas with past experiences that belong on the objective level, we identify abstractions of higher order with those of lower order, and set up confusions among the orders. These confusions Korzybski calls *objectifications* (for example, "He is a Red, and bad clear through!" or "Young people nowadays are spoiled!") (p. 417). They offer testimony to the primitive quality of much of our language and thought.

The result that Korzybski expects from this education in General Semantics is the realization, conveyed through "consciousness of abstracting," that the "unspeakable" object-level includes not only all ordinary objects, but all actions, functions, and processes going on "outside our skins," and also all immediate feelings, emotions, moods, and the like going on "inside our skins." These occurrences are not words, he asserts. The result of this awareness is that "the animalistic 'human nature' begins to be 'changed' into quite a different *human nature*" (p. 477).

The final stages of training are concerned with "the theory of natural evaluation based on natural order." Words must be considered in two categories: 1) descriptive, functional words, and 2) inferential words, "which involve assumptions." An important structural fact should be noted. One must remember that "human life is lived under conditions which establish a natural order of importance between different orders of abstractions. This natural order should be made the basis of natural adaptive evaluation . . ." (p. 478). We live our lives on the objective level; the verbal level is only auxiliary to it. At the verbal level description is more reliable than inference; all correct inference is based upon sound description. It might appear from this that poetry is closer to an expression of life than complex scientific inference. Korzybski does not mean this, however, for the ordinary macroscopic object is not so "important" as the scientific, submicroscopic object— that is, the inferred event. With this dogma, we have swung full circle, and are back to the fundamental belief upon which General Semantics is grounded: science is the basis of life. This is Korzybski's *summum bonum*, the metaphysics of dynamism as revealed by physical theory.

One wonders about the educative results of this method. Without question, something would happen. So far as I am aware, education against "allness" has been going on for some time—most effectively, perhaps, outside the classroom. One soon learns that "allness"—be it the "allness" of egotism or of the nature of truth—is unpopular. Yet there is a kind of "allness," a universality, that is with us constantly— the universality that inheres in every word we use when we are understood. If that "allness" were to be sacrificed on the alter of General Semantics, we would be without language in communication. Without it the chemist could not use his chart of elements, nor the physicist his second law of thermodynamics.

The process of abstracting, too, seems serviceable as a warning against confusion. However, one must not forget the lesson of the Structural Differential. It seems to be a matter of choice whether one interprets the submicroscopic event-level of science as the objective basis of fact, or as the highest abstraction that leaves out most of the characteristics of an object (see Figure 3). Whether one chooses to interpret a sunset as an event of light waves or as an experience of colored music seems to be a matter of attitude, purpose, and value. Korzybski elects the first interpretation; a poet might adopt the second. The rest of us may, on occasion, simply enjoy the sunset.

RETROSPECT

Korzybski is an eclectic philosopher of science. His general assumption of the factual world as process and change is based upon the findings of physical and chemical theory. The general description of meaning is drawn from physiology and neurology. The theory of extensional orientation is operationism. The belief that mathematics is structurally different from, and more "natural" than, natural language seems to have no scientific ground; it certainly is not based upon a knowledge of linguistics. (Korzybski's knowledge of spoken languages was extensive, but he was not a linguist.) The idea that the content of knowledge is structure (that is, is systemic) has been current for a long time. The fundamental tenet of non-identification was succinctly stated by the Hellenic Empirics, and is developed fully in Book III of Locke's *Essay Concerning Human Understanding*. There, too, in Chapter 4, is the semantic statement of basic undefined terms, in plain language. Locke holds that simple ideas cannot be defined, although complex ideas can. The reason is that the simple ideas are reduced to sensations. In Chapter 10 of the same book, entitled "The Abuses of Words," Locke anticipates most of Korzybski's polemics. The various devices for developing consciousness of abstracting are fresh, but not so illuminating as the general approach to the idea of abstraction in language. This is a process frequently more talked about than studied, and the theory of levels of abstraction, newly stated as it is, might offer a useful approach to a study of consciousness and logical relations. It is first cousin to Richards's theory of "delegated efficacy."

There is much more in *Science and Sanity* than has been presented here. Korzybski makes clear that he has studied long and hard in many departments of mathematics and science, and I do not hesitate to admit that I do not have the critical equipment to attend meaningfully to many of his disquisitions. No doubt, those of them that have substance will be handled appropriately by the specialists concerned. Some have been considered already—Korzybski's rejection of the "law of excluded middle," for instance. One mathematico-logician writes of Korzybski's view on this point:

> The author relies hopefully upon the work of the Intuitional School of mathematicians of whom the leading exponents are Brouwer and Weyl, but it seems that there is here a fundamental misunderstanding. It is commonly said, even by professional mathematicians who should know better, that the work of Brouwer and Weyl is essentially the denial of the excluded middle as applied to mathematical entities. This view is completely false, and its falsity vitiates some of the most important arguments advanced by Korzybski (Temple, 1935, pp. 246–247).

In this same vein Korzybski's devotion to multi-valued logics, accepted with enthusiasm in place of the "Aristotelian" two-valued logic, could be mentioned. There is evidently a use for multi-valued logic in physical theory, and in recent years much thought has been put to the business of perfecting a useful logic with at least three values. This is not to say that professional mathematicians have dispensed with the two-valued form, as Korzybski often implies. On the contrary, neither mathematical expert nor physical theorist as yet knows quite what to do with the newer possibilities. Far from being established, the implications of three-valued logic are only projected (Rosser, p. 212).

Aside from such special points, however, the essence of Korzybski's theory has been presented here. Several of his fundamental assumptions and assertions need more ventilation than they are given in *Science and Sanity*. Enough has been said of the attitudes that lead to scientism and mathematicism. This is not a new point of view, and Korzybski's particular version shares the weaknesses common to any single perspective. His metaphysics is colored by his assumptions, and he excludes by definition much of what he disagrees with. Some of the limiting factors of General Semantics are to be found in his theories of non-identification, of extensional orientation and its devices, of elementalism, and of meaning. Perhaps the most important of these is the doctrine of non-identification.

Korzybski frequently shifts his terms, and thus makes inferences that do not logically obtain. The most obvious example of this is his confusion of non-identification (of words with things) with the so-called "Aristotelian law of identity." Since non-identification is the foundation upon which his entire theory is built, this confusion is the source of much inconsistency in *Science and Sanity*. The law of identity has been given various interpretations, but its statement is agreed upon: *A* is *A*. Korzybski interprets this law in a striking fashion: *A*-the-first symbolizes a word, the copula stands for "absolute sameness," and *A*-the-second is an object. Therefore, according to Korzybski, *apple* = the actual object (genus *Malus*). This is an interpretation of the law of identity that is shared neither by Aristotle nor by any other responsible logician. Granted, there have been irresponsible logicians, and granted, the identification of words with objects is a deluding habit, but I doubt that any modern system of logic makes the identification claimed by Korzybski. He simply confuses one of the historical laws of thought with one of the seven or eight usages of the verb *is*. Nor does it require a multi-valued logic to develop a logical system based on primitive propositions other than these traditional ones. The *Principia Mathematica* uses several basic propositions, none of which is Aristotelian, but it does not dispense with logical identity, nor, for that matter, does multi-valued logic.

To illustrate the "'is' of identity" (or Lucifer to his Milton), Korzybski uses the sentence, "The apple is a fruit." The context is a discussion of the extreme difficulty of analyzing *is*. He writes:

> So I must be brief, and state but roughly, that in the Indo-European languages the verb 'to be' has at least four entirely different uses: (1) as an auxiliary verb, 'Smith is coming'; (2) as the 'is' of predication, 'the apple is red'; (3) as the 'is' of 'existence', 'I am'; (4) as the 'is' of identity, 'the apple is a fruit'. The fact that four semantically entirely different words should have one sound and spelling appears as a genuine tragedy of the race; the more so since the discrimination between their uses is not always easy (1933, p. 750).

Whatever Korzybski chooses to call "tragic," his distinctions here are by no means logical. On his principle of non-identification, sentence number four in these examples represents a linguistic usage that is false to facts. It is significant, however, that Korzybski does not demonstrate his thesis of non-identification with this sentence; instead, he uses "The map is not the territory" as the pièce de résistance of this fundamental semantic tenet. The basic fallacy of Korzybski's thinking lies in this shift of example. He persistently confuses syntactic and semantic rules of usage.

This is almost too obvious a point, but it evidently underlies the whole conception of General Semantics. "The apple is a fruit" is not comparable with "The map is a territory." The first is a defining sentence in which *is* stands for *means*; *is* is a true copula exhibiting the syntactic relation between *apple* and *fruit—apple* belongs to the class *fruit*. "The map is a territory" seems to be the same kind of sentence; syntactically it is the same. However, whereas there is a class, *fruit,* to which *apple* belongs in English, there is no comparable class, *territory,* to which *map* belongs. "The map is a territory" is syntactically possible in English, but, unless one especially interprets *is* to stand for *represents,* there is no semantic rule of usage that makes the sentence meaningful. How and why Korzybski insists that "The apple is a fruit" indicates the misuse of relations between words and objects is a logical mystery. One would suppose that Ogden and Richards and the logical positivists of the Vienna Circle, with whose work Korzybski professes familiarity, have made it sufficiently clear that definition is a verbal process, and that "The apple is a fruit" is a definitive proposition.

No doubt this confusion is related to his attitude toward identity. Korzybski recognizes only one connotation of the term—"'identity', defined as 'absolute sameness', necessitates 'absolute sameness' in 'all' aspects, never to be found in this world." This is a gratuitous specification of meaning that automatically limits his acquaintance with the term. He continues:

> Anything with which we deal on the objective levels represents a process, different all the 'time', no matter how slow or fast the process might be; therefore, a principle or a premise that 'everything is identical with itself', is invariably false-to-facts (1933, p. 194).

It is difficult to criticize this statement because it seems to be alogical. In his own terms, Korzybski is confusing two different levels of abstraction. Neither the law of identity nor any other logical postulate describes the objective level of existence. These are verbal laws, and without them symbolic manipulation is impossible. One wonders how Korzybski would go about defining the formal terms of language— *and, because,* and the like. One also wonders how he could be sure that in the equation "$1 + 1 = 2$" both of the "1s" are stable and thus additive, or that "$=$" correctly links the two major phrases. These are purely logical relations, and have no connection whatever with objects. Nobody condones the confusion between a word and the object that it symbolizes. However, this is by no means "the same thing" as Korzybski's evident confusion between syntactical and semantic aspects of language. Apparently, he does not recognize that an important meaning of "identity"—the meaning to which the logical law refers—is what William James called "the principle of constancy of the mind's meanings." That is, *"the mind can always intend, and know when it intends, to think of the same"* (James, 1890, p. 459). Korzybski might well have kept in mind James's observation that this *"sense of sameness* is the very keel and backbone of our thinking." Without it the mathematician could not use his numbers, nor the relational logician his symbols, nor the common individual his daily language. Korzybski believes, however, that this is the *only* meaning of "sameness." The critical conclusion to which one is forced by studying Korzybski's thinking on identification is that General Semantics is founded upon a logical idiosyncrasy that no amount of tinkering can correct.

There are other instances of intellectual myopia in *Science and Sanity.* The doctrine of non-elementalism, for instance, is easier to preach than to practice. Korzybski is only too well aware of the difficulties of referring to *feeling-thought* with consistency in a language in which *feeling* and *thought* are separate terms. Keyser suggests that one aspect of the problem might be crystallized by considering questions like, "Am I getting enough exercise?" or "Is this the proper food for me?" (1934, pp. 255–256). *I* and *me* have as their referent the personality of being of the speaker, but what is the referent of *enough exercise* or *proper food*? The speaker's organism-as-a-whole, the *I*? Korzybski does not answer such questions. They have no significance in his consideration of elementalism versus non-elementalism. Yet every adult knows how to answer them and how to respond to them; their references are within his ken. The idea of space-time is not so familiar to the "un-sane" Korzybski, and serves as a dramatic example with which to point up the thesis of non-elementalism. The trouble lies in the fact that he refuses to recognize the significance of connotation, and its logical implications. Prone to dichotomize, he must assume that "elemental" terminology cannot be used with consistency. He both overrates his theory and underrates man's symbolic dexterity. The whole question of elementalism versus non-elementalism is falsely put, and stems directly from Korzybskian assumptions about the nature of everyday language. Those assumptions, in turn, seem to be products of his intellectual self-righteousness.

This is also true with the dismissal of two-valued logic. It would be interesting to discover anyone, experimental scientist or poetic dreamer, who does not employ this system of thinking, or orientation, as Korzybski calls it. Is there any situation of choice in which two-valued logic is not a daily routine? *Science and Sanity* itself offers a case in point. In the workaday process of writing a dogmatic book, Korzybski uses two-valued orientation exclusively. Beginning with the subtitle and going on for eight hundred pages, one looks in vain for a single instance of three-valued, let alone infinite-valued, logic. The General Semanticist would do well to study the inconstancy of his own terms. Indeed, with the modern use of the computer many of his terms are denied.

There are other kinds of inconsistency in *Science and Sanity*, some born of misinformation, some of dogmatism, all of limited perspective. Discussing the treatment of elementalism by psychiatrists, Korzybski comments on Aristotle (pp. 86–88). Aristotle's work is summarized as the "gross empiricism" of the extrovert, "who projects all his internal processes on the outside world and objectifies them." Plato, on the other hand, was "the typical introvert, for whom 'reality' was all inside . . ." Now the psychotherapist aims to induce in his patient a balance between these two "elemental" extremes; the balanced person should be an "extroverted-introvert." It is easier, however, to re-educate an introvert than an extrovert. The introvert thinks; the extrovert has not developed his capacity to think (p. 88). The implication seems to be that Aristotle did not "think." This is not what Korzybski means, but it is what he says. The point is that neither he nor anyone else can express himself consistently in a given language without using "elemental" terms, thereby hoping to be correctly understood. *Appeals to the emotions* and *appeals to the intellect* are just as much, but no more, "elemental" for the rhetorician as are *introvert* and *extrovert* for the psychiatrist. As Bridgman suggests, the real test is how the terms are used. Korzybski frequently uses his language very badly, for example in the implied generalization about Aristotle as a "thinker." Observe what he does with these psychiatric terms:

> Now we shall be able to understand why Aristotle, the extrovert, and his doctrines have appealed, and still appeal, to those who can 'think' but feebly. The fact that the fuller linguistic system of the extrovert Aristotle was accepted in preference to the work of the introvert, Plato, is of serious semantic consequence to us. It is evident that mankind, in its evolution, had to pass through a low period of development; but this fact is not the only reason why the A [Aristotelian] doctrines have had such a tremendous influence upon the Aryan race. The reason is much more deeply rooted and pernicious. In his day, over two thousand years ago, Aristotle inherited a structurally primitive-made language (p. 88).

Statements like this one put the stamp of *crank* on Korzybski and vitiate the serviceability of some of his ideas. One hesitates to trust at all the thinking of a man who is capable of this sort of generalization. To classify Aristotle's Greek as a primitive language is simply linguistic misinformation, regardless of what connotation Korzybski gives to *primitive*. Moreover, he writes as if Plato inherited a better language. This is a troublesome idea. To assert that Platonic doctrine has not been influential in the world is to display a lack of acquaintance with history—philosophical, theological, and political— that is regrettable in an educator with Korzybski's scope. In the interests of decorum, I do not pursue this Korzybskian frame of mind further, except to remark that his dichotomies between intensional and extensional orientations, two-valued and multi-valued logics, subject-predicate and relational logic, and the like, exhibit much the same tone of crankiness and lack of familiarity with history and literature.

One is amazed to find this sort of dichotomizing in the work of a General Semanticist. Korzybski seems to live in an ivory tower of science and technology. He fails to recognize the significance of his own methods. All that is natural science is good, and all else is bad. Only a few mathematico-physicists are sane; most of the rest of the world is "unsane"—which is not even definable in terms of sanity. The "Aristotelian system," out of which grew modern logic and modern science, is bad; only its outgrowths are good. One might infer from reading Korzybski that the logic of relations was instituted in 1933, or that physicists employ no intensional orientation when they set up their hypotheses and try to prove or disprove them, or that there are no semantic rules in a natural language that control symbolic denotation. He is truly a devotee of "allness", and is utterly contemptuous of any perspective unlike his own. In short, he is unscientific in his methods. This is not a new trait in the proponents of technological supremacy, but it remains unfortunate. This sort of contempt seems to be one of the main reasons for the unintelligent split between the ideals of science and those of the arts that has been a notable failure of some men's understanding since the beginning of modern times.

Science and Sanity not only illustrates an inconsistent method, but it preaches an impractical doctrine, unempirical as a science, utopian as a way of life. Korzybski's system is predicated upon the belief that the evils of the world are the results of linguistic confusions. The corollary is that to abolish linguistic difficulties is to remove the evils of the world. One might agree that confusions of language could well be eliminated as a healthful step toward bringing problems and their causes into the open. To believe, however, that linguistic training will abolish our troubles is, as one critic of General Semantics has said, "as much a form of belief in verbal magic as the primitive's faith that his enemy can be slain by incantation" (Hook, 1942, p. 16). This belief, and the utopia that it engenders, is a faith, a kind of religion, that is far removed from the sphere of science. There is no doubt that many of Korzybski's followers look upon his system as a kind of religion, "a scientific mysticism." His ideas furnish the inspiration for such an interpretation. Based upon the limited perspective of natural science, founded on the principle that only natural science furnishes true inferences about the facts of the world, devoted to a rigorous mathematicism, and contemptuous of a humanistic tradition, the theory of *Science and Sanity* lacks a pragmatic view of existence and its problems. General Semantics is not an empirical science of man, but a normative system devoted to the education of man by a relatively narrow set of principles.

Both Richards and Korzybski underrate the purposive nature of the meaning-process. Both are positivists in their approach to the theory of symbolism in that they disregard or underestimate the social character of language. The next chapter deals with an attempt to bring together some of the virtues of positivism and the insights of pragmatism in such a fashion as to outline a genuinely descriptive science of sign analysis.

REFERENCES

Baugh, H., ed. General Semantics, Papers from the First American Congress for General Semantics. Lakeville, Ct.: Institute of General Semantics, 1938.

Bloomfield, L. "On Recent Work in General Linguistics. Modern Philology (1927) 211: 230.

———. Language. New York: H. Holt & Co., 1933.

———. "Linguistic Aspects of Science." In International Encyclopedia of Unified Science I: 4, edited by O. Neurath. Chicago: Univ. of Chicago Press, 1939.

Campbell, D. G. "General Semantics: Implications of Linguistic Revision for Theoretical and Clinical Neuro-psychiatry." American Journal of Psychiatry (1937) XCIII: 789–807.

Dewey, J. The Quest for Certainty: A Study of the Relation of Knowledge and Action. London: Allen and Unwin, 1930.

Hook, S. "Salvation by Semantics." Nation, 3 January 1942.

James, W. Principles of Psychology. 2 vols. New York: H. Holt & Co., 1890.

Jesperson, O. The Philosophy of Grammar. London: Allen and Unwin, 1924.

Johnson, W. Language and Speech Hygiene. Monograph I. Chicago: Institute of General Semantics, 1939.

Keyser, C. J. "Mathematics and the Science of Semantics." Scripta Mathematica (1934) II: 247–260.

———. "Mathematics and general semantics." In General Semantics, Papers from the First American Congress for General Semantics, edited by H. Baugh. Lakeville, Ct.: Institute of General Semantics, 1938.

Korzybski, A. The Manhood of Humanity. New York: E. P. Dutton & Co., 1921.

———. Science and Sanity: An Introduction to Non-Aristotelian Systems and General Semantics. Lancaster, Pa: Science Press, 1933.

———. "Outline of General Semantics." In General Semantics, Papers from the First American Congress for General Semantics, edited by H. Baugh. Lakeville, Ct.: Institute of General Semantics, 1938.

Myers, H. A. "Captain Ahab's Discovery." New England Quarterly, (1942) IV: 15–34.

Planck, M. "Causality in nature." In Science Today, edited by J. A. Thomson. London: Eyre and Spottiswood, 1934.

Reiser, O. L. The Promise of Scientific Humanism Toward a Unification of Scientific, Religious, Social and Economic Thought. New York: O. Piest, 1940.

Rosser, B. "On the Multi-valued Logics." American Journal of Physiology (1941) IX: 207–212.

Temple, G. "Review of Science and Sanity." Philosophy (1935) X: 245–247.

Trainor, J. C. "The Contributions of Alfred Korzybski." Psyche (1936) XVI: 165–177.

Chapter 6
SEMIOTIC

C. W. Morris

The suggestion is made in the Introduction to this work that the modern doctrine of "consistent empiricism" is closely connected with several ideas about theories of meaning. In these terms, one of the most compelling needs of modern thought has been the production of a consistent set of terms to describe meanings empirically, and to develop a critical metalanguage capable of expressing the theoretical aspects of diverse systems of knowledge. The New Encyclopedists envisaged a unification of methodology and supported a movement to this end in the 1930s and 1940s. There can be no correlation of knowledge, whether quantum theory or an aesthetic standard, without a unified terminology to describe meanings, a science of signs. The science of philosophy and the philosophy of science can meet in effective synthesis on this ground alone. Semiotic, the science of sign analysis, has been projected as the organon of rational analysis on the one hand, and of empirical confirmation on the other. Rooted in the analytic struggles of Hellenic philosophy, of medieval conceptualism, of Lockeian logic, and of C. S. Peirce's theory of signs, modern semiotic is interpreted by its analysts as a means of establishing a systematic universe of discourse for the study of meaning. It is best approached by way of the synoptic view offered by Charles W. Morris, an American pragmatist, and interpreter and editor of the writings and ideas of George H. Mead. Although he has published many articles on semiotic and its place in an empirical methodology, Morris's outstanding contribution to the subject is his *Foundations of the Theory of Signs* (1938).

Commenting on various recent interpretations of meaning, Morris remarks:

> Too much mystery is thrown around the analysis or clarification of
> meaning: the meaning of a term is completely specified when it is known

what objects the term designates, what expectations it produces in the persons for whom it has meaning, and what its connections are with other terms in the language of which it is a part (1937, p. 13).

This statement expresses the essense of semiotic, and suggests the nature of the approach to the complex relationships holding among thought, language, and experience. Whereas Cunningham is concerned with a definition of the term *meaning,* which he arrives at by a careful analysis of typical meaning-situations, Morris adopts the view that meaning is functional, and is to be described only in terms of the component relations active in the total complex of experience. The term *context* has no special significance in the theory of semiotic. A context is not sought after to illuminate meanings, because context is a result rather than a cause. It is the result of one's analysis of the triadic relations of a term, its references, the response of an interpreter to it, and its connection with the other terms with which it is used. Both Cunningham and Morris emphasize the relational character of meaning, but whereas Cunningham stresses the overall structure of this relationship, Morris analyzes the interlocked nature of its components. The two theories are not in opposition; they emphasize different aspects of the same problems, and, accordingly, serve quite different purposes.

SEMIOTIC: THEORY OF SIGNS

Rice suggests that the general movement for the unification of science is an attempt to weld pragmatism and a mature positivism. Pragmatism, he observes, has been contemptuous of precision, and has tended to neglect the abstract and systematic aspects of thought; positivism, on the contrary, has stressed these factors, but ignored or oversimplified the purposive elements of thinking (1939, p. 178). Morris specifies this blending of the two streams of thought, and makes clear the relations between the philosophical objectives of The New Encyclopedists and his theory of signs:

> The approach is made from the point of view of *scientific empiricism.* By this term is meant the temper which accepts propositions into the system of knowledge in proportion as they are verified by observation of the things or kinds of things meant, but which does not want to exclude from consideration whatever rationalistic, cosmological, or pragmatic factors prove to be integral parts of the scientific method or edifice. The *organon* of this temper is regarded as lying in the general theory of signs (semiotic). Analysis reveals that linguistic signs sustain three types of relations (to other signs of the language, to objects that are signified, to

persons by whom they are used and understood) which define three dimensions of meaning. These dimensions in turn are objects of investigation by syntactics, semantics, and pragmatics, semiotic being the general science which includes all of these and their interrelations (1937, pp. 3–4).

There is a familiar ring to these three elements of the meaning-relation; they appear to be very like the ancient Trivium in fresh garments. As a matter of fact they are, in Morris's words, "the modern forms of the Stoic-Medieval versions of grammar, logic, rhetoric." As this exposition proceeds, it becomes increasingly clear that semiotic is an eclectic theory that, true to the pragmatic tradition, draws heavily upon various doctrines of the past in order to develop an organic synthesis suitable for the purpose. Morris acknowledges a special debt to Peirce's insight on the central significance of semiotic for science and philosophy, and, in generalizing his theory, he observes that "formalism, empiricism, and pragmatism are simply emphases upon one or another of the three dimensions of meaning, that while neither is the whole story each is an important part." Morris's major aim is to furnish a three-lane highway along which the varied traffic of methodology and epistemology can proceed in the same direction. Semiotic is founded upon the observation that there can be no valid functional analysis of meaning that neglects the interlocked relationship among its three dimensions. In any particular instance, one of these elements might be closer at hand than the other two, but in no case is there only one instance to be considered.

Morris's definition of a sign is broad enough to meet Cunningham's restrictions. It includes all signs—natural phenomena, and linguistic or substitute (that is, mathematical) symbols. While he agrees with the general behavioristic explanation of meaning as it is stated in linguistic theory (Bloomfield, 1933, pp. 21–32), Morris specifies the three components of the meaning-function in terminology borrowed from Peirce:

> The process in which something functions as a sign may be called *semiosis*. This process, in a tradition which goes back to the Greeks, has commonly been regarded as involving three (or four) factors: that which acts as a sign, that which the sign refers to, and that effect on some interpreter in virtue of which the thing in question is a sign to that interpreter. These three components in semiosis may be called respectively, the *sign vehicle,* the *designatum,* and the *interpretant*; the interpreter may be included as a fourth factor. These terms make explicit the factors left undesignated in the common statement that a sign refers to something for someone (Morris, 1938, p. 3).

Morris characterizes the functions of a sign with simplicity:

> S is a sign of D for I to the degree that I takes account of D in virtue of the presence of S. Thus in semiosis something takes account of something else mediately, i.e., by means of a third something. Semiosis is accordingly a mediated-taking-account of. The mediators are *sign vehicles*; the takings-account-of are *interpretants*; the agents of the process are *interpreters*; what is taken account of are *designata* (p. 4).

A sign may—indeed, by definition, must—designate, but may not necessarily denote. Denotation is an empirical relation and necessitates an actual existent. Designation is a category of semiotic (one of the irreducible terms of semiosis) and may point at a nonexistent entity. In other words, the interpretant, the behavioral response of the interpreter's organism, may, as a matter of habit, be trained to an imaginative stimulus. "It thus becomes clear that, while every sign has a designatum, not every sign has a denotatum" (p. 5). This important observation on the functions of signs is too frequently overlooked by logical positivists and various semanticists.

Morris adduces three dimensions of semiotic, the science of signs:

> In terms of the three correlates (sign vehicle, designatum, interpreter) of the triadic relation of semiosis, a number of other dyadic relations may be abstracted for study. One may study the relations of signs to objects to which the signs are applicable. This relation will be called the *semantical dimension of semiosis* . . . and the study of this dimension will be called *semantics*. Or the study may be the relations of signs to interpreters. This relation will be called the *pragmatical dimension of semiosis* . . . and the study of this dimension will be named *pragmatics* . . . Certainly potentially, if not actually, every sign has relations to other signs, for what it is that the sign prepares the interpreter to take account of can only be *stated* in terms of other signs . . . Since many apparent cases of isolated signs prove on analysis not to be such, and since all signs are potentially if not actually related to other signs, it is well to make a third dimension of semiosis co-ordinate with the other two which have been mentioned. This third dimension will be called the *syntactical dimension of semiosis* . . . and the study of this dimension will be name syntactics (pp. 6–7).

It is worth noting that, in terms of usage in semiotic, *implicates* belongs to syntactics, *designates* and *denotes* to semantics, and *expresses* to pragmatics. These are, respectively, the logical, the referential, and the biosocial elements of communication. These three aspects of the meaning-function, so clearly expressed in Morris's theory, are either partially omitted or buried under a deluge of normative canons both in Korzybski's General Semantics and in the symbolic theorizing of Ogden and Richards. They are all present in Cunningham's account, but, whereas he derives his analysis from several types of meaning-situations, Morris concentrates on the communicative nature of the meaningful sign. In the theory of semiotic there is only one meaning-situation, and on this point Morris is considerably closer than Cunningham to a linguistic description of meaning.

In sum, semiosis is a process whereby signs function in situations where there are interpreters. Semiotic is the general science of signs, and theoretically presents the possibility of a critical metalanguage for the analysis of sign-situations. Semiotic is divisible into the subordinate sciences of semantics, pragmatics, and syntactics; the study of signs within each of these three fields of semiotic represents an abstraction from the actual sign-situation. Thus, the logician may concentrate on the implicative relations among signs, a study that has been undertaken by Carnap and many others. The semanticist may analyze referential relations, but he may not thereby undertake to develop an independent system of language, in the style of Korzybski. (Of course, he may do whatever he pleases; the question centers on whether what he does is generally informative and consistent.) The pragmatist (Mannheim, for instance) may concern himself with the purposive character of meaning. If Morris were to contribute nothing else to the consideration of meaning, this clear delineation of the systematic relations of meaning would mark him as a theorist worth attending to. "A sign is exhaustively analyzed when its relations to other signs, to what it denotes or can denote, and to its interpreters are specified" (1939, p. 133).

MODERN EMPIRICISM

Morris's analysis of semiotic offers a systematic outline. It is not a normative scheme, nor is it revolutionary. It does not prescribe a more definitive answer to problems of meaning other than that meaning has three elements, or dimensions, each of which must be considered. Empiricism has traditionally been negative, a defense against rational dogmatism; English empiricism of the seventeenth, eighteenth, and nineteenth centuries was subjective. Nineteenth- and twentieth-century positivism was also subjective. Morris conceives the task of modern empiricism to be the construction of a positive theory of mind and of the meaning-function, empirical in method, but stressing the intersubjectivity of meanings. He uses as his thesis the idea that philosophy and science are interrelated activities concerned with the interpretations of meanings. This is an exercise in methodological construction that finds its sanction in the demand to confirm all generalizations in experience. The ground was laid by Aristotle, but it was laid in his practices rather than in his scientific principles. An examination of Morris's synthesis makes it evident that his approach is inspired by the philosophy of pragmatism and directed by findings of linguistic studies. I find both these aspects of semiotic congenial. Too many semantic theories have neglected the purposive quality of speculation, and have been projected with an insufficient emphasis on the importance of language to whatever one chooses to call the nature of mind. (I am quite well aware that these are judgments.) The close relation of the theory of semiotic to the structure of the ancient Trivium is evidence that it is based upon the culture and learning of western civilization. The humanist finds himself on familiar ground throughout Morris's exposition. The positivist, of whatever degree, will find lessons to learn. In general, the theory of semiotic synthesizes the methodological lore of two and a half millenia. It systematizes an empirical theory of speculation in a fashion commensurate with the ideas, the language, and the experience of the twentieth century.

Morris suggests that syntactics, "the study of the syntactical relations of signs to one another in abstraction from the relations of signs to objects or to interpreters," is more fully developed than the other branches of semiotic. Students of language and logic have, since ancient times, studied inference, which "involves the study of the relations between certain combinations of signs within a language." Leibnitz developed a general calculus that has been extended within the last century and a half in the theory of symbolic logic, and, in the opinion of many critics, "has received its most elaborate contemporary development in the logical syntax of Carnap" (Morris, 1938, pp. 13–21). The theories of Wittgenstein and the Vienna Circle have been subjected to exhaustive analysis (Weinberg, 1936). Whatever may be said of the logical positivists, their theories are not sterile. Definitions, concepts, and analyses change with a baffling frequency. Indeed, much of what was undertaken by the group with Wittgenstein, and, later, in explication of "logical positivism" and "logical syntax," is quite foreign to the purpose of this book. These ideas have essentially nothing to do with experience, nor with communication. They are highly individual in precept and method, and quite without cognizance of "the social being" who communicates. Rudolph Carnap has been perhaps the most actively moving force of the earlier Vienna Circle, and he is the spokesman for the theory that is generally called "logical syntax."

SYNTAX AND POSITIVISM

It would be presumptuous to attempt a critique of Carnap's work, and of logical syntax in general, in the present context. Perhaps it is reasonable to let Morris's own summation demonstrate a connection between logical analysis as Carnap and others have expressed it, and semiosis. Logical syntax concentrates upon the logico-grammatical structure of language—that is, upon the syntactical dimension of semiosis. Morris states the point:

> In this type of consideration a "language" . . . becomes any set of rules related in accordance with two classes of rules: *formation rules,* which determine permissible independent combinations of members of the set (such combinations being called sentences), and *transformation rules,* which determine the sentences which can be obtained from other sentences . . . Syntactics is, then, the consideration of signs and sign combinations in so far as they are subject to syntactical rules. It is not interested in the individual properties of the sign vehicles or in any of their relations except syntactical ones, i.e., relations determined by syntactical rules (Morris, 1938, p. 14).

Logical syntax is mainly concerned with the consequences of statement. Its field is grammatical structure, and its medium is a kind of calculus.

One of the most thorough analyses of these points of view was undertaken by Weinberg in 1936 under the title *An Examination of Logical Positivism.* This discussion does not go far in an analysis of the efforts of Wittgenstein, Carnap, Tarski, Godel, and the others (this includes, as well, the Warsaw Circle). In many ways logical positivism (or "logical empiricism," "physicalism," and so forth) is inimical to the principal point of this book, which is a study of the dimensions of meaning. In several ways, which are admittedly borrowed interpretations, the basic system of the Wittgenstein group is a study of meaninglessness. It offers an unreal sense of meaning and scientism. If some of its basic postulates are true, they undermine the system of which they are a part. In effect, this provides a serious obstacle to communication. The system is anti-experiential.

Weinberg emphasizes that the system involves "the meaninglessness of epistemology and metaphysics." He continues: "Epistemology is out of the question because it consists of attempts to assert the relation between propositions and facts, whereas this can only be shown; metaphysics is impossible because it asserts the existence of entities which, by definition, cannot be specified in verifiable elementary propositions [the only ones allowed in the system]" (p. 291). Again, in summation: "That language is used for communication and that corroborative verifications occur is and must be an assumption. It is, however, the assumption that is almost universally made in scientific practice and in everyday life" (p. 307).

Many critics have pointed out that this sort of investigation—abstracting as it does from natural language, and referring solely to the formal structure of a language—has developed a vocabulary of analysis that might be of service to empirical research. Symbolic logic has long since been well established. This kind of consequential linguistic analysis is especially important in the construction of postulational systems, and, because so much of modern experimental method is concerned with inferential, as well as descriptive, statements, the protracted calculation of implications should be directly related to the ascertainment of truth-values.

Morris observes that the "formal logician differs from the grammarian only in his greater interest in the types of sentences and transformation rules operative in the language of science" (1938, p. 21). Perhaps a further difference, that is not appreciated by many positivists who have written in the past several decades, is that the logician is abstracting from normal language whether he knows it or not. He omits the pragmatic element of meaning. (Possibly he does not care about it.) To some linguists, however, as, indeed, to most scientists, this pragmatic element is of major importance. It is here, incidentally, that Bridgman's operational theory of meaning is most significant. Operationism can reasonably be described as a method by which the experimental scientist can control the purposive factor of his language. Within this category of semiosis, the linguist finds the historical basis and the descriptive relations of all natural languages. The linguistic habits of a community furnish him with the speech forms, the raw material, upon which his science is based. The linguist recognizes speech as a social phenomenon, and whether he is studying morphological structure, change of meaning, or the relations between them, he must inevitably give emphasis to all phases of the pragmatic dimension of signs. Unlike the formalist of whom Morris writes, the linguist cannot limit his interests to scientific discourse. For him, language is a human pattern, every facet of which should be important; his "rules" are derived not from postulates but from the habits of human behavior.

This comparison between formalist and linguist is not entirely a digression. It may serve to aid in understanding the scope of semiotic as a science. The positivists, historically notorious as empirical extremists, have frequently been castigated for making untoward claims both as to the finality of their work and as to the nature of philosophy. It is only when their ideas on logical analysis are examined in the light of research in linguistics that the logical positivists can be shown to overlook the importance of the users of a language. (See the discussion below on Chomsky's ideas.) The formal logician may, of course, limit his attention to the formal element of language, but this by no means provides him with the knowledge to lay down dicta about the nature of philosophy, the ends of science, or the conduct of communication. Morris's system offers no new explanation of logical positivism, nor of the theory of syntactical analysis, but it does a service to recurrent philosophical disputation. Semiotic supplies an adequate niche for the theoretical study of syntax, and thereby gives it a relatively undistorted position in epistemological theory. For anyone acquainted with the verbal warfare in the philosophical journals of thirty or forty years ago, this is a happy state of affairs.

SEMANTICS

With regard to the second dimension of semiotic, the scope and the achievements of semantics are not quite so clear-cut as those of syntactics. Perhaps this state of affairs reflects in part a tendency to use the term semantics as a synonym for *meaning* or meanings. Morris writes:

> Semantics deals with the relations of signs as their designata and so to the objects which they may or do denote. As in the case of the other disciplines dealing with signs, a distinction may be made between its pure and descriptive aspects, pure semantics giving the terms and the theory necessary to talk about the semantical dimension of semiosis, descriptive semantics being concerned with the actual instances of this dimension. The latter type of consideration has historically taken precedence over the former; for centuries linguists have been concerned with the study of the conditions under which specific words were employed, philosophical grammarians have tried to find the correlates in nature of linguistic structures and the differentiations of parts of speech, philosophical empiricists have studied in more general terms the conditions under which a sign can be said to have a denotatum (often in order to show that the terms of their metaphysical opponents did not meet these conditions), discussions of the term 'truth' have always involved the question of the relation of signs to things—and yet, in spite of the length of this history, relatively little has been done in the way of controlled experimentation or in the elaboration of a suitable language to talk about this dimension (Morris, 1938, pp. 21–22).

Morris believes that behavioristic experimentation "offers great promise in determining the actual conditions under which certain signs are employed," and that the critical language of semantics has been aided by recent attempts to define the doctrine of empiricism. He emphasizes the idea that the development of pure semantics, that is, a metalanguage relating to the semantical dimension of semiotic, must inevitably wait upon "a relatively highly developed syntactics." This follows from the nature of language. As Carnap puts it: "It is especially important to be aware of the fact that the rules of designation do not make factual assertions as to what are the designata of certain signs. There are no factual assertions in pure semantics" (1942, p. 25). It was pointed out in the last chapter that Korzybski's confusion between syntactic and semantic elements of a language leads him to make preposterous claims for his semantic theory.

The importance of usage is made clear in Morris's discussion of semantical rules:

> In considering this dimension, the most important addition to the preceding account lies in the term '*semantical rule*'. Unlike the formation and transformation rules, which deal with certain sign combinations and their relations, 'semantical rule' designates within semiotic a rule which determines under which conditions a sign is applicable to an object or situation; such rules correlate signs and situations denotable by the signs. A sign denotes whatever conforms to the conditions laid down in the semantical rule, while the rule itself states the conditions of designation and so determines the designatum (the class or kind of denotata) (1938, p. 23).

It seems apparent that a semantical rule is one of the biosocial phases of language; it is part of the conventional assignment of names within any speech community. This relation of rules to the speech community is a particularly interesting aspect of language. Morris does not fail to notice that the science of semantics has some serious shortcomings in respect to this category of rules:

> Rules for the use of sign vehicles are not ordinarily formulated by the users of a language, or are only partially formulated; they exist rather as habits of behavior, so that only certain sign combinations in fact occur, only certain signs are applied to certain situations. The explicit formulation of rules for a given language requires a higher order of symbolism and is a task of descriptive semiotic; it would be a very difficult task to formulate, for instance, the rules of English usage, as may be seen if one even tries to formulate the conditions under which the words 'this' and 'that' are used. It is natural, therefore, that attention has been chiefly devoted to fragments of the common languages and to languages which have been deliberately constructed (pp. 23–24).

The delineation of semantical rules for the various kinds of signs is aided by Peirce's vocabulary:

> The semantical rule of an indexical sign such as pointing is simple: the sign designates at any instant what is pointed at. In general an indexical sign designates what it directs attention to. An indexical sign does not characterize what it denotes (except to indicate roughly the space-time co-ordinates) and need not be similar to what it denotes. A characterizing sign characterizes that which it can denote. Such a sign may do this by exhibiting in itself the properties an object must have to be denoted by it, and in this case the characterizing sign is an *icon*; if this is not so, the characterizing sign may be called a *symbol*. A photograph, a star chart, a model, a chemical diagram are icons, while the word 'photograph', the names of the stars and of chemical elements are symbols. A 'concept' may be regarded as a semantical rule determining the use of characterizing signs. . . . The semantical rule for the use of symbols must be stated in terms of other symbols whose rules or usages are not in question, or by pointing out specific objects which serve as models (and so as icons), the symbol in question then being employed to denote objects similar to the models (p. 24).

Of special interest here is the term *concept*. It is a function of the interpretant; it is the individual's habit of response to certain sign-situations. In other words, a concept is the connotation by virtue of which a person uses a symbol as a characterizing sign. Since scientific discourse must eliminate all private habits of response and meaning, it becomes necessary for the semantical rules governing a concept to be rigidly limited and publicly demonstrable—thus the need for operationism in experimental science.

In his concluding remarks on the relations between sign and object, Morris stresses a truth too frequently forgotten in many discussions of meaning:

> If pragmatical features have appeared frequently in pages belonging to semantics, it is because the current recognition that syntactics must be supplemented by semantics has not been so commonly extended to the recognition that semantics must in turn be supplemented by pragmatics. It is true that syntactics and semantics, singly and jointly, are capable of a relatively high degree of autonomy. But syntactical and semantical rules are only the verbal formulation within semiotic of what in any concrete case of semiosis are habits of sign usage by actual users of signs (p. 29).

One may well believe that many of the theorists in syntactics and semantics overstate the case for the autonomy of these two fields of investigation. The more one analyzes the terminology of semiotic, the more obvious a linguistic truism becomes: the behavior of the users of a language is by all means the controlling influence at any level of abstraction. The language men speak is little affected by theory. Mathematics, symbolic logic, any of various schemes of notation that are subsidiary to natural language, are only apparent exceptions to this fact. Any valid rules of language are simply purposive generalizations. Yet the world is still full of the misapprehensions of eighteenth-century grammarians who labored under the delusion that normative laws of grammar must somehow be right and proper. Many of the syntacticians, as represented by certain extreme positivists, have seriously mistaken the nature of their work. The positivist who rules metaphysics out of the field of philosophy has a metaphysics, whether he knows it or not. Otherwise, he would exhibit the inhuman anomaly of negative behavior. The obvious aim of the student of pure syntactics and pure semantics is the delineation of the laws of consequence and of truth-values. These laws can be of service only to empirical science, itself presupposing a metaphysical "slant" that may quite possibly be at variance with other metaphysical views at certain times and in certain places. The essential point is that the rules of any language are laid down not by some rarified encyclopedia called "science" but by the users of that language. Rules reflect values, and values are teleological. This is the reason for rejecting that subtle metathesis offered by Reiser—"Scientific Humanism" (1940, 1942). If this brand of "humanism" is grounded in science, it is only a part of the whole that is the study of man. If it is a religion, as Reiser suggests, it abstracts from its empirical sanction.

This disquisition on the importance of the biosocial element of language is not a criticism of Morris. I believe that he agrees, in principle, with an insistence upon the primacy of pragmatics. His monograph makes clear the need for recognizing various levels of semiosis. At the descriptive level of analysis that he employs, the three dimensions are interlocked. At a critical level, the history of human behavior underlies any description of signs.

PRAGMATICS

The pragmatical dimension of semiosis is perhaps the easiest to understand. Certainly it is the most obvious of the three categories of sign analysis. Morris acknowledges that his term reflects a recognition of the achievements of Peirce, James, Dewey, and Mead in the field of semiosis. During the decades following World War I there was much owlish criticism of the pragmatic view of life. A favorite device of some anti-pragmatists has been to append the label of Babbitry on whatever they reject as an unaristocratic pursuit of purposive existence. This is not the place for a commentary on the ideas, genuine or apparent, that have attached themselves to pragmatic theory. It is perhaps sufficient to suggest that Morris's debt to the four leading American pragmatists has little relation to Ludwig Lewissohn's gusty damnation of the "success story" that he finds so typically ingrained in pragmatic thinking.

"It is a plausible view that the permanent significance of pragmatism," writes Morris, "lies in the fact that it has directed attention more closely to the relation of signs to their users than had previously been done and has assessed more profoundly than ever before the relevance of this relation in understanding intellectual activities" (1938, p. 29). Pragmatics deals with "the relation of signs to their interpreters," and has for its subject matter "the biotic aspects of semiosis, that is . . . all the psychological, biological, and sociological phenomena which occur in the functioning of signs." (Thus, we currently have a keen interest in psycholinguistics.)

As a historian of "scientific empiricism," Morris suggests the general background of this branch of semiotic. Historically, "rhetoric may be regarded as an early and restricted form of pragmatics." Since he does not indicate what he means by rhetoric, it is difficult to judge the weight of this qualification. The point is that the reference to interpreter and interpretation is common in the classical definition of signs. It is hoped that enough was said in the first chapter of this essay to establish the idea that in classical terms the interpreter of the sign is the mind, while the interpretant is a thought or a concept "common to all men." Modern experimental science has little use for such a doctrine. It furnishes no handles for the grasp of laboratory techniques. The mind as the interpreter of signs is a locked house to which the faculties furnish no descriptive keys. The theory is not untenable—rather it is sterile, a dead end—and modern empiricism, theoretically at least, recognizes no hypotheses that are not experimentally useful.

Morris briefly traces the history of the change from this traditional view of pragmatics. Of special importance to the theoretical relations between signs and their interpreters is Darwinian biology. A notable theoretical revision came with the loss of uniqueness in the status of man's mind and the emphasis on means of survival. Peirce concluded that "the interpretant of a symbol must reside in a habit and not in the immediate physiological reaction which the sign vehicle evoked or in the attendant images or emotions" (Morris, 1938, p. 31).

James believed that a concept was "a way in which certain perceptual data functioned representatively . . . a highly selective process in which the organism gets indications as to how to act with reference to the world in order to satisfy its needs or interests." Mead examined the social-behavioristic aspects of sign usage, believed by Morris to be "the most important study from the point of view of pragmatism of these general aspects of semiosis." Dewey's instrumentalism "is the generalized version of the pragmatist's emphasis upon the instrumental functioning of signs or 'ideas'."

The general significance of all this speculation is to concentrate the analysis of meaning within the category of expectation. The function of meaning is described in dynamic terms of evaluation, a characterization of meaning that is implicit in modern linguistics. Morris adopts these more recent pragmatic interpretations in his description of sign usage. For his purpose, the account runs as follows:

> The interpreter of the sign is the organism; the interpretant is the habits of the organism to respond, because of the sign vehicle, to absent objects which are relevant to a present problematic situation as if they were present. In virtue of semiosis an organism takes account of relevant properties of absent objects, or unobserved properties of objects which are present, and in this lies the general instrumental significance of ideas. Given the sign vehicle as an object of response, the organism expects a situation of such and such a kind and, on the basis of this expectation, can partially prepare itself in advance for what may develop. The response to things through the intermediacy of signs is thus biologically a continuation of the same process in which the distance senses have taken precedence over the contact senses in the control of conduct in higher animal forms; such animals through sight, hearing, and smell are already responding to distant parts of the environment through certain properties of objects functioning as signs of other properties. This process of taking account of a constantly more remote environment is simply continued in the complex processes of semiosis made possible by language, the object taken account of no longer needing to be perceptually present (pp. 31–32).

Here is a broad behavioristic hypothesis of the relationship between mind and language, that is consistent with psychological and physiological findings and methods. In specifying thoughts as habits, it removes the necessity, explicit in the theory of Ogden and Richards, of appealing to a mental entity that is not available to experimental research. True, Morris's account is only a simplified outline, but this is a genuine virtue, for it directs attention to the social aspects of meaning that, at least for language, are of primary importance.

Morris's conception of pragmatics is at one with the linguistic view that the structure of language is a system of behavior. "In general," he writes, "from the point of view of behavior, signs are 'true' in so far as they correctly determine the expectations of their users, and so release more fully the behavior which is implicitly aroused in the expectation or interpretation."

This point is worth purusing briefly, because it is at the core of the diversity among several semantic theories. The question is one of terminology, which for operationism is quite important. In her *Philosophy in a New Key* (1942), Langer refers to "terms," that may be "signs" or "symbols." Her analysis generally agrees with that of Morris, but her description includes what is often dismissed as "mentalism." Langer asserts that symbols "are not proxy for their object, but are *vehicles for the conception of* objects." The same can be said of Morris's "sign vehicle." However, Langer continues, "To conceive a thing or a situation is not the same thing as to 'react toward it' overtly, or to be aware of its presence." Here the pragmatist would take exception. Langer appears to draw a line (the skin of the interpreter?) that somehow implements a clear cut separation of overt and covert response. Langer insists that "signs announce their objects to him, whereas symbols lead him to conceive their objects." Truly enough, some such explanation serves to account for *displaced speech,* but what is this process or activity of "conceiving"? Is it a habit, with or without imagery, or something more, or something different? Langer states that the "connotation of a word is the conception it conveys," and observes that because "the connotation remains with the symbol when the object of its denotation is neither present nor looked for, we are able to *think about* the object without reacting to it overtly at all." The crux of the question lies in this last idea. The linguist (Bloomfield, for instance) believes that we do react to *displaced speech* in exactly the same fashion that we react to direct signification. Language, uttered or not, is simply a sign vehicle, with no accompanying gross biological effect, "mediating between the more practically important stimuli and responses" (1939, p. 17). A description that satisfies the philosopher is not acceptable to the linguist.

With the explanation of pragmatics, the full scope of semiotic is circumscribed:

> Syntactical rules determine the sign relations between sign vehicles; semantical rules correlate sign vehicles with other objects; pragmatical rules state the conditions in the interpreters under which the sign vehicle is a sign. Any rule when actually in use operates as a type of behavior,

and in this sense there is a pragmatical component in all rules. But in some languages there are sign vehicles governed by rules over and above any syntactical or semantical rules which may govern those sign vehicles, and such rules are pragmatical rules . . . The statement of the conditions under which terms of syntactical and semantical rules, constitutes the pragmatical rules for the terms in question.

The full characterization of a language may now be given: *A language in the full semiotical sense of the term is any inter-subjective set of sign vehicles whose usage is determined by syntactical, semantical, and pragmatical rules* (Morris, 1938, p. 35).

It becomes obvious that the science of semiotic finds its primary sanction in the science of linguistics. Semiotic is broader than linguistics in that it is not limited to the study of speech forms. Semiotic is a science of empirical methodology that encompasses the inferences of all science, including the formal logics, within its three categories.

DESCRIPTIVE SEMIOTIC

Morris's account of language is not so much normative as normal, within the compass of common experience:

> To understand a language is to employ only those sign combinations and transformations not prohibited by the usages of the social group in question, to denote objects and situations as do the members of this group, to have the expectations which the others have when certain sign vehicles are employed, and to express one's own states as others do—in short, to understand a language or use it correctly is to follow the rules of usage . . . current in the given social community (1938, p. 36).

Some such analysis of the use of language underlies the basic assumption of linguistic science, that "in every speech community some utterances are alike in form and meaning." This familiar, and, to date, sound statement of the social character of communication offers a striking contrast to Korzybski's singular contention that the structure of a natural language is out of keeping with the known facts of the structure of the world.

It is interesting, too, to apply this behavioristic description of knowledge to Mannheim's theory of the sociology of knowledge (see below), an application made by Morris in a sketchy form. The theory of pragmatics fits Mannheim's contention that an individual's complex of habits is initiated, usually, within the activity of a social group. Once this fact is recognized, he argues, an observer could acquire a perspective sufficient to enable him to make an objective interpretation of the group's values. Or, in Morris's terms:

When a sign produced or used by an interpreter is employed as a means
of gaining information about the interpreter, the point of view taken is
that of a higher process of semiosis, namely, that of descriptive pragmatics (p. 38).

Moreover, if one may interpret Cunningham's term *context* to refer to
this body of group habits, his theory of knowledge as penetration into
the significance of reference at once supports the sociology of
knowledge and is describable within the theory of semiotic. As Morris
remarks, psychoanalysis, pragmatism, and the sociology of knowledge
"have made this way of looking at signs a common possession of educated persons." He might well have added that rhetoric, among the
arts, has so employed descriptive pragmatics for long ages past.

Regarding the psychological aspect of semiosis, Morris notes
that, together with the social character of language, there is "a further
stipulation often made in connection with the linguistic sign: it must
be capable of voluntary use for the function of communicating." (I
am aware that the opinion reflects a strong bias, but I do believe that
any involved study of language and its uses simply must be related to
communication. Without this, there is only an exercise in an
intellectual vacuum.) For the explanation of the psycho-sociological
activity of communication, he relies on Mead's characterization of
language as "vocal gesture" and the resulting development of individual "self" and "mind" in the now familiar theory of "role-taking"
(Mead, 1934, pp. 354–378). Mind is thus given an empirical explanation: "having a mind" is equated with "using linguistic signs."
Accordingly, the two phases, sociological and psychological, of pragmatics are brought together:

> Since the linguistic sign is socially conditioned, Mead, from the
> standpoint of his social behaviorism, regarded the individual mind and
> self-conscious self as appearing in the social process when objective
> gestural communication becomes internalized in the individual through
> the functioning of vocal gestures. Thus it is through the achievements of
> the community, made available to the individual by his participation in
> the common language, that the individual is able to gain a self and mind
> and to utilize those achievements in the furtherance of his interests
> (Morris, 1938, p. 38).

The pertinent point here is that the use of language is purposive. This
is not to say that truth and utility are one. Pragmatics is only one aspect of semiosis, and the relations between a sign and its designatum
can be specified only in the semantical dimension of sign analysis.

At least one of Morris's critics challenges his theory of semiotic
on the ground that it evades the crucial question of meaning (Roelefs,

1939, p. 179). One can only wonder how the critic could fail to make such an obvious connection. It is true that Morris develops the basic description of his system without using the term meaning, but his intent is clear throughout, and in one section he specifies it: "Semiotic does not rest upon a theory of 'meaning'; the term 'meaning' is rather to be clarified in terms of semiotic" (1938, p. 44). Morris cautions against looking for meanings as one would look for rabbits (Whitehead's "fallacy of location"), or in a special realm of subsistence, "perhaps grasped by a special faculty for intuiting 'essences'," or in any sort of mental entities. The history of philosophy is full of such attempts to grasp the Protean *meaning*, most of which are inimical to empirical methodology. Morris meets the traditional rationalistic views directly:

> As a matter of fact, none of these positions has proved satisfactory and none of them is demanded. As semiotical terms, neither 'sign vehicle,' 'designatum,' nor 'interpretant' can be defined without reference to one another; hence they do not stand for isolated existences but for things or properties of things in certain specifiable functional relations to other things or properties. A "psychical state," or even a response, is not as such an interpretant but becomes such only in so far as it is a "taking-account-of-something" evoked by a sign vehicle. No object is as such a denotatum but becomes one in so far as it is a member of the class of objects designatable by some sign vehicle in virtue of the semantical rule for that sign vehicle. Nothing is intrinsically a sign or a sign vehicle but becomes such only in so far as it permits something to take account of something through its mediation. Meanings are not to be located as existences at any place in the process of semiosis but are to be characterized in terms of this process as a whole. 'Meaning' is a semiotical term and not a term in the thing-language; to say that there are meanings in nature is not to affirm that there is a class of entities on a par with trees, rocks, organisms, and colors, but that such objects and properties function within processes of semiosis (pp. 44–45).

Many theories of semantics and symbolism—those of Korzybski and Ogden and Richards are reasonably typical—emphasize the subjective, individual phases of communication while taking very much for granted the communal elements of language. Yet aside from a rare instance of "private reference," linguistic signs are manifestly public property. Their initiation and change lie within the domain of communal usage. Morris attacks the belief that "meaning is in principle personal, private, or subjective."

> Such a view historically owes much to the assimilation of the conceptualistic position within an associational psychology which itself uncritically accepted the current metaphysical view of the subjectivity of

experience. Persons such as Ockham and Locke were well aware of the importance of habit in the functioning of signs, but as the associational psychology came more and more to reduce mental phenomena to combinations of 'psychical states,' and to conceive these states as within the individual's "mind" and only accessible to that mind, meaning itself came to be considered in the same terms. Meanings were inaccessible to observation from without, but individuals somehow managed to communicate these private mental states by the use of sounds, writing, and other signs (p. 45).

A more brutal criticism would be that historically meaning has been, and still is being, subjected to and developed ex cathedra, from armchair psychology. The verbal nature of purely rational analysis is always apt to result in circular argument around the hub of the analyzer's own preconceptions, which are not always made explicit and are frequently unavailable for experimental techniques.

Morris's answer to the historical associational argument—the subjectivity of English empiricism—is expressed in the thesis that every experience and every meaning is potentially intersubjective. This thesis hinges upon two premises: first, that experience may be direct or indirect; second, that indirect experience might offer knowledge of another person's meanings. Morris's argument is that *experience,* like *meaning,* is a relational term. He remarks that "to experience something is to take account of its properties by appropriate conduct; the experience is *direct* to the degree that this is done by direct response to the something in question, and *indirect* to the degree that it is done through the intermediacy of signs." The fact that there may be subjective direct experiences is not in opposition with the intersubjectivity of meaning:

The fact that y_1 and y_2 do not stand in the relation of direct experience to each other's respective direct experience of x_1 does not prevent them both from directly experiencing x_1, or from indirectly designating (and so indirectly experiencing by the use of signs the experience relations in which the other stands—for under certain circumstances an object which cannot be directly experienced can, nevertheless, be denoted. Applying this result to the case of a particular sign, y_1 and y_2 may differ in their direct experience of the meaning situation and yet have the same meaning in common and, in general, be able to decide what the other means by a particular sign and the degree to which the two meanings are the same or different. For the determination of the meaning S_1 (where S_1 is a sign vehicle) to y_1 it is not necessary that an investigator become y_1 or have his experiences of S_1; it is sufficient to determine how S_1 is related to other signs used by y_1, under what situations y_1 uses S_1 for purposes of designation, and what expectations y_1 has when he responds to S_1. To the degree that the same relations hold for y_2 as for y_1, then S_1 has the same meaning to y_1 and y_2; to the degree that the relations in question differ for y_1 and y_2 then S_1 has a different meaning (p. 47).

This is not to say that the logical referential, and purposive elements of our language are automatically apprehended. On the contrary, in our daily communications, these attributes of meaning are apt to be taken for granted, or subsumed as part of the general state of affairs. Morris hastens to add that "in practice the determination of meaning is difficult."

Having said this much of meaning, he sloughs off the term as sterile and confusing—a judgment with which one might not agree. In its place he suggests *sign analysis*:

> Sign analysis is the determination of the syntactical, semantical, and pragmatical dimensions of specific processes of semiosis; it is the determination of the rules of usage of given sign vehicles. Logical analysis is, in the widest sense of the term 'logic,' identical with sign analysis; in narrower usages, logical analysis is some part of sign analysis, such as the study of the syntactical relations of the sign vehicle in question. Sign analysis (i.e., descriptive semiotic) can be carried on in accordance with all recognized principles of scientific procedure (p. 48).

From the demonstration that meaning refers not to an entity but to a complex relationship—in behavioristic terms, to a mediating process—it follows that meaning can be thoroughly characterized by a study of the elements that support the relationship. That is to say, so far as the study of behavior is concerned, meaning is not a relationship among three entities—mind, content, and object. Nor does Cunningham's later description of the meaning-situation—"one in which a content refers to a referent for a perspective and because of a context"—clearly specify the nature of the behavioral situation. According to Morris, any situation in awareness is a meaning-situation, and all such situations are describable as a mediating process in which a sign vehicle signifies a designatum (referent, real or imaginary) to the degree that an organism takes account of the designatum through the presence of the sign vehicle. A man, on leaving his house, notices gathering clouds overhead, returns for an umbrella, and then sets out. This is significant behavior. Nothing more than the three elements of semiotic is necessary to describe it as a meaning-situation. "Content" is the sign vehicle, in this case the gathering clouds; the designatum is rain, or the possibility of rain; the interpretant is the habit that directs the activity of returning for the umbrella—the actual "taking-account-of" the possibility of rain as signified by the gathering clouds. There is no need to postulate a context; the causal character of the behavior resides in no special element or system. It is the cumulative habit of the interpreter. It is not a cause, but a result of all his similar "takings-account-of" situations in the past, conditioned further, no doubt, by various details in the immediate present. Behavioristically speaking, the causal element exists only in the history of past expectations. There is considerable theoretical simplification in the removal of the *context* from the meaning-situation, or, in the present terms, from the sign-situation. Context cannot be satisfactorily explained except by means of the logical, referential, and anticipatory elements of the behavioral situation, and once these elements are admitted into the argument, there is no need for a context. The theory of semiotic is genuinely systemic; the three basic elements seem sufficient to characterize any meaningful behavior that is oriented to signs.

Granted that, point by point, there is little in Morris's work that is entirely new, his analysis of semiosis provides a useful synopsis of a vast amount of speculation on meaning and methodology. Designed to serve the empirical sciences, semiotic emphasizes, as many theories do not, the socially objective character of meaning, and offers a consistent terminology for studying the various aspects of sign usage. Morris suggests that the implication becomes "ever clearer that meaning is not only socially conditioned in genesis and practice, but that potentially every meaning is intersubjective, so that meaning becomes an objective phenomenon to be studied as are all other phenomena" (1937, p. 61). In light of the fact that empirical confirmation is the sine qua non of twentieth-century methodology, this approach to meaning is timely. Many thinkers today believe that "every empirical science is engaged in finding data which can serve as signs." Whether or not this observation is too extreme, it is certainly true that every empirical science must eventually generalize its results in linguistic signs. The implication of this fact is inescapable: some method of sign analysis is a methodological necessity. This is a world of meanings; meanings imply signs, and signs imply interpretation. An appreciation of these factors of knowledge clarifies the often misunderstood observations that the conclusions of science are inconclusive and that truth changes.

PURE SEMIOTIC

Pure semiotic is distinguishable from descriptive semiotic in that it is the development of a metalanguage where the three dimensions of sign analysis are discussed and interrelated. Serious difficulties unquestionably stand in the way of the consistent use of language to talk about language. The linguist knows this only too well, and has no hesitancy in creating terminology with an utter disregard for personal connotations. The precision of scientific terminology is, after all, not a matter of etymology but of restricted reference. Some of Korzybski's difficulties in this matter have been noted. There is no need, however, to employ Korzybski's normative approach to the problem of meaning. Morris is content to let pure semiotic develop from the regular channels of discourse; language develops and meanings are assigned as the need appears. Within the subordinate fields of pure semiotic, this metalanguage is in various states of development. The field of syntactics is currently receiving much attention; here belongs the entire vocabulary of logical analysis. Semantics is more poverty-stricken. Since the Hellenistic disputes over "indicative" and "ad-monitive" signs, there has been little success in attempts to work out a consistent language for the relations holding among gestures, words, and referents. Morris uses Peirce's language; Korzybski's diction has been discussed; Carnap, Tarski, and others have been at work on fresh definitions. Pragmatics has a wealth of language, a rich heritage from rhetoric and the psychological and social sciences, not all of which is sufficiently restricted in reference to be useful. Fortunately, one does not have to be a registered semiotician to feel at home in some aspects of pure semiotic. Like Monsieur Jourdain, one discovers that one has been talking in semiotic all one's life.

There is nothing in the use of critical prose per se, however, to ensure oneself of employing language with consistency and in purely empirical terms. This insurance is precisely the point of Morris's theory. If all knowledge is ultimately conveyed by means of linguistic signs, the organon both of scientific experimentation and of philosophical synthesis had better be a genuinely empirical system of sign analysis. One who is devoted to the metaphysics of empiricism can only agree with Morris on the utility of semiotic.

There is wisdom, however, in an attempt to divorce sign analysis from various other aspects of the movement to unify the sciences. Such a movement has a long tradition, and its fruition must remain a hope for the future. Whatever may be the outcome of this particular encyclopedic effort, and however much the theory of semiotic may contribute to it, Morris has put the methodological stress where it belongs—on the study of signs. There is good ground for believing that, if the sciences are ever to be unified, the formula must be evolved from some such system of sign analysis as he describes.

Regardless of the connection between his theory and this unifying movement, and regardless of the status of pure semiotic, Morris's explanation can be judged solely on its merits as an empirical theory of meaning. What is frequently forgotten or mislaid by many theorists in the field is made adequately clear in Morris's study. Meaning is a functional process of behavior, and there can be no comprehensive discussion of any one element of this process that does not implicate the other elements. Meanings imply habits, and habits are behavioral responses. Or, to put it differently, meanings imply signs and symbols. These imply rules, and rules imply interpreters. Any syntactician can evolve some kind of a logical system. The important point is that his theoretical work relates at all stages to a particular kind of behavior. The semanticist may study word-fact relations, but unless he is content to develop a normative set of rules, his findings depend upon the usage of the community. The study of pragmatics considers signs as they are interpreted, but the interpreter and his habits must sooner or later be accounted for in terms of logical relations and objective reference—real or imagined, natural or supernatural. Morris's scheme is founded on the evident truth that all human activities are reflected in the signs that mediate them. So long as one dedicates oneself to empirical methods, there is virtue in trying to avoid confusion of the various ways in which signs work. Whether one chooses to adopt any special metalanguage is a matter of utility, choice, and, probably, group habit. More important is the fact that here is a simplified method of interpreting meaning that is systematic. Each of the three elements of sign behavior is fully definable in, and only in, terms of the other two.

It is perhaps disappointing to discover that the theory of semiotic is simply an outline for sign analysis. If one begins with the usual assumptions of empiricism, however, this result should be reasonably satisfying. The scientific confirmation of experience is almost entirely relatable to the interpretation of sign situations. Semiotic claims no normative function as a method of settling the problems of the world. Morris's work is aimed solely at the elimination of verbal confusions in matters of observation, critical judgment, and system building. His goal is the development of socially objective scientific discourse based on behavioristic techniques, a rigorously empirical methodology for giving an account of interpretations of the universe. His methodological sanctions are found in the tenets of pragmatism; he adopts some of the methods, but not the anti-metaphysical values, of positivism. As a behavioristic theory, semiotic seems to successfully eliminate the need for referring to *thought* and the other "mentalistic" properties of mind, all of which exist as terms in our language, but which are not available for confirmation by experience in their "pure" forms. The theory of semiotic carries *mind* into the laboratory of experience in transposing the "content" of mind into sign vehicles, and in removing the need to pay tribute to context as a causal system somehow outside of, or different from, the individual's habits. How it continues to fare there is a question for the future; that it must be there is a necessity of empirical methodology.

GENERALIZATIONS

There are, evidently, no limits to the scope of semiotic, provided one remains in the realm of signs. Morris's principal monograph is admittedly concerned in the main with sign analysis for scientific purposes. Yet he does not envision the utility of semiotic principles as limited to the scientific universe of discourse. In an article entitled "Theory of Discourse—Science, Art and Technology" (1939), he examines the possibility of applying semiotic to other frames of reference. The observation of the role of signs in human behavior draws one's attention to the idea that human culture is a "web of sign-sustained and sign-sustaining activities." Morris writes:

> The project naturally suggests itself of approaching the nature and relations between the dominant forms of human activity through a study of the forms of discourse which are components and products of the activities in question. This approach has the method of concreteness, since in comparing, for instance, art and science it directs attention to the work of art and the piece of scientific writing, searching in them for the reflection of the differences between art and science as human activities (1939b, p. 409).

A "form of discourse" is defined as "a specialization of language for the better accomplishment of some specific purpose." Morris finds the three primary forms of discourse to be the scientific, the aesthetic, and the technological, relatable to the three elements of semiosis: "scientific discourse brings into prominence the relations of signs to objects;" "aesthetic discourse accents in a distinctive way the sign-structure itself;" "technological discourse emphasizes the efficacy of the signs in the practice of the users." The first stresses referential language and the need for confirmation, the aim being accurate prediction. The second is a language of values, and the third is concerned with inducing a mode of action. For the sake of illustration, let us observe Morris's treatment of aesthetic discourse.

Aesthetic discourse is "that specialized type of language which is the actual work of art"—a poem, a painting, a piece of music, and so forth. The idea of art as a language goes back to Plato. The ancient theory of imitation as defined by Plato and Aristotle means that the work of art is a sign, "indeed, a sign of a specific character: an image or an icon 'imitating' what is designated by embodying in itself the characters of any object the sign could be said to denote" (p. 413). In these terms, from the standpoint of sign analysis, poetic discourse is aesthetic discourse. Morris's principal suggestion is that a modern theory of signs should be able to make explicit what was no more than implicit in classical poetics, the interpretation of meaningful relations in the artistic sign-situation. The main question turns on the nature of the sign vehicle and its possible designatum. Morris advances the theory that:

> the aesthetic sign designates the value properties of actual or possible situations and that it is an iconic sign (an "image") in that it embodies these values in some medium where they may be directly inspected (in short the aesthetic sign is an iconic sign whose designatum is a value) (p. 415).

Regardless of the particular theory of values that one may hold, all objects have value properties, and aesthetic media are values. The designated value is embodied in the work of art itself, "so that in perceiving a work of art one perceives directly a value structure and need not be concerned with other objects which the aesthetic sign might denote (technically, other denotata than the sign vehicle itself)." It follows that this iconic sign "has a different truth-status from a predictive statement." It is here that Morris's theory of semiotic, when applied to aesthetics, proves itself superior to the discomforting distinction between the two major uses of language advanced by Ogden and Richards. Morris writes:

> Since the work of art does designate, and in many cases denotes the value properties of actual situations, aesthetic discourse is by no means a mere "expression of emotions"; value properties are objectively relative properties of objects and in dealing with them aesthetic discourse is concerned with the same world with which science and technology are concerned (Morris, 1939b).

The distinction, then, between art and science comes in the fact that the presentation of values is not the same thing as making statements about values. Science makes statements; art "presents values for direct experience." "It is not a language about values, but the language of value."

This sign analysis of aesthetic discourse seems to make sense. It has a long tradition and, of course, offers nothing intrinsically new to students of aesthetics and ethics. However, it can offer a genuine service to the world in an age wherein, as Eastman once suggested, the theoretical mind does obeisance to science and looks to art to justify its existence. Moreover, it is not simply traditional, for, as Morris remarks, semiotic "should be able to free the sign theory of art from the Platonic metaphysics of universals which has enshrouded the doctrine from Plato to Schopenhauer and Santayana and which itself arose out of inadequacies in existing theories of signs." Sign analysis appears to offer a method of handling value properties with all the accuracy of natural science's methods of dealing with space-time properties. The terminology of semiotic, incidentally, suggests the possibility that critics of art can clean their Augean stables of several varieties of jargon and cant; it proffers a means of scientific aesthetic and "a language in which to talk simply and clearly about art and its relations to other components of culture."

A similar approach is made to technological discourse, the distinguishing signs of which are *ought, should, do,* and *do not.* In sum, Morris writes of his theory of three primary types of discourse:

> If interests are to be satisfied and values realized it is helpful to present vividly what has been attained and what is being sought, and aesthetic discourse provides such presentation. It is also desirable to know the consequences of proposed courses of action under the conditions which have to be met, and scientific discourse favors such accuracy in prediction. Technological discourse gives the stimulation to act upon the techniques deemed effective in the realization of the values sought.

This is a synthesis of human behavior with which I have no argument. If one agrees that signs play a vitally important role in human behavior, a conviction that the modern mind seems to share with the ancient Greek, the principles of sign analysis should serve well in the rational consideration of the humanity of man.

Aiming at the consistent exposition of man's activities, the theory of semiotic delineates a practical means of eliminating confusions from critical discussion. It is not an answer to the world's ills, but rather a method to promote an understanding of them. As a science it is neither new nor mature, but a synoptic idea dedicated to empirical methodology. So far as systemic knowledge is concerned, semiotic is eclectic. It encompasses mathematics, symbolic logic, and linguistics. It utilizes the methods and the findings of social psychology, rhetoric, the sociology of knowledge, and psychoanalysis. Devoted to the task of systematizing the rules of sign usage, semiotic is, in Morris's opinion, "the framework in which to fit the modern equivalent of the ancient trivium of logic, grammar, and rhetoric" (1938, p. 56). It can be of service to science, to art, and to philosophy. Indeed, if philosophy is described as the effort to systematize the knowledge of any given period, a theory of signs may well serve as the organon of philosophy, because it directly implements what seems to be unique in philosophical speculation—the apprehension of the metaphysical object. It is extremely doubtful that the army of investigators interested in the theory of signs and the apprehension of meaning will adopt the particular terminology suggested by Morris. People do not learn linguistic habits by theoretical dicta. There is no doubt, however, that a consistent language for reference to meaning and the various elements of sign usage is necessary. To build such a language is not easy, and to use it is even less so. Semiotic at least points the way to metalingual consistency, and does so, I believe, with laudable directness.

One particular feature of Morris's treatment of sign analysis stands out—the importance of the pragmatical element of meaning. Whatever may be said of the various categories of semiotic, and however useful Morris's linguistic synthesis may prove, it is clear that sign analysis as an empirical methodology is keyed to the behavior of the individual. Neither logical relations nor truth-values have any status outside of the voluntary activities of the individual. This was the burden of Protagoras' protestation of the relativity of all things. The modern mind emphasizes an aspect of the individual, however, that does not seem to have been given special consideration in ancient speculation—that is, man's partnership in group activity. The further one searches in the modern analyses of meaning, the more evident the importance of the concept *social* becomes. There may be certain elements of behavior that are distinctly private, but empirical methods are concerned, in the main, with public responses and the intersubjectivity of meanings. Man's habits as a user of signs are governed by rules, and rules are social properties. They represent more or less definitive strains of behavior within conventional limits. It is only in the realm of the social that the controlling force of rule arises.

The comment has been made several times in the course of this work that the approach of individual psychology is probably insufficient to deal with the function of meaning. This is a behavioral function, truly enough, but one that is conditioned at every stage of social forces. The problem of meaning has been, therefore, under mass attack by social psychologists and sociologists. One of the most provocative theories of recent times is that known as *the sociology of knowledge,* already referred to as a contributor to the science of pragmatics. Among the principal explicators of the sociology of knowledge is Karl Mannheim, of the University of London, and the discussion now turns to his theses for a more detailed treatment of this major aspect of the study of meaning.

REFERENCES

Bloomfield, L. Language. New York: H. Holt & Co., 1933.
————. "Linguistic Aspects of Science." In International Encyclopedia of Unified Science I IV, edited by O. Neurath. Chicago: Univ. of Chicago Press, 1939.

Carnap, R. Introduction to Semantics. Cambridge: Harvard University Press, 1942.

Langer, Susanne K. Philosophy in a New Key. Cambridge: Harvard University Press, 1942.

Mead, G. H. In, Mind, Self and Society from the Standpoint of a Social Behaviorist, edited by C. W. Morris. Chicago: University of Chicago Press, 1934.

Morris, C. W. 1937. Logical positivism, pragmatism and scientific empiricism. In Exposes de Philosophie Scientifique, Paris.
————. "Foundation of the Theory of Signs." In, International Encyclopedia of Unified Science I, ii, 1–59, edited by O. Neurath. Chicago: Univ. of Chicago Press, 1938.
————. "Esthetics and the Theory of Signs." Journal Unified Science (Erkenntnis) (1939a) VIII.
————. "Theory of Discourse—Science, Art and Technology." Kenyon Review (1939b). I.

Reiser, O. L. The Promise of Scientific Humanism Toward a Unification of Scientific, Religious, Social and Economic Thought. New York: O. Piest, 1940.

Rice, P. B. "The New Encyclopedists: Considerations, Part 3." Kenyon Review (1939) I.

Roelefs, H. D. 1939. "The New Encyclopedists: Contra, Part II." Kenyon Review 1939 I.

Weinberg, J. R. An Examination of Logical Positivism. New York: Harcourt Brace, 1936.

Chapter 7
THE SOCIOLOGY
OF KNOWLEDGE
Karl Mannheim

Mannheim's major work was published in English in 1936 under the title of *Ideology and Utopia*. The main idea of the book is that thought, especially thought functioning in political action and ethical choice, can be understood adequately only in terms of the habits of the group to which the individual belongs. Mannheim undertakes to describe perspectives in social terms; he is interested in developing an empirical science capable of classifying the social genesis of thought— a method of analyzing what Morris calls the pragmatical dimension of meaning. He considers meanings from a historico-social approach, and the implications of his concepts and methods for the problem of meaning are stimulating to a high degree.

Only two aspects of Mannheim's theory are considered here: First, his proposed formula for examining the social backgrounds of meaning-in-action, that is, his treatment of perspectives; and, second, his analysis of the relation between social perspectives and the theory of knowledge. The detail of the historical background of the sociology of knowledge, its problems as a special science, and Mannheim's proposal of a science of politics are not the concern in this essay. Interesting as these ideas and details may be, their inclusion would only further complicate the subject under consideration. Most of the material of this chapter is taken directly from Mannheim's work. Sociology is a relatively new field of inquiry, and its progenitors have been verbally prolific. Their multiple theses are both voluble and extensive, but need not detain us overlong. Most of those with whom I am familiar acknowledge Mannheim as a major spokesman for the sociology of knowledge, although they do not always agree with his views.

(The most complete critical review of *Ideology and Utopia* in English is von Schelting's in *American Sociological Review*, I, 1936. See also, Gerard de Gré, "The Sociology of Knowledge and the Problem of Truth," *Journal of the History of Ideas*, II, 1941; G. H. Sabine, "Logic and Social Studies," *Philosophical Review*, XLVIII, 1939. For an extension of these ideas, see Werner Stark's book, *The Sociology of Knowledge*, Routledge and Kegan Paul, London, 1958).

Mannheim's theory is apparently derived from the Continental sociology of the past century and the philosophy of pragmatism. Some elements of his approach are traceable to Bacon's discussion of the "idols"—a source that Mannheim specifies—while more recent influences are the doctrines of Kant, Marx, Scheler, and Weber in Europe, and, in America, those of Peirce, James, Mead, and Dewey. The resulting theory presents both an empirical methodology and a philosophy of knowledge, a state of affairs that has troubled some of Mannheim's professional colleagues, who feel strongly that the sociological science must be kept apart from the epistemological thesis that he upholds. However, this theory of knowledge has many similarities with the ideas of Morris and Cunningham, and is perhaps not so far off the empirical track as some critics believe.

In general, the root proposition is apparently derived from Marx—"man's consciousness is derived from his social being." A key concept is that ideas serve as weapons for social interests. According to some commentators, Max Scheler might be thought of as the "inventor" of the general approach:

> The sociology of knowledge, then, is the procedure by which the socio-historical selection of ideational contents is to be studied, it being understood that the contents themselves are independent of socio-historical causation and thus accessible to sociological analysis (Berger and Luckman, 1966, p. 8).

There was reportedly much discussion, primarily Continental, about this "new discipline." "Out of this debate emerged one formulation that marked the transposition of the sociology of knowledge into a more narrowly sociological context" (p. 8). This was what was carried to the English-speaking world. The commentators write, "It is safe to say when sociologists today [1966] think of the sociology of knowledge, *pro* or *con*, they usually do so in terms of Mannheim's formulation of it."

This formulation is based in large part on the thesis that society determines the content of human ideation. The only exception would be mathematics and various aspects of the natural sciences.

> With the general concept of ideology the level of the sociology of knowledge is reached—the understanding that no human thought (with only the aforementioned exceptions) is immune to the ideologizing influences of its social context. By this expansion of the theory of ideology Mannheim sought to abstract its central problem from the context of political usage, and to treat it as a general problem of epistemology and historical sociology (pp. 9–10).

The next task is to determine how Mannheim does this.

Ideology and Utopia is a study of thought "as an instrument of collective action." Its principal thesis is that modes of action cannot be understood if their social origins are obscured. In short, as a social historian, Mannheim is interested in exposing the roots of group participation in experience. He is a student of the perspective of society:

> It is imperative in the present transitional period to make use of the intellectual twilight which dominates our epoch and in which all values and points of view appear in their genuine relativity. We must realize once and for all that the meanings which make up our world are simply historically determined and continuously developing structure in which man develops, and are in no sense absolute.

Here is a familiar pragmatic position. Mannheim believes in no such transcendental entity as a group mind. Yet it is a fact that the individual speaks the language of his group, and therefore, in the field of political action, must think as the group thinks. Nor is there any such phenomenon as original, individual thought unconditioned by society. At best, "individually differentiated thought only very gradually emerges" from the historico-social biography of the group. For the most part, political activity is carried on by "men in groups who have developed a particular style of thought in an endless series of responses to certain typical situations characterizing their common position." For example, at any given date Labor's attitude toward Capital is conditioned by the history of Labor's attempts to protect its interests in a competitive system. Moreover, Mr. John L. Lewis, Nietzschean figure though he may have been in his own mirror, emerged from the group interest; he neither created that interest nor shaped the attitudes that made possible his rise to leadership. This seems quite as true of his successors. The individual mind only extends the group's perspective, asserts Mannheim. "Every individual is therefore in a two-fold sense predetermined by the fact of growing up in a society; on the one hand he finds a ready-made situation and on the other he finds in that situation preformed patterns of thought and conduct." These ideas suggest a workable basis for understanding meaning-in-action. On the thesis that thought is language, or even on the less radical hypothesis that thought and language are never separable, Mannheim's approach fits very well into Morris's scheme of sign analysis, and with Sapir's discussion of the nature of language (Sapir, 1921). The sociology of knowledge may be treated as a method for discriminating various socially causal factors of sign usage; it is the study of the social bases that underlie the rules of interpretation. In Cunningham's language, Mannheim's system offers a method for revealing the nature of the context operating within the perspective.

This study of perspectives constitutes the major element in the analysis of meanings in political action. This study ignores Mannheim's explanation of the historical development resulting in the twentieth-century concept of *the social,* and bringing about our current consciousness of perspectives. It is enough to assume that there is an awareness of *the social* as a conditioning element of experience, and that people do evaluate ideas in terms of perspectives.

The fact that this kind of evaluation exists, at least in the realm of politics and ethics, leads Mannheim to observe that people attempt to change the world or to maintain it according to the attitudes, the social position, and the reasoning processes of the groups to which they belong. "It is the direction of this will to change or to maintain, of this collective activity, which produces the guiding thread for the emergence of their problems, their concepts, and their forms of thought" (Mannheim, p. 4). On this hypothesis Mannheim develops what might be called his operational concepts—*ideology* and *utopia.* He believes it is by the analysis of group experience according to the ideological and utopian yardsticks that the nature and direction of political action can be understood.

These two concepts furnish the sociologist of knowledge with the means of systematizing various interpretations of political reality. Both of these extreme rationales are products of "the collective unconscious"—they represent attitudes that are out of step with concrete existence. Mannheim epitomizes the account of his two archetypes in this fashion:

> Viewed from the standpoint of sociology, such mental constructs may in general assume two forms: they are "ideological" if they serve the purpose of glossing over or stabilizing the existing social reality; "utopian" if they inspire collective activity which aims to change such reality to conform with their goals, which transcend reality (1937).

The importance of considering the social factors that control meanings follows directly:

> There is thus a close bond which connects the social process itself with intellectual development and the formation of the mind. Not only the mental structure of existing social groups but the destiny of an entire social scheme may depend upon the nature of the unreal or reality transcending concepts originally embraced by these groups, upon the manner in which the original ideas have been assimilated into the social stream and, finally, upon the ultimate outcome of the inter-action between the utopian element and the other elements and the mind.

It is Mannheim's judgment that the social group that dominates the existing order determines what is to be regarded as utopian. On the other hand, the group still in the process of emergence attacks ideologies as false interpretations of the fact of existence. *Existence* in this usage means "what is concretely effective." A group's status in society is indicative of the imaginative quality of its thinking.

> In a word, all those ideas which do not fit into the current order are "situationally transcendent" or unreal. Ideas which correspond to the concretely existing and *de facto* order are designated as "adequate" and situationally congruous. These are relatively rare and only a state of mind that has been sociologically clarified operates with situationally congruous ideas and motives. Contrasted with situationally congruous and adequate ideas are the two main categories of ideas which transcend the situation—ideologies and utopias (1936, p. 183).

It is instructive to examine these two categories in some detail.

"Ideologies are the situationally transcendent ideas," writes Mannheim, "which never succeed *de facto* in the realization of their projected contents." They represent value-judgments that are out of keeping with "the functioning social order . . . according to which people really act" (p. 174). Brotherly love, for instance, in a social order founded on serfdom "remains an unrealizable and, in this sense, ideological idea, even when the intended meaning is, in good faith, a motive in the conduct of the individual" (p. 175). The individual simply has to fall short of his own good intentions.

> The fact that this ideologically determined conduct always falls short of its intended meaning may present itself in several forms—and corresponding to these forms there is a whole series of possible types of ideological mentality.

The first type is that in which the individual's convictions are such that he is prevented from realizing the lack of congruity between them and the social order in which he lives. This is the state of mind customarily described as "old-fashioned" or "hyper-conservative."

Second is the "cant mentality," "characterized by the fact that historically it has the possibility of uncovering the incongruence between its ideas and its conduct, but instead conceals these insights in response to certain vital-emotional interests" (p. 176). Third, Mannheim suggests the kind of mind that employs conscious deception, "where ideology is to be interpreted as a purposeful lie." The field of political action seems to abound in adequate possibilities for illustrating this mode of action; one's choice would depend largely upon one's point of view. In sum, the ideological mentality may range from attitudes built upon good intentions, through cant, to deliberate falsehood. These mental states are surely too familiar as types to warrant further explication. They are notable mainly insofar as they are distinguishable from the utopian mind:

> The concept "ideology" reflects the one discovery which emerged from the political conflict, namely, that ruling groups can in their thinking become so interest-bound to a situation that they are simply no longer able to see certain facts which would undermine their sense of domination. There is implicit in the word "ideology" the insight that in certain situations the collective unconscious of certain groups obscures the real condition of society both to itself and to others and thereby stabilizes it.
>
> The concept of *utopian* thinking reflects the opposite discovery of the political struggle, namely, that certain oppressed groups are intellectually so strongly interested in the destruction and transformation of a given condition of society that they unwittingly see only those elements in the situation which tend to negate it . . . They are not at all concerned with what really exists; rather in their thinking they already seek to change the situation that exists . . . In the utopian mentality, the collective unconscious, guided by wishful representation and the will to action, hides certain aspects of reality. It turns its back on everything which would shake its belief or paralyze its desire to change things (p. 36).

"A state of mind is utopian," Mannheim believes, "when it is incongruous with the state of reality within which it occurs" (p. 173). Not every wishful thought, however, is to be defined as utopian. The term is applicable only to intentions that have genuine revolutionary possibilities, to ideas that are inorganic, inharmonious, not integrated with the characteristic predilections of an epoch. The relation between the utopian mind and the existing order is dialectical in the Hegelian sense: "every age allows to arise (in differently located social groups) those ideas and values in which are contained in condensed form the unrealized and the unfulfilled tendencies which represent the needs of the age" (p. 179). For his justification of the concept of the utopian mind, Mannheim leans heavily upon the implications of Lamartine's assertion: "Les utopies ne sont souvent que des verités prématurées."

Mannheim describes several "ideal types of utopian mentalities," and traces their development in modern history. These types, like the ideological, are simply working models created by the sociologist of knowledge for the sake of outlining past and present complexities of political thought.

The first form of utopian mentality is the Chiliastic. Historically, the Anabaptist Chiliasm (anticipation of the millenium) was combined with the attitudes of the oppressed strata of society in such a way as to educe the "spiritualization of politics" that resulted in the Peasant Wars (pp. 190–191). This fusion between Chiliasm and social dissatisfaction brought about a state of mind that is perhaps clarified if one thinks in some such terms as Nietzsche's concept of Dionysian ecstasy. In political jargon, the Chiliastic-ecstatic element produced anarchy—political chaos for its own sake, truly a political religion. This utopian mind, perfectly exemplified in Bakunin's, "The will to destroy is a creative will," knows only the ebb and tide of time; it has no sense of "becoming." Such a dynamic sense is the special mark of the second type, actively opposed to the Chiliastic, called the Liberal-Humanitarian Idea, the product of the rationalism of those who set out after the French Revolution to reform the world. The idea of progress is an evaluation of existence according to a forward-looking attitude. There is a controlling principle, but the nature of the progress is indeterminate. This quality suggests a third utopian view, Conservatism, the mental pattern of which gives "positive emphasis to the notion of the determinateness of our outlook and our behaviour." Its utopian character emerges only as a counter-attack on the liberal idea. Not normally concerned with ideas, the conservative mentality is imbedded in the reality of the established order, and is activated by a sense of the uniqueness of events. Pressed by the liberal idea, it becomes utopian in trying to wish away all change in existence. The conservative mind has a sense of time in which durability is made normative. In contrast to the lack of any temporal sense in the Chiliastic mind and to the liberal's awareness of duration only in terms of progress, the conservative perspective judges the value of existence primarily as a very gradual past evolution. (Shades of Darwin and Huxley's admonitions to the contrary!) "Consequently not only is attention turned to the past and the attempt made to rescue it from oblivion, but the presentness and immediacy of the whole past becomes an actual experience" (p. 212). In judging history, this turn of mind describes existence in cyclical terms.

The fourth form of the utopian mentality is the Socialist-Communist, which presents a Janus face to the other three. The socialist-communist attitude is a synthesis of other utopias that have struggled together in the past. "On the one hand, socialism had further to radicalize the liberal utopia, the idea, and, on the other, to render it impotent or in a given case to overcome completely the inner opposition of anarchism in its most extreme form" (p. 215). Both liberal and socialist believe that the future holds their answers, but whereas liberalism postulates a vague point in the future, socialism sets a more definite date-line—the breakdown of the capitalistic system. In addition, whereas the liberal believes in the indeterminate nature of events, the socialist insists upon the determinate quality of existence: the *economic* is as important as the *social* in the structure of society. On these grounds, socialism is not an absolute utopia. It shifts its point of attack and changes its "idea" as existence shifts and changes, an attribute that brings it into conflict with conservatism. "While conservative mentality naturally connected the feeling of determinateness with the affirmation of the present, socialism merges a progressive social force with the checks which revolutionary action automatically imposes upon itself when it perceives the determining forces in history."

These various types of mentality—the one group "unreal," the other "transcending reality"—represent the constant flux of behavioral habits in political action. Within this pattern of ideologies and utopias, the sociologist of knowledge inquires into the social foundations of experience, or into what Mannheim calls "the situational determination of existence." (Compare this state with deGré, pp. 112–114.)

> Are the existential factors in the social process merely of peripheral significance, are they to be regarded merely as conditioning the origin or factual development of ideas (i.e., are they of merely genetic relevance), or do they penetrate into the "perspective" of concrete particular assertions? (p. 243).

In Mannheim's opinion the latter occurrence is true, and he looks upon the examination of perspectives as the core of the sociological analysis of thought. Perspective signifies "the manner in which one views an object, what one perceives in it, and how one construes it in his thinking" (p. 244). In supporting his theory, he sets up analogy between the understanding of perspectives and the criticism of fine art. He argues that the history of art shows that particular art forms can be dated accurately according to their style; each form is possible only at the time it appears, and each reveals the characteristics of that time. "What is true of art," Mannheim asserts, "holds *mutatis mutandis* good for knowledge."

Hence the thesis that the historico-social process is of essential significance for most of the domains of knowledge receives support from the
fact that we can see from most of the concrete assertions of human
beings when and where they arose, when and where they were formulated
(p. 243).

Cubistic sculpture and surrealism are, then, like the sociology of
knowledge itself, children of the widely diversified and overt assertive-
ness of the twentieth century.

There are many traits by which perspectives may be
characterized. Mannheim adduces seven criteria that may enable an
observer to attribute an assertion to a given epoch or situation:
"analysis of the meanings of the concepts being used; the phenomenon
of the counter-concept; the absence of certain concepts; the structure
of the categorical apparatus; dominant models of thought; level of
abstraction; and the ontology that is presupposed" (p. 244). The
application of these criteria should expose the significance of the
ideas, whether they be ideological or utopian, applied in any situation.

The first criterion is familiar enough—definition by referent.
"Freedom," for instance, meant "inner freedom" to the early
nineteenth-century German conservative and to the member of the
Protestant movement, or *"the qualitative conception of freedom"*—the
right of a man to regulate his life by his own set of values, and to
think as he chooses. The contemporary liberal conception, however,
was "an *equalitarian conception of freedom,"* the meaning conveyed
in the phrase "all men are created equal."

> That the liberal saw only one, and the conservative only another side of
> the concept and of the problem was clearly and demonstrably connected
> with their respective positions in the social and political structure (p.
> 244).

Something of the same shift in perspective is observable in the
American confusion between "rugged individualism" and "the rights
of the individual."

Much in the same vein is the phenomenon of the counter-concept.
The conservative *Volksgeist,* says Mannheim, was probably brought
into being to answer the challenge of the progressive concept of *Zeit-
geist.* The same is true with "states' rights" versus "federal centraliza-
tion" and the like.

The third criterion is perhaps less familiar.

> The absence of certain concepts indicates very often not only the absence
> of certain points of view, but also the absence of a definite drive to come
> to grips with certain life-problems. Thus, for example, the relatively late
> appearance in history of the concept "social" is evidence for the fact that

the questions implied in the concept "social" had never been posited before, and likewise that a definite mode of experience signified by the concept "social" did not exist before (p. 246).

Basic categories of thinking, too, may differ, resulting in a difference between two groups in their interpretation of existence. Modern conservatism, which is exhibited in the principles of Landon's party in 1936 or even of Eisenhower's in 1952, is apt to think in synthetic wholes that tend to preserve "the concrete totality of experience" in all its uniqueness—that is, in terms of "the American way of life," "freedom of competitive enterprise," and the like. The groups of the political left, on the contrary, tend to think according to analytical parts, a categorical structure that helps to break down the uniqueness of a situation into its components, to the end of building anew.

A fifth device to help characterize perspectives is the "thought-model," the image of an object that a man has when he begins to reflect on it. Here Mannheim subscribes to the Jamesian theory that most people think in terms of images. (*Image* in this sense does not mean pictorial representation; it may be "visual," "aural," or simply a conception, a formed idea.) He gives special emphasis to this criterion for discovering perspective:

> Behind every question and answer is implicitly or explicitly to be found a model of how fruitful thinking can be carried on. If one were to trace in detail, in each individual case, the origin and the radius of diffusion of a certain thought-model, one would discover the peculiar affinity it has to the social position of given groups and their manner of interpreting the world. By these groups we mean not merely classes, as a dogmatic type of Marxism would have it, but also generations, status groups, sects, occupational groups, schools, etc. Unless careful attention is paid to highly differentiated social groupings of this sort and to the corresponding differentiations in concepts, categories, and thought-models, i.e. unless the problem of the relation between super- and sub-structure is refined, it would be impossible to demonstrate that corresponding to the wealth of types of knowledge and perspectives which have appeared in the course of history there are similar differentiations in the substructure of society. Of course we do not intend to deny that of all the above-mentioned social groupings and units class stratification is the most significant, since in the final analysis all the other social groups arise from and are transformed as parts of the more basic conditions of production and domination (p. 248).

If one may interpose a critical aside, it is interesting to observe that in the category of audience-analysis, rhetorical theory, both ancient and modern, has developed precisely this conception of perspective. Whether one defines rhetoric from Aristotle as "the faculty of discovering in every case the available means of persuasion," or from Campbell as "the adaptation of discourse to its end," or from the *New English Dictionary* as "the art of using language so as to persuade or influence others," the writer of rhetorical discourse always, as Hudson puts it, "has his eye upon the audience and occasion" (1923, p. 177). In Aristotelian terms, the speaker offers the audience appropriate grounds of inference—logical, ethical, and emotional. In more modern psychological terms, he offers the necessary stimuli for the appropriate responses. It is a fair generalization to say that the speaker is successful to the extent that he is acquainted with the thought-models of his audience, and furnishes grounds of inference that are appropriate to the ways his audience looks at existence. This idea has been at the core of rhetorical theory since fourth-century Athens; the awareness of the thought-model is the coat hanger of rhetorical clothes (and now is part of sociological apparel).

Mannheim's sixth criterion has to do with the level of abstraction to which a given pattern of thought pertains. For instance, the "bourgeois-liberal mode of thought" never got beyond the point of "an abstract and generalizing mode of observation in its theory." Marxism, on the contrary, is principally concerned with the concrete problems it sees:

> It can be shown in the case of Marxism that an observer whose view is bound up with a given social position will by himself never succeed in singling out the more general and theoretical aspects which are implicit in the concrete observations that he makes (p. 248).

It follows in this instance, of course, that to have done so would have exposed Marxism to the same sort of examination that its adherents applied to their political opposition. Mannheim is interested in this criterion of abstraction to the extent that, on one hand, "there is a tendency to abide by the particular view that is immediately obtainable," while, on the other, some perspectives are so generalized that they remain unaware of concrete problems.

The last criterion, the ontology presupposed by the man-in-action, is not elaborated. "It is precisely because the ontological substratum is fundamentally significant for thinking and perceiving that we cannot deal adequately in limited space with the problems raised thereby . . ." The critic may infer that Mannheim subscribes to no theory that does not take into consideration the findings of the sociology of knowledge. Or, to put it another way, Mannheim's fundamental position is that knowledge in political action is founded on the social structure and governed by the social processes.

In sum, the particular meaning given to a term, the opposition of meanings, the absence of certain ideas, the categories of reasoning, the thought-model, the level of abstraction, the state of reality presupposed—all these characteristics of the perspective supply means for analyzing thought-in-action and for arriving at judgments on the nature of perspectives. In studying perspectives according to Mannheim's formula, the sociologist of knowledge builds up the data of an empirical science of sociology: his interpretations are open to the same process of confirmation that obtains in any modern science. Wirth adduces six objectives of such a "discipline" (Mannheim, pp. xxix–xxxi):

1. Determine the shifts in intellectual interest which accompany changes in social structure;
2. Study the thought of a social stratum with particular attention to the reasons why a certain group accepts or rejects ideas;
3. Discover how the interests of groups give rise to various types of knowledge;
4. Study the force which certain developments in knowledge (technology, for instance) exert in bringing about shifts in social relationships;
5. Analyze thoroughly the agencies and devices through which ideas are diffused;
6. Analyze "the institutional organization within the framework of which intellectual activity is carried on."

The implications of these objectives for a theory of meaning are almost self-evident. Mannheim's methods offer the possibility of systematizing the connections between language (thought) and behavior in a thorough-going fashion. The emphasis is placed squarely on the social bases of meanings. This is a pragmatic stress. "Our new ways of thinking" mark men as an actor, and Mannheim marshalls his arguments for the sociology of knowledge with keen insight. In Morris's terms, the sociology of knowledge relates to an understanding of the character of the interpretant; in Cunningham's terms, Mannheim's formula would help to expose the conjoint relation between perspective and context. This is Beard's point when he writes:

> The system of cross-references employed in dictionaries to indicate that the definitions are really not so clear and neat as they seem is developed by the sociology of knowledge into a wide scheme of thought, thus making knowledge a living, growing thing, rather than a collection of isolated ideas (words) held in the mind like eggs in a basket (1934, pp. 118–119).

Mannheim's theory of perspectives emphasizes an aspect of word-magic that marks his method as empirical, in contrast with the normative tone assumed by some semanticists. It is not a mistaken relation between words and things, but the inevitable operation of "the collective unconscious" that is the important fact about the process of meaning. The sociologist of knowledge, unlike the normative semanticist, does not set out by assuming a theoretical set of values. He works with the actual symbols of thought, regardless of whether the thought-pattern of the individual who uses the symbols is real or imaginary, rational or irrational, ideal or practical, pejorative or ameliorative. He works with signs as they are interpreted. Like the rhetorician, he is interested in the images with which people shape their judgments. It is probably true that most people have a set of personal terms ready at hand for the problems of the day. Mannheim suggests that for the most part these are group images. In political activity people use the words of their group; they must do so, because these represent the habits that compose the group's perspective. The aim of the sociology of knowledge is a systematic understanding of the influence of social forces upon meanings. Within the limits of Mannheim's formula, the views of a particular group can be studied to the end of determining why it accepts certain facts and rejects others; that is, to the end of determining a more precise equation between the imagery of a group and the active experience associated with this imagery.

The suggestion was made above that several of Mannheim's colleagues think well of his formula for a descriptive science, but reject his theory of knowledge. In order to understand this theory, we must turn back to the characteristics of perspectives. These he has called the qualitative ingredients of thought "which must necessarily be overlooked by a purely formal logic." However, if all perspectives contain these limiting qualities, one may well ask how it is possible for the "collective unconscious" to rise to the level of the conscious. Mannheim's answer comes in his idea of the detached perspective, itself a prerequisite for the sociology of knowledge. This detachment may come about in three ways:

(a) a member of a group leaves his social position by ascending to a higher class, (emigration, etc.);
(b) the basis of existence of a whole group shifts in relation to its traditional norms and institutions;
(c) within the same society two or more socially determined modes of interpretation come into conflict and, in criticizing one another,

render one another transparent and establish perspectives with reference to each other (p. 253).

A fourth possibility always obtains—education. Mannheim has much to say of "the socially unattached intelligentsia." Indeed, on this educated group—called "the one unifying bond between all groups of individuals"—he pins his his hopes for a scientific politics.

It is only a short step from the thesis of a detached perspective to that of *relationism*. When the individual leaves his original group for another whose outlook he adopts, and learns to criticize the beliefs and opinions of his native group, "he no longer discusses these opinions as a homogenous participant, that is, by dealing directly with the specific content of what is said."

> Rather he relates them to a certain mode of interpreting the world which, in turn, is ultimately related to a certain social structure which constitutes its situation. This is an instance of the "relational" procedure (p. 253).

Relationism is not to be confused with philosophical relativism. Relationism recognizes criteria of true and false references, but insists that "it lies in the nature of certain assertions that they cannot be formulated absolutely, but only in terms of the perspective of a given situation."

This is the reason, in Mannheim's opinion, why the methods of the sociology of knowledge relate to an epistemological theory that differentiates between knowledge that classifies data and knowledge oriented toward action. The idea of relationism implies what he calls *particularization*. What can the relational process tell us about the truth-values of an assertion, he asks, that we would not know if we have been unable to relate the assertion to a particular point of view? "Have we said anything about the truth or falsity of a statement when we have shown that it is to be imputed to liberalism or to Marxism?" Mannheim believes that the sociology of knowledge offers three paths of analysis.

First, the "absolute validity" of an assertion can be denied on the ground that it *is* bound up with a particular mode of existence and a particular perspective:

> This is the answer of those who take their criteria and model of truth from other fields of knowledge, and who fail to realize that every level of reality may possibly have its own form of knowledge (p. 166).

Second, one may conclude that the sociology of knowledge tells nothing about the validity of an assertion. It simply establishes the social equation by specializing in the "task of disentangling from every concretely existing bit of 'knowledge' the evaluative and interest-bound element, and eliminating it as a source of error with a view to arriving at a 'non-evaluative', 'supra-social', 'supra-historical' realm of 'objectively' valid truth." That this is the opinion of many critics has already been suggested. (See deGré and Sabine.) Third,—and this is Mannheim's belief—the sociology of knowledge seems to make it possible to assert that the genesis of an idea may have relevance not only to the pragmatic nature of, but also to the validity of, a judgment.

The historico-social observer is concerned not only with the purposive element of an individual's meanings, but also with the rela-tions between those thought-patterns and the world of reality, as the plurality of knowledge presents this world. The idea of importance here is that semantic rules, governing the relations between sign vehicle and denotatum, are rules (habits), and are therefore products of psycho-social behavior. In the process of relating the factual genesis of meanings to their background in the social group

> the sociology of knowledge goes a step further than the original determi-nation of the facts to which mere relationism limits itself . . . it reaches a point where it also becomes a critique by redefining the scope and the limits of perspective implicit in given assertions (p. 256).

The technique is familiar enough to the literary critic. A person sees the world according to the state of his perceptual apparatus. The observed and the observer cannot be separated—the traditional cliché of thinking about thought. However, if the observer knows this and makes allowances for his own bias, he can be said to penetrate beneath the simple factual surface of the meanings he is observing. The critic not only classifies, but, as Cunningham tries to make clear, also evaluates. This much pragmatism seems inevitable in criticism. Mannheim does not think of his observer as an omniscient being, however, nor of the sociology of knowledge as a super-science, because he recognizes no "absolute truth." His major philosophical demand is the insistence upon doing away with the concept of a supra-empirical truth of pure forms, or pure ideas, or pure meanings. Nor, in his opinion, can there be an empirical concepts of dualistic truth. Yet Mannheim does not claim that his methods of analysis will "reveal the truth":

> The mere delineation of the perspectives is by no means a substitute for the immediate and direct discussion between the divergent points of view or for the direct examination of the facts.

He generalizes his position thus:

> The function of the findings of the sociology of knowledge lies somewhere in a fashion hitherto not clearly understood, between irrelevance to the establishment of truth on the one hand, and entire adequacy for determining truth on the other. This can be shown by a careful analysis of the original intention of the single statements of sociology of knowledge and by the nature of its findings. An analysis based on the sociology of knowledge is a first preparatory step leading to direct discussion, in an age which is aware of the heterogeneity of its interests and the disunity of its basis of thought, and which seeks to attain this unity on a higher level (p. 256).

It becomes evident that Mannheim's epistemological position is based upon the belief that there can be no knowledge that is divorceable from the perspective of the knower, that truth is a function of meaning, and that there is a vital activistic element in all political and ethical knowledge that has no empirical connection with a suppositional "world of pure thought." Granted that the type of knowledge concerned only with classification can well employ validating grounds outside the realm of factual items, there are certain kinds of knowledge that are enmeshed inextricably with the intentions of the knower. This is another way of saying that a "fact" is not "truth," and that any conception of truth depends upon the way in which the knower connects his thoughts (terms, words, images) with what he recognizes as the "fact" of existence. "Not purpose in *addition* to perception but purpose *in* perception," Mannheim asserts, with strong support from the pragmatists, ". . . reveals the qualitative richness of the world in certain fields" (p. 265). The "certain fields" are politics and ethics.

Here is the basis of Mannheim's philosophy of knowledge. In insisting upon the importance of perspective to knowledge, he rejects absolute truth and supports pluralistic knowledge. His assault on the dualism of "real" and "ultimate" truth is a familiar one. In the physical sciences, for instance, the laws of validity are determined by the methods and findings of those sciences:

> The theory of knowledge takes over from the concrete conditions of knowledge of a period (and thereby of a society) not merely its ideal of what factual knowledge should be, but also the utopian conception of truth in general, as for instance in the form of a utopian construction of a sphere of "truth as such" (p. 261).

There is no absolute of knowledge or of truth. Yet, though there may be changing conceptions of truth, its nature is not shaped by chance.

This is a product of the times. In the terminology of semiotic, semantical rules control the nature of truth in any given period, and, insofar as all rules are aspects of human purposes, truth-values are the products of behavioral habits. As Morris suggests, even formal logic has its empirical side, a state of affairs not always understood by the positivists. There is always present in thinking an "*a priori* variable," a set of meanings that govern the use of empirical data and outline the structure of logical inference (Morris, 1937, p. 51). In Mannheim's opinion:

> We see, therefore, not merely that the notion of knowledge in general is dependent upon the concretely prevailing form of knowledge and the modes of knowing expressed therein and accepted as an ideal, but also that the concept of truth itself is dependent upon the already existing types of knowledge. Thus . . . there exists a fundamental although not readily apparent nexus between epistemology, the dominant forms of knowing, and the general social-intellectual situation of a time. In this manner the sociology of knowledge at a given point, through its analysis by means of the particularizing method, also penetrates into the realm of epistemology where it resolves the possible conflict among various epistemologies by conceiving of each as the theoretical substructure appropriate merely to a given form of knowledge (p. 262).

This means simply that knowledge is pluralistic and, accordingly, truth is relative—an insight voiced by Protagoras, shared on occasion ever since his time, and often forgotten.

Mannheim believes that this observation of the social bases of knowledge and truth implies that an acquaintance with the genesis of a proposition can tell us something about its validity. True, the dualism of "being" and "meaning"—the separation of the known from the act of knowing—is necessary for the quantitative sciences. Political and ethical knowledge cannot be characterized within any such dichotomy, however. Here knowledge is activistic, qualitative, revealing "purpose in perception."

> 'Social existence' . . . an area of being, or a sphere of existence, of which orthodox ontology which recognizes only the absolute dualism between being devoid of meaning on the one hand and meaning on the other hand takes no account (p. 264).

In other words, states of being in "social existence" carry within themselves their own particular brand of consistency. In summary:

> The next task of epistemology, in our opinion, is to overcome its partial nature by incorporating into itself the multiplicity of relationships between existence and validity (*Sein und Geltung*) as discovered by the sociology of knowledge, and to give attention to the types of knowledge

operating in a region of being which is full of meaning and which affects the truth-value of the assertions. Thereby epistemology is not supplanted by the sociology of knowledge but a new kind of epistemology is called for which will reckon with the facts brought to light by the sociology of knowledge.

Mannheim, who wrote this paragraph in 1931, does not seem to recognize that this "new epistemology" was well under way. This is precisely the field, and at least one of the aims, of the intensive study of signs and of meanings that goes back more than forty years. Some speculators pay special attention to problems of symbolism in the belief that the symbol is the only datum of the thought. Some use other approaches. All are concerned with the relations between meaning and knowing. Cunningham's thesis that all meanings are significant is clearly echoed in Mannheim's requirement. Morris's theory of semiotic is dedicated to the development of a unified language of epistemology. Bridgman's theory of operational meaning is aimed specifically at the exposition of experimental limitations in physical research. Ogden and Richards earlier took some tottering steps toward Mannheim's goal. Korzybski's system includes some pertinent points, but in general only exemplifies Mannheim's strictures on "the utopian conception of truth." In short, most of the modern theories of meaning examined thus far are dedicated to a knowledge of existence, and therefore should include the empirical findings of the sociology of knowledge. Moreover, this "new epistemology," as outlined or implied in the systems considered here, equates knowledge with penetration into the process of meaning, and therefore includes Mannheim's epistemological principles. In fact, as Morris suggests, the entire field of the sociology of knowledge can well be incorporated under semiotic. Mannheim offers no systematic theory of meaning, but some methods for studying the pragmatic element of meanings, for understanding perspectives.

Whether his explication of the sociology of knowledge entails an exact science, a highly conditioned science, or a pragmatic philosophy, has bothered some of Mannheim's critics more than it does this one. More important is the fact that critics of all colors and designations find Mannheim's methods for studying social forces significant and fruitful. He adds a strong voice in support of the principle of pluralistic knowledge. His historical analyses are carried out with a keenness of insight that is refreshing in an age of mathematical equations and statistical tables.

Even his normative recommendations are offered with restraint. For the most part, his thinking about education has been passed over in this discussion, but it may be in order to include here a brief summary of his prescription for social rehabilitation. "The attempt to escape ideological and utopian distortions," he writes, "is, in the last analysis, a quest for reality." The awareness of these distortions, possible only on the part of a "displaced perspective," provides the basis for a sound skepticism. One must read, watch, and interpret with suspicion. These habits "can be used to combat the tendency in our intellectual life to separate thought from the world of reality, to conceal reality, or to extend its limits." Insofar as a man can bring his group perspective into consciousness, he can negate the force of it, and, ultimately, it might be possible to so broaden the sociological basis of knowledge as to achieve a higher degree of cooperation in the interaction of social groups. Mannheim puts much faith in the technique of problem-solving by group discussion. Like Dewey, he believes that it is here that "creative thinking" exists. When we know our own particular usage of symbols and that of others with whom our existence is interactive, we are better able to modify our ideas for the sake of concerted action on common problems. Mannheim's hope rests in the education of perspectives. People must learn to stop "talking past one another." They must learn the technique of problem-solving. He cannot say whether the application of his methods

> . . . will ultimately lead us to a fully rationalized world in which irrationality and evaluation can no longer exist, or whether it will lead to the cessation of social determination in the sense of freedom through a complete awareness of all the social factors involved. This is a utopian and a remote possibility and is therefore not subject to scientific analysis (p. 170).

There are grounds for believing that such a state of affairs is truly utopian. The techniques of group discussion have been utilized for various purposes, but there remains a legitimate doubt that an understanding of another's perspective is sufficient warrant for adopting his values. The ability to apprehend other perspectives may help to evoke the issues at stake, but it does not usually remove the conflict of interests that creates those issues.

I take leave of Mannheim's theory with the observation that it stimulates a better acquaintance with the social forces that control the individual's apprehension and evaluation of existence. The sociology of knowledge does not touch directly on many problems—communication, for instance—that are vital for a complete understanding of the nature of meaning. Even within its own limits it is as yet undeveloped.

At the present stage of development, we are still far from having unambiguously formulated the problems connected with the theory of the sociology of knowledge, nor have we yet worked out the sociological analysis of meaning to its ultimate refinement . . . These studies are attempts to apply a new way of looking at things and a new methods of interpretation to various problems and bodies of fact.

Both Mannheim and Morris emphasize the status of *the social* in the study of meaning. Within this category are subsumed both the conventional background of sign usage and the overtly pragmatic idea of expectation as the domicile of meaning-in-action. Whereas Mannheim limits his attention to the critical evaluation of social phenomena as meaningful situations, Morris is much concerned with the development of a metalanguage to encompass the entire field of sign usage. Morris's work might appropriately be characterized as an attempt to evolve a language with which to speculate on communication. He treats the general aspects of the process, but does not anatomize it.

There is one book, however, that is apparently dedicated to this end—Karl Britton's *Communication: A Philosophical Study of Language*. Britton offers nothing to the development of a critical language, but he attempts with varying success to epitomize the communicative process. The subtitle means simply that he employs the methods of propositional analysis. Actually, he is rather more interested in debating technical logical topics of importance some years ago than in providing fresh insights to the problem of meaning. Much of his book is dialectic to answer the extreme positivists and the devotees of the theory of physicalism. He adopts several principles of behaviorism and phenomenalism, and uses the "Cambridge technique" of logical analysis to examine "normal" communication within the Ogden-Richards categories.

REFERENCES

Beard, C. A. The Nature of the Social Sciences in Relation to Objectives of Instruction. New York: C. Scribner's Sons, 1934.

Berger, P. L. and T. Luckmann. The Social Construction of Reality. New York: Doubleday, 1966.

deGré, G. "The Sociology of Knowledge and the Problem of Truth." Journal History Ideas, (1941) II.

Hudson, H. H. "The Field of Rhetoric." Quarterly Journal of Speech (1923) IX.

Mannheim, K. Ideology and Utopia: An Introduction to the Sociology of Knowledge. Translated by L. Wirth and E. Schils. New York: Harcourt, Brace & Co., 1936.

————. In Encyclopedia of the Social Sciences (1937) XV: 201.

Morris, C. W. 1937. "Logical Positivism, Pragmatism, and Scientific Empiricism." In Exposes de Philosophie Scientifique, Paris.

Sabine, G. H. "Logic and the Social Studies." Philosophical Review (1939) XLVIII.

Stark, W. The Sociology of Knowledge. London: Routledge & Kegan Paul, 1958.

von Schelting, A. "Ideologie und Utopie." American Sociological Review (1936) I.

Chapter 8
THE ANALYSIS
OF PROPOSITIONS
Karl Britton

Karl Britton was among those who, some years ago, turned to various communicative aspects of the study of meaning. He did this not as a rhetorician but as a commentator who set up a scheme for the analysis of propositions that seem to communicate in different ways. His main argument is that there are four different kinds of language—empirical propositions, necessary principles, moral and ethical judgments, and poetry. All these forms of communication can be explained by one or both of the two principal categories of linguistic usage: language "may inform and it may affect the emotions." Britton's debt to the *Meaning of Meaning* is obvious. However, he is devoted to the doctrine of commonsense, and avoids a few of the theoretical pits into which Ogden and Richards fall in their early work. It is to be doubted that Britton deserves special credit for this, however. His method is to avoid any questions that cannot be answered by propositional analysis. Consequently, he oversimplifies the analysis of meaning and advances no further as to conclusions than did Ogden and Richards.

In lieu of a bibliography, Britton lists his theoretical antecedents in the preface to *Communication: A Philosophical Study*, and to know them is to go far toward understanding the author's "philosophy" of language. The group includes Bertrand Russell (*The Analysis of Mind*), Ogden and Richards (*The Meaning of Meaning*), Richards (*Principles of Literary Criticism*), C. I. Lewis and C. H. Langford (*Symbolic Logic*), L. Wittgenstein (*Tractatus Logico-Philosophicus*), R. Carnap (*The Unity of Science*), L. S. Stebbings (*Logical Positivism and Analysis*), W. Empson (*Seven Types of Ambiguity*), and articles by John Wisdom, L. J. Russell, O. Neurath, and M.

Schlick. Logical analysts are overwhelmingly present here; linguists are conspicuously absent.

According to Britton, the general purpose of *Communication* is "to give an account of the principal uses to which language . . . is commonly and properly applied" (p. 1). One may or may not wish to accept this statement, even as a truncated version of "communication." It is rather grandly self-limiting; this tends to be habitual in Britton's approach. These "uses" are equated with those of Ogden and Richards, but whereas the latter specify them as "symbolic" and "emotive," Britton selects the terms "informative" and "dynamic" to describe his dichotomy. With regard to the four kinds of language, it is clear that he refers to the functions of language in much the same manner as do Ogden and Richards. In other words, the rough outlines of the early "science of symbolism" are used by Britton to trace his observations on communication.

The explanation of reference and the two uses of language is grounded in the same kind of quasi-behaviorism that is exhibited in *The Meaning of Meaning:* "words mean thoughts." A thought is a "mental state" that has an object; one person communicates with another when he provokes in him a thought of the same object that serves as a referent for his own thought.

> Words are used to provoke in people thoughts of objects of a certain sort—propositions, logical possibilities (p. 18).

Words are used purposefully to call up propositions.

> And here we meet . . . the two sorts of purpose for which words may be used: the words are used to inform, by the communication of propositions; or they are used to *move*—either by the communication of propositions or by other means. But very often the same words are used with the two sorts of intention at once.

It is plain why Britton's theory is fundamentally only quasi-behavioristic. If words mean thoughts that are propositions, the obvious conclusion is that a proposition is simply a series of words. Accordingly, there is no need to draw the term *thought* into the discussion. It serves only as a "mentalistic" entity that cannot be studied by empirical means.

At least the purpose of moving is not made alogical here, as it is in *The Meaning of Meaning.* Britton believes that words operate symbolically even when the purpose is "to move." Yet what of the activity of purpose in informative discourse? In any commonsense account, purposive communication seems to include some set of attitudes.

Many people agree with Delacroix that there is some sort of affective element in all speech. When one is indifferent, one remains silent. If it is true, as it seems to be, that "very often the same words are used with the two sorts of intention at once," one must continue to wonder about the usefulness of the distinction. It is one thing to agree with Cicero that the speaker's purpose is to inform, to conciliate, and to move. It is quite another thing to insist that language is informative or dynamic. Again—as in *The Meaning of Meaning*—there is a fundamental confusion between the uses of speech and the functions of language. Campbell was closer to the mark when he outlined the utility of speech for "explaining, convincing, pleasing, moving, and persuading" (Campbell, 1776, p. 17). Explanation, conviction, and persuasion are all subsumed in the term "informative." Pleasure and emotion are evoked in the "dynamic" use of words. But, according to Britton, propositions may also be called up when the purpose is to move. The further one takes the analysis of this bifocal view of language, the more its fictional character becomes evident.

The actual point toward which Britton is driving is that the "informative intention" implies consistency and verifiability, while the "dynamic intention" does not—or, at most, is not open to the same logical tests. This point is considered again later.

Britton defines a set of terms with which he constructs three senses of meaning. The *reference* of a sentence is its effect on the behavior of a person who understands it—"who has proved himself able, in a regular way, to identify the objects indicated by the separate words in the sentence, and who is acquainted with the relevant syntax" (p. 24). This statement seems to define not reference but understanding. *Belief* is "reference which involves special feelings and special behavior." The referent is "the object of thought"—the situation, always physically experiential, toward which the hearer is oriented. *Significance* is a blanket term for private responses—"mental processes." Finally, as a reminder, truth-values are testable by the "abstract facts of fully concrete events." These definitions suggest why Britton describes his attitude toward communication as behavioristic (pp. 23, 78,). Actually, he is only saying what Morris has expressed with greater precision: sign usage has three elements—word order, word-fact relations, and the psychological state of the interpreter, for whom words act as attention-getters.

It follows from these definitions that meaning becomes a generalized process including these elements, but Britton chooses never to synthesize the process. Instead, he discusses three kinds of meaning—reference, significance, and definition. He suggests three stages of informative communication: utterance, understanding, and verifiability. "The reference of a sign is that state of bodily adaptation which enables the body to pick out a certain definite class of objects." (The definition of this class of objects is, of course, formulated by agreement among the majority of users of a language; it is determined within the traditional range of meaning in the speech community.) The distinction between reference and significance is that reference is the effect of a sign upon the body of the listener, while significance "may also affect his immediate experience." "A sign has significance for . . . the listener if it leads to . . . an expectation." This somewhat oblique observation seems to mean that both reference and significance are phases of the situation in which speaker and hearer are active. Each is, in a sense, private meaning that is made public by verifiability, that is, by considering the semantical rules that are applicable, and by noting whether or not anticipation is satisfied. If a person states that a piece of fruit looks yellow to him, he may be telling us "something about the character of *his experience now,* and of how it resembles *past experience of* his for which he agreed to use the sign 'yellow-looking'." Britton's point is that "what he tells us, no other observer can either refute or confirm" (p. 31). The upshot is, as Morris and Weinberg have stated, that the intersubjectivity of meanings is the prevailing sanction for accepting reports in scientific discourse (Weinberg, 1936, p. 307). This is in direct opposition to much positivist opinion that insists upon referring to a world of events, but says precious little about the way words and their objects are connected.

Britton's third sense of *meaning* is definition. This is simply lexical meaning, either within the traditional range or as particularly specified by the speaker. He remarks that "meaning by definition" has both informative and dynamic aspects:

> Besides conveying information about customs actually prevailing amongst a certain group of people, [when we define a term] we are trying to command or persuade our audience to follow that custom and not to use words in any other way (p. 36).

Here is a statement of the obvious linguistic point that all languages are normative.

In general, Britton's explanation of meaning makes no contributions to our knowledge, but it does furnish the possibility of considerable confusion. His distinction of three kinds of meaning is misleading, and he seems unable to decide whether meaning is an object, a state of affairs, or a process. One can only conclude that his thinking on meaning is choppy and incomplete. Moreover, he makes no clear-cut discrimination between the meaning of a word, developments and changes of which can be traced historically, and the meaning of a total utterance. The two are blended—perhaps this is only a verbal confusion—and meet only within the smoke screen of arm-chair psychology. He admits that "everywhere in this book problems of 'meaning' have had to be over-simplified. . ." The simple truth is that not all problems of meaning can be solved by logical analysis; recourse must be had to empirical facts, the most important of which come from the fields of linguistics, sociology, biology, and psychology.

Yet it is upon this foundation of two uses of language and three kinds of meaning that Britton builds his theory of communication. It is not surprising that the net results are simply a normative brand of commonsense.

Britton observes that an important function of language is the assertion of empirical propositions, of which there are five subordinate types (this material is discussed in Chapters 3 and 4 under the heading "Theory of Contingent Propositions"):

1. Physical Property Sentences.
   The moon will be full tonight.
   This radiator is very hot.
2. Emotional Property Sentences.
   The moon is looking lovely [the moon looks, lovingly?].
   This radiator is a nuisance.
3a. Sensation Reports.
   I see a bright circle high up.
3b. Emotion Reports.
   I feel tired.
4. Perception Sentences.
   She tasted the dish with approval.

Britton subjects these five types of assertions to an exhaustive, and frequently digressive, analysis.

He labels Type 1 informative: these assertions suggest sensory experience that might be shared by any normal person in the speech community. They are verifiable, so long as one remains within the traditional range of English. They "make possible an exchange of information about physical objects." They carry the implication that "all normal people have very similar sense-experiences." This reasoning seems unimpeachable.

Sentences in Type 2 are essentially dynamic in meaning; they convey information only to those whose values are similar to the values of the speaker. Britton habitually associates value-judgment with emotional response, but has nothing to say of the semantic nature of values.

Types 3 and 4 are informative in a special sense:

> In my opinion, the use by A of a sentence of either type would at once suggest to me that A is immediately acquainted with the sort of experience (color, smell, feeling), that leads me to make use of the words he utters, or other words closely connected with these in the syntax of the language (p. 75).

Thus, the intersubjectivity of meanings makes introspective reports useful to science. Type 3a is difficult to verify, and is rarely used except in psychological laboratories. Type 3b can give no accurate information, and, like Type 2, is essentially an emotive expression. The reason for this is that the "average" person does not have the terms with which to develop a very accurate description of his own physiological activity.

Type 4 is also an example of sentences "often taken to mean a proposition that could be *more directly expressed* in a combination of sentences of Type 1. and Type 3., between which a causal implication holds."

Britton's general conclusion about contingent propositions is that it is logically possible for one person to be aware of another person's experience, but causally impossible. In spite of this, one may accept other people's reports as factual on the ground that perception is standard; all normal people are physiologically similar. Moreover, beliefs about the nature of the world are grounded in social forces: one can prove an assertion of Type 1 by observing that other people say the same thing under similar circumstances. In other words, the facts are abstracted from publicly observable objects, and the probability of truth increases with the numerical progression of similar reports. All of this is simply a rather plodding account of the principles of induction. Here, too, however, the facts are oversimplified. Britton thinks that certain assertions are readily verifiable because perception is standard—this is public meaning. Other assertions are not so readily verifiable because feelings are not standard—this is private meaning. The implication is that perceptions and feelings are nicely separable, a state of affairs that Britton assumes, but does not demonstrate. In the last analysis, the public quality of meaning resides in the nature of the referential habits of any group of people, and nowhere else. Britton's last word on contingent propositions is the pragmatic observation that "an expression conveys information if it gives rise to suggestions about possible future experiences in certain possible circumstances;" ". . . the test for truth lies always in the immediate experiences of the person who tries to verify the proposition" (p. 142). These cannot be said to be fresh insights; like most modern empirical generalizations on meaning, their net effect is to combat the doctrine of absolute truth.

Britton's second kind of language is that of necessary propositions ("All white swans are white;" "All white swans are birds;" "All men are mortal"), self-evident by nature, and useful as systemic postulates. These are a priori propositions that serve as hypotheses. The main thesis is that "all Necessary Propositions that are really valid can be expressed by explicit tautologies." To this he adds two others:

(1) That necessary propositions give us information, not about the objects designated by their terms, but about language—about the signs that are used to express the necessary propositions. So that they give us no information at all about all possible worlds, nor (apart from language) about the actual world; they give us information about our use of *words*.

(2) That necessary propositions are not merely informative but regulative or legislative. They command or recommend a certain usage of words—they have a dynamic, as well as informative, use (p. 146).

Various squabbles over the Aristotelian "laws of thought" indicate that the "commands" occasionally fall upon deaf ears. Again, there is nothing startling in these generalizations. The proposition that "all men are mortal" refers to the world only in that it specifies the use of the term *mortal;* this is what has been called a definitive proposition that has no substantial reference. In other words, logic is normative; it deals with the ways in which terms may be combined. Its subject matter is form, not content. As hypotheses, necessary propositions furnish a needed step in demonstration, but by no means the final step.

This discussion of necessary propositions leads to a treatment of the "Structure of Language and Structure of Fact" (Chapter 8). Britton observes that questions of reference are answerable by the specific sciences, while questions of consistency—of the use of formal signs—belong to the logician's interests. The structure of fact—our abstractions from concrete events—must, in the realm of informative language, be self-consistent, must avoid contradiction. A fact is "that in events to which we make a learned discriminating response determined in part *by the understanding of statements*" (p. 204). The world is not deterministic. Events per se have no structure. Facts do have structure, and something can be learned about the structure of facts from the formal laws of language. In other words, say, the "critique and theory of scientific speech is the task of logic" (see Bloomfield).

In his treatment of a third kind of language, Britton undertakes to determine "what references are made by sentences which—as Kant would say—'are used to express Rules, Counsels, Laws.'" This chapter is a meandering exegesis of what Morris calls technological discourse. Britton determines that moral and ethical judgments are both informative and emotive:

> They make statements about the relation between the interests of the audience and certain events or objects and they make them in such words that the audience is moved immediately to feel in a certain way towards or against the objects concerned: they very words used to describe these objects tend to make a momentary interest for or against them (p. 213).

(One might almost suppose from this that Britton is becoming a rhetorician.) In other words, moral and ethical judgments are intimately related to the pragmatic element of sign usage. They express attitudes, serve as commitments to behave in certain ways, and induce people to share these attitudes toward certain objects (see Kaplan, 1942, pp. 283 ff.). Value judgments appeal from and to beliefs about the nature of the world. Yet, though the diction of technological discourse inevitably has emotive repercussions, "we have not here something quite different from information;" on the contrary

> to assess the value of something cannot be contrasted sharply with describing its properties: for value-propositions do tell us certain properties of things, viz. the way in which they may help or hinder human happiness. But they convey information in words which inevitably affect our attitude towards the things described—tend to make us favour them or oppose them, seek them or shun them. So that a value-proposition may be highly persuasive—whether it happens to be a true statement or a false one (Britton, p. 277).

There is no need to dispute these various observations. It is difficult to understand, however, how, on these principles, Britton or anyone else can successfully distinguish between informative and dynamic language in a political debate, for instance, or in any other sphere of human experience in which the participants face action and choice.

Britton's treatment of the language of poetry in Chapter 10, is less satisfactory. Although he goes beyond Richards's early exclusion of referential meaning from poetry, his general conclusions are only too similar to those of Richards. He writes:

> My conclusion then must be that imaginative writing has its quite distinctive 'truth' and 'falsity', its 'reasonings' of the heart that Reason does not know; its 'meaning'. But for these different features of imaginative writing, the terminology of science and history is inappropriate and positively misleading. For the 'truth' *that is peculiar to poetry*—its *validity*—is simply its value for men: this can be assessed, and statements *about* the value of poetry are themselves either true or false in the straightforward sense of those words. And the 'reasons' of poetry are those emotional connections which are fundamental to poetry; they are not founded upon any relations of implication. And the 'meaning' that is peculiar to poetry is not reference to an identifiable object, but a certain definite effect upon the feelings. . .
>
> We are left, then, with no grammar, no logic that is a genuine alternative to the logic and grammar of scientific and historical language. When we use language that is *exempt* from the canons of scientific and historical writing and has its own canons, we find that *we are not using words to convey information at all* (p. 275–276).

True, Britton limits his attention to lyrical poetry, and therefore seems to limit the scope of his conclusions, yet he means these observations to be applied to all forms of poetics. The type of thinking exemplified here persistently puts the cart before the horse. One is led to believe that poetry is somehow "about" a world that is quite different from the world of science. Nothing could be further from the truth, and no amount of juggling with logical principles could produce two worlds— one of the "mind," the other of the "heart." Like Richards, Britton underestimates the intellectual quality of literature. The trouble seems to have a dual source: first, the belief that the accomplishments of science are somehow outside of human values; second, the belief that value-properties are not just as much a part of objects as are space-time properties. One gets the feeling from Britton's approach—and from all others like it—that the scientist never works with discretion and that the poet never writes objectively.

This is a strange bifurcation of human activities. True, the object of scientific discourse is prediction, while that of poetic (or aesthetic) discourse is the exemplification of values. However, how can it be that there is an informative use of words in moral and ethical value-judgments and yet none in the arts, which are devoted to the conveyance of these judgments? As Morris suggests, there is much more to aesthetic language than an appeal to the emotions. There is only one world about which both scientist and artist speak, and value-properties can scarcely be dismissed as emotional effusions. If so, what is the value of scientific prediction? The evidence for the statement demonstrates life, and therefore the breadth of human behavior. This seems fairly conclusive. It follows that there is quite as much "logic" in poetry as there is in existence. One concludes that Britton is far off the track of "truth" when he insists that in "poetry we are not using words to convey information at all." Considering how little is known of human emotional activity, one must observe that the Richards-Britton generalization errs in its initial assumption.

This assumption is the conviction that the informative-dynamic dichotomy offers a sufficient description of linguistic activity. Furthermore, in the belief that these two uses of language are clearly distinguishable, the theorist must put into one category whatever does not fit cleanly into the other. By so doing he is free to talk about statements that give information and statements that express or inspire emotional responses. But what about *experience*? Both Britton and Richards (notably in his *Principles of Literary Criticism*) lean heavily upon this term, but neither undertakes to define it. In this oversight each begs the question of the utility of the two primary categories. Britton writes in his chapter of summary: "My principal conclusion about Informative Language is that all such language is about what we may experience" (p. 227). We have just taken note of his statement that poetry gives no information about the world. Is the corollary the assertion that poetry has no relation to experience? It follows logically, but Britton probably does not mean this. I suspect the trouble is mainly verbal, and that the verbosities begin and end with this theory of the dual usage of language. It seems apparent that *experience, like meaning,* is a complex and treacherous term, and that everywhere in Britton's book complexities are oversimplified and terminology is loose. Perhaps the entire question can be laid to rest with one of Britton's final remarks:

> It is hard, certainly, to separate the informative from the dynamic, expressive, emotional uses of language; they are seldom met with in pure forms (p. 279).

Britton's style and methods of approach are loose and inexact. His style is extremely skittish; his diction varies haphazardly from colloquialism to technical logical jargon. His explanation of communication suffers not only from the shortcomings of his assumptions, but also from the limitations of conversational language. The "Cambridge School" of analysis, to which Britton belongs, is devoted to the dissection of facts according to the usage of correct English. One commentator suggests that there is a climate of opinion present there that is hostile to metaphysics and speculative philosophy, and devoted to the dogma of commonsense (Black, 1939). The only sign of Britton's metaphysical hostility is his utter lack of attention to metaphysical questions. Yet his work is representative of this climate of opinion. He rings the changes of colloquial usage until the problems disappear. Of course, they do not really disappear; they simply fade into the haze of oversimplification. So far as his methods can take him, Britton says much that is sound, pertinent, and well authenticated by the traditions of Western culture. Accordingly, it is perhaps unfair to expect anything more than commonsense from his analysis of communication. There is some reason to believe, however, that the language of the man-in-the-street is not sufficiently refined to handle the complexities of meaning and experience. A long exposure to a methodology based on "correct" rules of English and the "proper" use of words inclines one to the opinion that Britton is here concerned with a world of dreams, presided over by the grammarians of eighteenth-century England. People do not talk or think in "proper" language according to "correct" rules. They use the language they have learned from their group. The problems of meaning and communication are not limited to the educated group. The average man does not deliberate about meaning—he means. He does not analyze experience—he lives it. There is little about speculation on these problems that is clarified by the loose diction of daily speech, and Britton's explanations suffer from the lack of a clear critical language. In general, he offers a few commonsense answers to various aspects of the nature of communication.

Communication is "the use of sounds and shapes to prepare us for features in future events, towards which we are able to make a selective discriminating response." Physical language refers to what anyone may experience; "'a physical property' just *is* that to which the great majority of people can learn to make a uniform linguistic response." The statements upon which scientific conclusions rest are simply "reports uttered or written by people under certain conditions." The probability-value of these reports is contingent upon the possibility that most people under similar circumstances would make the same report. That is to say, the accuracy of protocols has its sanction in linguistic conventions. Meanings are intersubjective mainly because we believe that other people have the same experiences that we do under similar conditions. Rules of language are important, and if one wishes to avoid talking nonsense one is under obligation to put words together in conformity with the conventional rules. This involves certain normative considerations. Consider the following assertions:

1. Mount Everest is 29,141 feet high
2. Mount Everest is a soul-stirring sight
3. Mount Everest is sick at heart

The first gives information about an object that is verifiable—this is public language. The second seems to be an objective statement, but actually refers to private feelings—these might be shared by people who enjoy the same set of values. The third is nonsense—it violates the rules of English.

Britton is not so clear on dynamic language. He believes that feelings are evanescent and do not have a high predictive value, but beyond this he does little except to point out how difficult it is to keep informative and dynamic language apart.

Britton's anatomizing of communication does not take one far. The biosocial factors of meaning are lumped together under the generalization that people are bound by common linguistic rules. Nowhere in his discussion of the "philosophy of language" does Britton consider the diverse social factors that distinguish various brands of value-judgments. He makes a strong case for the simplicity of apprehending physical properties, but does not recognize that the perception of values is quite as much an intellectual activity as the perception of space-time relations. Although he finds that moral and ethical judgments are value-judgments, and are at least partially informative, he does not recognize that poetry, the language of value, is at least similarly informative. Scientific discourse and aesthetic discourse are unquestionably different, both as to ends and means. The first is referential language that begins and ends with publicly discriminable objects; here communication is exact. The second is value-discourse that relates to private psycho-physiological events; here communication is exact only to the degree that the communicants enjoy a common set of values toward the object of discussion. To say that this value-discourse is uninformative, however—to say that it says nothing about the world we experience—is to make a topsy-turvy assertion. Aesthetic discourse is by far the more concrete of the two types, closer to the psycho-physiological behavior to which Britton refers; herein lies its evanescence and its inexactness. Poetry demonstrates life—not a scientific abstraction, but a continuum of events. This truth Britton does not appreciate.

His theory furnishes a good antidote to the doctrine of absolute truth. He enlarges upon some of the pragmatic features of meaning in communication. Yet he offers little that is not stated with more philosophical discernment in Aristotle's *Rhetoric* or Campbell's *Philosophy of Rhetoric*. A fundamental criticism of Britton's work amounts to the observation that his basic dichotomy is neither factual nor useful. The distinction of the two uses of language that he employs, after Ogden and Richards, is a critical fiction, and his discussion of the several types of propositions would suffer no loss without it.

The comment has been made from time to time in this essay that, although the nature of the meaning-process is at all stages closely connected with language, few of the theorists whose work we have examined pay tribute to the findings of modern linguistic science. There are reasons for this neglect. In the first place, some of the more popular modern theories of meaning are normative in means and ends, and linguistics does not lend itself to normative constructions. In the second place, only one element of meaning—the symbol—is given special attention in linguistic science. For the rest—whatever one chooses to call the activity of the mind—one must depend upon the biosocial sciences. In the third place, the study of speech forms is a slow, undramatic anatomization of usage, and linguistic usage is apt to be taken for granted—so much so that logic is often considered basal to language. Strange things have happened where the facts of language have been considered in the theory of meaning. Cunningham seeks a "proper" definition of meaning. Ogden and Richards inveigh against word-magic as though it were simply a persistent bad habit, never before understood, and open to theoretical correction. Korzybski seems to think that we all speak the Attic dialect of the fourth century B. C., and that this was the speech of the Neanderthal man. Britton evidently believes that "correct usage" is a sufficient determinant of communicative principles, and that the meanings of words, phrases, and statements can all be understood within the same categories. Cunningham, Bridgman, Morris, Mannheim, and Britton all recognize the significance, in greater or lesser degree, of the pragmatic element of meaning. The last three named pay special attention to the importance of linguistic habits that control the rules of language. Richards comes around to a recognition of this approach in his later theory. Korzybski, so far as I am aware, stays with his normative dicta.

Because the study of speech forms is so much a part of the empirical study of meaning, and because so many appeals are made in modern speculation to the traditional range of word-usage, the next consideration is an interesting book on meaning written by a linguist in the tradition of Michel Breal, who first wrote on "semantics." Gustaf Stern's *Meaning and Change of Meaning* is one of the few expositions undertaken in the 1930's within the range of our subject that adheres more or less strictly to the facts of language.

REFERENCES

Black, M. "Relations Between Logical Positivism and the Cambridge School of Analysis." Journal Unified Science (Erkenntnis) (1939) VIII.

Britton, K. Communication: A Philosophical Study of Language. New York: Harcourt Brace Jovanovich, 1939.

Campbell, G. (1776) 1873. The Philosophy of Rhetoric. New York: Harper & Bros., 1873.

Carnap, R. The Unity of Science. Translated by M. Black. London: K. Paul, Trench, Trubner & Co., Ltd., 1934.

Empson, W. Seven Types of Ambiguity. New York: Harcourt Brace Jovanovich, 1931.

Kaplan, A. "Are moral judgments assertions?" Philosophical Review, (1942) LI.

Lewis, C. I. and C. H. Langford. Symbolic Logic. New York: The Century Co., 1932.

Ogden, C. K. and Richards, I. A. The Meaning of Meaning: A Study of the Influence of Language Upon the Thought and of the Science of Symbolism. 4th rev. ed. New York: Harcourt Brace Jovanovich, 1936.

Richards, I. A. (1926) 1938. The Principles of Literary Criticism. New York: Harcourt Brace Jovanovich, 1938.

Russell, B. The Analysis of Mind. New York: Macmillan, 1921.

Stebbings, L. S. Logical Positivism and Analysis. London: H. Milford, 1933.

Weinberg, J. R. An examination of Logical Positivism. New York: Harcourt Brace Jovanovich, 1936.

Wittgenstein, L. Tractatus Logico-Philosophicus. New York: Harcourt Brace Jovanovich, 1922.

Chapter 9
SEMASIOLOGY
Gustaf Stern

Stern's major book was published in 1931. He undertook a difficult task and made a considerable contribution both to the theory of meaning and to the descriptive science of semasiology. As a linguist, he reinterpreted and extended the semantic categories of Breal and others who have classified change of meaning. Breal developed his study of semantics around laws of specialization and differentiation. He considered analogy a means of linguistic change and discussed polysemia (multiple meanings of the same linguistic form). Stern rephrases, modernizes, and extends Breal's ideas. As a student of the psychology of language, he attempted to develop a theory of meaning correlative with his analysis of change. His "mentalistic" theory is, of course, open to attack on the usual grounds; yet he makes few overt claims and, I suspect, would meet objections with genial disagreement and ask to be given a better explanation of the linguistic facts. Stern's scholarly care and the reasonableness of his presentation are noteworthy. His book is a monument of neat organization, and he employs his central terms with clarity and caution. Unlike many writers on the theory of meaning, he is careful to qualify his views according to the limitations of the facts available. He labels his assumptions, and consistently emphasizes the tentative nature of many of his conclusions. This combination of linguistic scholarship and modest theorizing is a breath of fresh air amidst the humidity of speculation on meaning.

Stern explains in his opening paragraph that his method is to make a historical study of words (he is particularly concerned with English in this book) in an attempt to discover more or less regular patterns in change of meaning. He relies mainly upon the *New English Dictionary* (*N.E.D.*) for his source-material—that is to say, he works with dated meanings according to the contexts supplied in the *N.E.D.*—and has already made an extended analysis of change of meaning in a considerable number of English words.

It is an obvious linguistic fact that sense-change occurs. Stern is interested in why it occurs, and in determining how its contexts and the theoretical explanation of the psychology of sense-changes merged, and Stern checked them one against the other. In general, his attitude is that his investigations constitute only an initial step in the analysis of sense-changes and should, ideally, be followed by an exhaustive study of vocabulary.

The significance of his work for the present study is that it furnishes a bridge between the theoretical approach to the problem of meaning and the historical study of language. It is obvious that many modern writers on meaning pay little or no attention to the details of the living language that is the real subject of their theories. On the other hand, students of comparative linguistics are prone to side step a detailed treatment of meaning, and concentrate on the forms of a language. Stern's work falls somewhere between the labors of the philosopher and psychologist, and those of the linguist. This midpoint has for some years been called the science of semasiology (*semantics* is Breal's term), the study of "the intellectual causes which have influenced the transformation of our language" (Breal, 1900, p. 5).

Stern relates his work to psychology in that meaning is a psychic phenomenon, and to linguistics in that the facts of meaning and change of meaning must always be interpreted within the traditional range of a language (Stern, pp. 1 ff.). This relation between two fields of knowledge is made clear in his initial discussion of the functions of words and speech. He distinguishes three functions of words—the communicative, the symbolic, and the expressive. All three are essential, although "in individual instances one or the other may predominate." The main function of speech, however, is "the promotion of purposes":

> No trace of this function is found in the meaning of the single word, when analysed alone, and it should therefore probably be regarded as a peculiarity of the psychic complex that constitutes the meaning of a complete utterance (p. 22).

This distinction between the three functions of words and the single function of speech seems simple enough. Yet the confusion of verbal functions with the purpose of an utterance as a whole has led to some extreme views in the theory of meaning. The diversity of opinion on the definition of language by a plurality of functions is a major bugaboo of some modern theories of meaning (see McGranahan's discussion of the psychology of language). I suspect that the particular description of functions is not so important as the distinction made by Stern between functions of words and the functions of speech (or writing).

The purposive function of speech is the keystone of Stern's theory. He seems unwilling, however, to undertake, as others have done, the impossible task of setting up subcategories under purpose. If Stern is judged by omissions as well as by inclusions, his position is simply the common linguistic generalization: the speaker's purpose, inevitably affected by the hearer's understanding, is an integral part of the speech situation, and, since speech situations possess infinite variety, the purposive function of speech cannot be specified. He writes:

> The uses to which a tool is put, naturally react on the tool itself, especially in the case of a tool so sensitive and flexible as language. In a great number of cases we have therefore to regard sense-changes as successive phases in the attempt, intentional or not, to adapt language to the purposes for which speakers make use of it (p. 23).

However, he does not neglect the importance of the hearer in the speech situation. He observes that the speaker's purposive use of language is under certain definite limitations. His choice of words is limited by traditional range, and, in consideration of the hearer, "understanding is as important a factor for the development of language as speaking is."

Stern's discussion of the way in which words become signs offers nothing that is new or extraordinary. He is committed to the general theory of the conditioned response, and refers to the explanation of it by Ogden and Richards. His generalization of this theory is straightforward. He states that:

> To be a symbol or a sign is to involve a reference to another entity, to some thing symbolized, and . . . this is equivalent to having meaning. Such a reference is founded on the fact that the entities are members of recurring contexts. The possibility of communicating by signs is dependent on similar references being made by speaker and hearer (p. 26).

Stern distinguishes between symbols used as signs and symbols used as signals, that is, nondistinctive features of language. He points out, too, that symbols may be used as substitutes (mathematical signs, for instance). In using these, we do not think about what they symbolize; "they completely lack the expressive function." One of Korzybski's problems is that he is unable to understand this point emphasized by Stern. Mathematical signs (symbols) cannot be discussed except in translation into ordinary language (symbols), which is purposive. Stern's study is limited to words used as symbols.

Chapter 3 contains the definition of meaning and the core of his theory. He adduces five factors of meaning:

1. A thinking and language-using *subject* (speaking, writing, hearing, reading.)
2. The *acts of thinking* taking place in the mind of the subject.
3. The *thoughts* forming the content of these acts of thinking.
4. The *word-forms* to which the thoughts are associated and which express them more or less completely.
5. The subject, the acts of thinking, and the thoughts are referred (in the widest sense of this term) to some object, which I shall call the *referent* (p. 29).

By combining the acts of thinking with the thoughts in the term *mental content,* and "by excluding the subject as a separate factor, since he is represented by his mental content," these five factors are reduced to three:

1. The *word,* expressing the mental content and denoting the referent.
2. The *mental content,* connected with the word, and involving a reference to the referent.
3. The *referent.*

It is probably unnecessary to review here the detail of Stern's approach to the definition of meaning. He assumes that word and meaning never coincide, and suggests that "when the referent is a material object, it can evidently not coincide with meaning, which is a psychic entity" (p. 33). The rather special terminology of Ogden and Richards is revised so that in Stern's usage" the word *expresses* the mental content (meaning, thought) and *names* or *denotes* the referent" (p. 38). These terms are somewhat more consistent with ordinary usage than are the particular senses of *symbol* and *symbolize* developed by Ogden and Richards.

Stern's theory of meaning is by all means empirical. He offers a commonsense explanation of the fact—so painfully anatomized by Korzybski—that a referent may be unique, but it is still the object of a common reference. Two people may talk about a camera, one a layman who knows only that the thing takes pictures, the other an expert in photography, and understand each other quite well:

The word cannot reasonably be said to have the same meaning for the two persons, yet they are able to discuss *camera* because they refer to the same thing by the same word, although they do it in different ways (p. 40).

Stern concludes that "the meaning of a word is determined by the characteristics of the referent, which is thus a necessary factor in the differentia specifica of meaning."

As to the third factor of meaning, the word, Stern has much to say under the heading of "traditional semantic range." This range is the indispensable condition of *communication*. Stern says:

> The existence of a traditional range for all words in a language makes the language a normative system for the meanings, and it is this fact that makes semasiology a branch of linguistics; it would otherwise fall under the heading of psychology, since the two other determinants, the objective reference and the subjective apprehension, are purely psychological in nature (p. 43).

Further implications of the importance of traditional range belong in the discussion of the analysis of sense-change.

For the sake of accuracy and brevity, it is probably best to follow Stern's own capable summary of the factors of meaning that underlie his definition. There are three determinants of meaning:

> We have found, in the first place, that the objective reference is an indispensable element in any meaning, and that the qualitative characteristics of meaning are conditioned by the actual characteristics of the referent which the word is employed to denote. This factor conditions the symbolic function of the word . . .
>
> We have found, secondly, that the meaning of a word is determined also by the subject's apprehension of the referent that the word is employed to denote, that is to say, the subject's thoughts and feelings with regard to the referent. This factor conditions the expressive function of the word . . .
>
> We have found, thirdly, that the traditional range of a word serves to discriminate its meanings from concomitant elements of mental content, or mental context. This factor conditions the communicative function of the word (pp. 43–45).

On the basis of these generalizations, explained in detail and fully documented, he proceeds to define meaning:

> I conclude that the meaning of a word, in any individual case of actual use in speech, is completely determined by its relation to the three factors, word, referent and subject. Each of these three factors conditions one of the three functions of words. No other determinant is necessary for the definition of meaning, but all three must be embodied in the definition. I propose the following formulation:

The meaning of a word—in actual speech—is identical with those elements of the user's (speaker's or hearer's) subjective apprehension of the referent denoted by the word, which he apprehends as expressed by it.

The definition is applicable to prefixes, suffixes, and stem syllables, in so far as these carry a distinctive element of meaning.

It is not applicable to speech as a whole (utterance) owing to the purposive function not being included.

It is further not applicable to signals or substitute signs (p. 45).

With the exception of the caveat to exclude the purposive function, this definition is in tune with Bloomfield's view that the meaning of a linguistic form is "the situation in which the speaker utters it and the response which it calls forth in the hearer." (Bloomfield would, of course, look with distaste upon Stern's "mentalistic" explanations.) In general, Stern presents an instrumental definition of verbal meaning that is a fitting counterpart to his pragmatic view of communication as a whole.

In Chapter 4, he discusses some of the elements of *mental content.* His definition of context is a familiar one:

I have stated above that the meaning of words comprises only a portion of the total mental content present in the mind of a person when they are pronounced or comprehended; and I have used the term context to denote such elements as are not expressed by the words (p. 62).

He presents an eclectic discussion of imagery, agreeing with much current psychological opinion that images may or may not accompany utterance. He concludes that "images seem to belong to mental context," and notes that they "sometimes function as supplementary signs." His treatment of the emotional and volitional elements of meaning is particularly impressive. It is marked by a "sweet reasonableness," the lack of which has been noted with regret in certain other theorists on meaning.

Stern follows Delacroix in asserting that "there is some sort of emotive element in all speech; if a thing were quite indifferent to me I would not say it." His generalization on this aspect of communication is succinct:

The emotional elements of meaning correspond to the subjective attitude taken up by a speaker or hearer towards the referent and the interlocutor. The attitude may vary indefinitely: the same referent may be spoken of with doubt, concession, desire, questioning, pleasure or the reverse, contempt, irony, derision, confidence and so on. How these varying attitudes are expressed and how they influence the meanings of the words used is an immense and complex problem that has as yet scarcely been touched by scientific investigation. It is therefore impossible to give anything like an adequate account of the matter (p. 54).

"How forcible are right words!" Stern mentions two methods of expressing emotional elements: 1) the emotion may be the referent of the word ("I am annoyed at your coming here") and 2) "some words possess an emotive colouring as a permanent element of their meaning" (compare *house—hovel, horse—steed*). Nonverbal signals, he decides, belong to context. He pays some attention to phrase-meaning (distinct from word-meaning); changed order of words, incomplete expressions, and the like have emotional significance. Volitional attitudes are described as specific kinds of emotional attitudes, whose purpose is not merely to influence a hearer's state of mind but to get him to act.

Because of its significance for an attempt to understand sense-change, Stern is much concerned to discover at what point the word arises in the speaker's mind (see Chapter 5). This stage of the theory makes use of Head's findings in aphasia. Head classifies aphasic defects in four categories—verbal, syntactical, nominal, and semantic—and Stern assumes, from the evidence of Head's data, "the existence of four groups of automatic functions" that relate to verbalization. Stern believes that the basic temporal step in speech is the adjustment to the situation. He writes: "My conclusion is that the production of speech normally begins with an adjustment, comprising determining tendencies arising from the intentional awareness" (p. 117). This elliptical statement can be interpreted to mean that, because the purposive function is the major determinant of all speech, the speaker attempts to express himself (and ideally the hearer will so understand him) according to what he wishes done. A more detailed explanation of purpose is impossible, insofar as every speech situation is unique. Against this uniqueness, however, the native speaker of a language will bring to bear upon the situation this four-fold habit of automatic (intuitive?) pre-adjustment. It is doubtful that Stern's explanation tells us much more than that the native speaker, because he is a native, has learned from childhood to use speech purposively. The argument is, in a way, circular.

Stern does not go beyond this point of fixing an initial step of adjustment. The stages between this automatic adaptation to the speech situation and the ultimate verbalization cannot be fixed in terms of temporal relations. If the intermediate stages could be ordered, we would have a neatly wrapped package of the relations between words and thoughts.

One does not have to look far to determine the reason for this concern with the point at which the word arises in the speaker's mind. The historical study of sense-change depends for accuracy upon the fact that the interpreter can know when a sense-shift has occurred. Unless he can date the initial change, he is helpless to determine the relations between the new and the old meanings. Obviously, Stern's theory of an initial adjustment to the speech situation is helpful in interpreting the nature of the context involved (to the extent, that is, that the context is clear in the historical dictionary). It is worthwhile to quote Stern at some length on this point:

> A sense-change may be said to occur at the moment when the word arises in mind and is connected, as its symbol, with a sufficiently determinate item of mental content, with which it has not previously been connected. Since this may happen at any phase of development, an analysis of sense-change has to reckon with the whole complex of normal speech functions as being, potentially, operative at the moment of change; and, moreover, not only with the context really expressed in the surrounding words, but with any other perceptual or mental context that may happen to exist simultaneously. The polysemy of words connects most of them with many different items of experience, any of which may act as stimulus for their evocation. All these circumstances taken together provide an infinite variation of contexts in which the word may appear, subjected to a variety of influences, by which its meaning is moulded to suit the momentary purposes and environment (p. 119).

Aside from the fact that Stern's views of automatic functions cannot as yet be verified in the laboratory—perhaps will never be verified—and are therefore not admissable as evidence, they seem to agree reasonably well with common experience. At the very least, it can be said that Stern is not laboring under serious delusions. He realizes rather more than most the tenuous quality of his "mentalistic" explanations.

The second part of the book is devoted to the direct treatment of meaning. There is no need to do more here than outline the relation of his classifications to his theory. He begins his explanation with some comments on change and stability. Every utterance is momentary and purposive; it is also part of a linguistic system, a fact that tends to hold utterance within a traditional frame.

> The actual course of semantic development emerges as the result of these conflicting tendencies; and according as one or the other of them prevails with regard to a complex of word and meaning, we find that the complex remains stable throughout long periods, or, conversely, that it offers a picture of constant change.
>
> Change and stability are equally normal phases in the history of language; only the total absence of either would be abnormal (p. 162).

The precise definition of change of meaning has been foreshadowed by the theoretical discussion:

> I define change of meaning as the habitual modification, among a comparatively large number of speakers, of the traditional semantic range of the word, which results from the use of the word (1) to denote one or more referents which it has not previously denoted, or (2) to express a novel manner of apprehending one or more of its referents (p. 163).

This definition is apparently broad enough to include all phases of the purposive use of language. All variance of reference does not, however, indicate change. In the example of the two speakers who talk about a camera, for instance, one may think "Kodak" while the other thinks "reflex, extension, swing-front, focal-plane, anastigmatic hand-camera." This is not change of meaning but *fluctuation*. There is no change in the traditional range of the word. Moreover, even a change in the cameras themselves (that is, in the referents) would have to be quite extensive to set up a significant subcategory of *cameras*.

Stern emphasizes the resolution of the apparent discrepancy between the opposing tendencies of language towards stability and change. He insists that

> a change of meaning must involve a *habitual modification* of the traditional semantic range of a word among a *comparatively large* group of speakers. In other words, the change must have been incorporated in the language system of the other group (p. 165).

On the basis of his historical analysis of meanings, Stern distinguishes seven classes of sense-changes. The immediate cause of change is a shift in the three factors of meaning—word (verbal relation), mental content (subjective relation), and referent (referential relation). If only two of these factors are stable, the meaning varies with the third; fundamentally, change of meaning rests in the adaptation of speech to new purposes. With these ideas in mind, we may observe the correlation between factual classification and theoretical explanation in Stern's scheme:

CHANGE OF MEANING

I.   External, non-linguistic causes.

   Class 1:   *Substitution*—the difference in meaning, for instance, between *ship* in 1840 (clipper) and *ship* in 1977 (tanker); the category remains; language only *registers* the change.

II. Linguistic causes.
  A. Changes resulting from a shift of verbal relations.
      Class 2: *Analogy*—borrowed meanings.
      Class 3: *Shortening*—a simple loss of part of an earlier linguistic form.
  B. Changes resulting from a shift of referential relations.
      Class 4: *Nomination*—metaphor, an intentional transfer of referents.
      Class 5: *Transfer*—an unintentional shift caused by a similarity between the original and the secondary referent, e.g., *the bed of a lathe.*
  C. Changes resulting from a shift of subjective relations.
      Class 6: *Permutation*—for instance, because of the act of saying prayers with a rosary, prayers are associated with balls, and balls with beads; the result, by permutation, is the phrase *counting his beads.*
      Class 7: *Adequation*—"an adaptation of the meaning to the actual characteristics of the referents which the word is employed to denote, but in contradistinction to *substitution,* the cause of the shift lies in the subjective apprehension of the speakers" (e.g., the musical instrument called a *horn*).

Stern's findings present a simple pattern. One can read him without the sensation of violet swirling in a maelstrom of verbalism. His theory is generalized, his data are extensive, and his inferences are well documented. He does not claim verification of his analysis of meaning to any greater extent than that his findings in historical language appear to support it. His method is empirical, and his general view of meaning is pragmatic. He makes ample allowance for both subjective and objective relations in meaning, and stresses the social factors of communication. He is primarily a linguist, and is not in haste to utter his theory as the final word. In short, he is not an apostle of normative semantics, but attempts to describe the patterns of meaning in a living language.

Once one agrees with Stern that the traditional range of meaning changes, that these changes are part and parcel of the individual's use of language (that is to say, of his behavioral mechanism), and that speech as a whole has the single function of "the promotion of purposes" (although any and all words can be analyzed in terms of the three functions communication, symbolization, and expression), one has gone some way toward a clear understanding of the relations between language and experience. (That is quite a sentence!) Stern's work produces some interesting results as an exercise in definition. *Meaning* as a noun has two principal referents: it refers to the user's psychic complex of verbal usage—that is, it constitutes his behavioral habits of symbolism—and it refers to the purposive nature of speech as a whole. Aside from the rare use of holophrasis, the purposive function of speech resides in the complex of the situation. This distinction between the function of words and the function of communication is by no means clearly maintained by many semantic theorists, and, once it is understood, the Ogden-Richards-Britton dichotomy of linguistic usage breaks down. So far as word-meaning is concerned, all words have communicative, symbolic, and expressive aspects, and, although the general purpose in a particular situation might be to inform, emotive or dynamic expression is by no means a parallel category of general purpose. The expressive quality of a word—its subjective reference—is as much a part of its normal function as is the symbolic quality. Stern expresses the idea, in terminology that is consonant with Morris's theory, that verbal meaning is determined by the three relationships of objective reference, subjective apprehension, and traditional range. Situational purpose is something else. The conclusion is that the Ogden-Richards-Britton dichotomy confuses the functions of a word with the function of communication, thereby reducing nonscientific discourse to the plane of "merely" evaluative, nonintellectual expression.

The epistemological significance of this confusion is far-reaching. Only science handles facts, informs, demonstrates the "truths" of existence, and gives knowledge. Literature alone expresses the emotions and signifies values. Perhaps the issue here is just verbal: *knowledge* is a vague term, highly abstract, and useful at many different interpretative levels. I have used it in this essay to represent broadly the more or less stable gleanings from man's attempt to understand the nature of existence. This attempt usually employs language as a means of understanding. It does not necessarily employ language as a conveyor of the results of this understanding because there are other means of communication than the verbal, other arts than the literary. So far as knowledge is expressed in the sounds and symbols of language, however, there is a purposive dichotomy of linguistic usage that is too rarely examined by modern semantic theorists. Langer suggests it in her division of the source of knowledge according to "discursive" and "intensive" reasoning. The higher educational system recognizes it in the academic structure of "arts and science." Morris notes it in his distinction between the language of reference and the language of value. It is implicit in Mannheim's theory of knowledge. Few modern theorists are much concerned, however, with a detailed explanation of a literary universe of discourse that is on an epistemological level with scientific discourse. There is need for a "scientific" theory of literature. It was with the idea of contributing to the satisfaction of this need that T. C. Pollock wrote *The Nature of Literature,* the next of the semantic theories discussed.

REFERENCES

Breal, M. Semantics. Translated by Mrs. Henry Cust. New York: Henry Holt, 1900.
McGranahan, D. V. "The Psychology of Language." Psychology Bulletin (1936) XXXIII.
Stern, G. Meaning and Change of Meaning with Special Reference to the English Language. Goteborg: Elanders, 1931.

Chapter 10
THE THEORY
OF LITERATURE

T. C. Pollock

In the author's words, Pollock's *The Nature of Literature* (1942) is a map-making enterprise—he offers a chart to student, teacher, and critic of literature. His theory is based upon the science of linguistics and the psychology of language. In essence, it postulates a literary use of language that is in every degree the counterpart of a scientific use of language. He distinguishes these two purposive operations according to the nature of the activity that each performs. Science employs a referential language that abstracts from experience; literature employs a reproductive language that controls experience. Each of these uses represents one phase of the dual means whereby man employs symbols to understand existence. Neither is superior nor inferior to the other. The behaving Man is the user in both instances. Perhaps it is unnecessary to offer the caveat so frequently made in this essay: there is probably not a single idea in Pollock's book that is new. Whatever novelty is in it rests upon the timeliness of the author's conception of literary theory.

In this twentieth-century age of science, literature and its devotees are too often on the defensive. The fault here, if there is a fault, must be shared. On the one hand, the modern humanist does not always include a scientific attitude among his values. On the other hand, there are many individuals and groups in modern society who are unaware of the value of literature. A theory of literature is needed, Pollock affirms, to distinguish clearly between the "use of language which is literature . . . he use of language which is scientific communication without obscuring either" (Pollock, 1942, p. 164). Moreover, says Pollock, there are strategic reasons for basing a literary theory upon the science of language. In the first place, literature is "something which occurs linguistically and depends upon the existence of language." The science of linguistics furnishes verifiable premises for a theory of literature, something that a more traditional, "spiritual" approach to literary has not done. Second, the analysis of signs is and has been for some years a dominant intellectual interest. A theory of literature might well be consonant with this interest. Third, perhaps most important, a linguistic basis for literary theory "will make our theoretical understanding of literature . . . more readily available to educational theory."

Pollock is extremely suspicious of modern educationism. The traditional methods no longer prevail. Education today is conducted on current theories, and, whereas the construction of a sound literary theory may be no more than an intellectual pastime for those who have learned to read literature, "for those whose adolescence lies ahead, it may be a dominant factor in determining how and what they learn to read." That is to say, literature in modern education must either sink or float with the theoretical current. If it is not to sink, it had better have an acceptable theory for a life belt. In general, then, Pollock writes with two broad purposes in mind, both of which are constantly reflected in his methods. First, he wishes to resolve the apparent disparity between the sciences and the literary arts. Second, he wishes to combat the critical flatulence—the "floating generalizations and irrational explanations"—so frequently a part of the litterateur's stock in trade. He believes that both these ends are served by an analysis of the purposive functions of language. "The point is that human beings, no matter how 'objective' or how 'imaginative,' live in terms of actual experiences, . . . frequently very complex; the semantic problem is to determine whether the meanings they try to express verbally are composed of abstractions from these experiences . . . or of something at least closer to the stuff of life itself" (p. 101).

Pollock's criteria of success or failure throw some additional light on his objective:

> It this theory more or less successful than other theories of literature: (1) As a basis for our present generalized knowledge of literary phenomena, such as metrics, fictional theory, and dramactic theory? (2) As a basis for further investigation into the theory of literature? (3) As a basis for further investigation into the history of literature? (4) As a basis for the investigation of individual works of literature, in their character as such? (5) As an explanation in general terms of the reader's direct (i.e., "experiential" or "intuitive") knowledge of works of literature? (6) As a general explanation of the semantics of literature (i.e., of the way in

which words, individually and cooperating in groups, convey meaning in literary units)? (7) As a basis for educational theory in the field of literature? (8) As a general explanation of the nature of literary phenomena which can be correlated with general knowledge in other fields of inquiry?

Here is the material of a scientific theory of literature, an idea that many members of the old guard will dismiss with a shudder of abhorrence. Aside from the practical nature of the writer's objective, there are two points that the literary traditionalist might well bear in mind. The essence of modern scientific theory is not content but method, not substance but relations. Inasmuch as literature is a part of active language, perhaps the use of the facts of linguistic science and of the language of psychology can help to explain, more clearly and more consistently than has been done, just what the nature of literature is. This is the gist of Pollock's presentation, and there is quite enough "literary loose talk" around to warrant hearing him out.

In his first projective chapter, Pollock attempts to fence off the term *literature* so that it will be complementary to the term *science*. *Literature* ordinarily has two meanings in general usage: 1) the whole body of writings of a field, a nation, or a period, or 2) "writing which has claim to distinction on the ground of beauty of form or emotional effect." These definitions are taken from the *New English Dictionary*, (*N.E.D.*), and neither definition antedates the nineteenth century. *Poetry* might have remained useful for the second sense, except that *poetry* could not comfortably embrace the increasingly important arts of prose. In addition, under the ministrations of the romanticists and the transcendentalists, *poetry* inherited value-definitions that extolled its qualities instead of classifying it as a use of language. (Here Pollock is referring to Shelley's "A Defense of Poetry" and to the transcendentalist's view as it is expressed by Emerson in "The Poet.") The modern definition of *science* had come into being during the eighteenth century, and by 1812, according to the *N. E. D., literature* was used to indicate all kinds of writings, including poetic and scientific. De Quincey's distinction between the "literature of knowledge" and the "literature of power" was made in 1823, and, observes Pollock, "in succeeding decades the writings which De Quincey referred to as the 'literature of power' were spoken of with increasing frequency simply as *literature.*"

The upshot of the historical development and shift of meaning is that there is now a field called *literature,* the boundaries of which are not very certain:

Whatever other characteristics this field has . . . I suggest (1) that it includes at least certain types of prose, especially prose fiction, as well as much verse, and this without prejudice; (2) that it does not embrace simply the most excellent specimens of its kind, but includes the poor as well as the good, the minor as well as the great; and (3) that it is distinguished from scientific communication by essential characteristics, not quality of value: the field of literature, in other words, though different from that of scientific communication, is not ipso facto superior, or inferior, thereto (p. 9).

Pollock interprets these characteristics of literature in formulating a "satisfactory analytical definition of literature, in the restricted sense":

Such a definition must, whatever else it does (1) include prose as well as verse, (2) avoid the pit-falls of value-definition, and (3) distinguish the essential characteristics of literature from those of science (p. 9).

He can find no existing definition that satisfies these requirements. For this reason he writes "*literature (L)*" throughout the rest of the book. Readers who think he is misusing the term *literature* are asked to remember that he is referring to *L*, a term that includes the properties and distinctions outlined above. *The Nature of Literature* is, in a sense, a definition of literature and an analysis of the implications of that definition.

Pollock begins his analysis with a discussion of the elements of language. The broad outlines are apparent:

The most certain fact in the study of literature (L) is the persistence through time of the book. The next most certain is that the book contains language . . . Whatever else literature (L) may be, it is unquestionably something which occurs linguistically; and we may state as two essential requirements of a satisfactory literary theory, first, that it be grounded on the best knowledge we have concerning the nature of linguistic phenomena, and second, that it makes a satisfactory discrimination between uses of language which are literature (L) and uses of language which are not (p. 12).

The definition of language is a familiar behavioral description current in at least some aspects of linguistic science. Language is a human activity, learned by habit, for the sake of communication, a process that culminates in the understanding of response of the hearer (reader) (p. 15). Or, in Bloomfield's words, "Language enables one person to make a reaction when another person has the stimulus" (1933, p. 24). The important point is that linguistic signs are mediators between two phases of human behavior. Accordingly, no activity of language, with the exception of purely emotive sounds, is simply expressive. One might expect that the writer considers only himself and his words; the reader, himself and the words; and the critic, only the words. Literary history is full of examples of all these slightings of the linguistic process. Insofar as the dramatist usually remembers his audience, Pollock suggests that the study of drama is a particularly good springboard for the student of literary theory. It seems to me that the study of rhetoric, of which Pollock's work is clearly one aspect, might be quite revealing.

Pollock's next undertaking is a rapid survey of sign functions, and he determines that a major characteristic of sign systems is the presence of time-order. He then redefines language as "a process through which one individual makes *in a certain time-order* signs which enable him to communicate with another individual" (p. 20). He is not interested in a philological comparison between analytic and inflectional languages.

Under the heading "Elements of Semantics," he considers the central question of communication. How is it possible for signs to have meaning, that is, serve as mediators between speaker's stimulus and hearer's response? His approach is genetic. By way of introducing this discussion, he calls attention to five misconceptions concerning the nature of words, the delineation of which serves here as a review of a modern attitude about semantics.

The first of these is the semanticist's whipping boy, word-magic—the belief that a sign "naturally" has meaning, that the name is inherent in the thing. "A second naive misconception is that a sign has a certain meaning because a dictionary says it has." The error lies in the misapprehension of what a dictionary is, and of the nature of its recordings. Third is the windblown conception of meaning from etymological sources—a word must have a primary or original meaning, because all changes in meaning are corruptions. In these three misconceptions, says Pollock, the controlling assumption is that the meaning is *in* the sign. Two others are more subtle. One, which Pollock calls *reification,* is "the error of assuming that a word necessarily means or refers to a thing," as opposed to a process or an event. Whitehead's phrase for this misconception is "misplaced concreteness." Lastly, Pollock refers to "the cognate fallacy of hypostatization." "To reify is to assume that the sign means a thing; to hypostatize is to assume that there necessarily is in existence some thing to which the sign refers." This last is the assumption that a sign cannot be meaningless; it is reification plus.

There are two phases to the genetic description of the semantic elements of language—individual and group habits. Pollock follows Bloomfield in concluding that a sign "gains meaning for an individual . . . by becoming habitually associated with other events in his experience." A *symbol* is defined as "a sign which has meaning," that is, as a sign that has habitual behavioral associations. Pollock offers the data of the conditioned response (quoting extensively from Pavlov and Razran) and of Head's clinical findings on aphasia, to furnish generalizations about the individual's semantic habits. To characterize this process, he adopts the phrase "conditional response":

> To emphasize the fact that human responses to "conditioned"stim-
> uli . . . are not automatic, but are instead "conditional" on a great many
> other psycho-physiological factors, such as the attitude of the individual,
> competing "thoughts," and his "will," it is helpful to take the suggestion
> of Korsybski and to speak of *conditional,* instead of conditioned,
> responses (p. 36).

The second phase of word-meaning, the traditional range of a sign for a group of people, has already been discussed at some length in the chapter on Stern's work. In Pollock's terminology, "a sign comes to have meaning for a speech-community because a number of individuals are conditioned to respond in similar ways to the same sign." This is the social factor of communicative learning to which reference has been made several times in this book. This is clearly behavioristic psychology, with the emphasis on social aspects of behavior.

In sum, "the major part of the reality of language lies not in the external signs, which through the mechanics of writing may be isolated and indefinitely preserved, but in the experiences of the human beings by whom the signs are produced and received" (p. 48). The pragmatic events of sign analysis is by all means the most important.

From the elements of meaning, Pollock turns to a consideration of the tendencies of language. He makes a recommendation that seems fundamental: that we learn to think about language in terms of Hermann Paul's axiom—"all purely psychical reciprocal operation comes to its fulfillment in the individual mind alone" (Paul, 1890, p. xxxvii). It has been noted that this is a major idea in Cunningham's analysis of the meaning-situation and in Morris's theory of semiotic.

There are deterrents to an acceptance of this as truth. In the first place, the very method by which people learn to talk concentrates their attention on the relations between signs and things. The result is that language is mistakenly supposed to consist of "external signs whose meanings are external objects . . ." (Pollock, p. 49). "A second difficulty arises from the fact that if we are to use Paul's axiom as an instrument of thought, we must penetrate behind certain of the useful working assumptions of students of language." Pollock refers to Bloomfield's view of meaning, and observes that Bloomfield's basic assumption—"in every speech community some utterances are alike in form and meaning"—is satisfactory for the phonologist, but that for a theory of literature we "should base our assumptions . . . on the facts on which the linguist bases his, and not, second-hand, on his simplifications" (p. 52). The third difficulty in thinking with Paul's axiom is that there is no simple language for the discussion of mental events; the possibility of misunderstanding is forever present. One cannot avoid using inexplicit psychological terminology if one wishes to discuss what goes on in his mind.

All these difficulties become apparent in any treatment of *experience,* one of the main terms of Pollock's system, the ambiguity of which he well understands. As with "literature (L)," he adopts the device of writing "experience (E)": "*E* is used to mean the full psychophysiological experience of any individual at any particular time." The time may be long or short. "Each human being lives in a series of psycho-physiological experiences (E). Together they form the total reality of his sentient life." Pollock offers a final warning about the use of the term experience in a somewhat ponderous summation:

> In what follows it is important to remember (1) that *all* mental events occur at total complex individual experiences (E) or as elements therein; (2) that human psychophysiological experiences (E) are not open to direct observation; and (3) *that they are not the same as generalizations from particular experiences (E) or the words which refer to these generalizations*—although the processes of generalizing and of uttering signs always take place as parts of actual human experiences (E) (p. 56).

Here is an emphasis on the complexity of experience that is sometimes forgotten in discussions of meaning. Britton, for instance, seems to assume that propositional analysis on the basis of introspection is sufficient to illuminate the nature of verbal reports. Using the study of phonemes as an illustration, the point is that analysis can never accurately portray the continuum of experience, for the obvious reason that events occur in continuum; a phoneme is an abstraction from the phonetic series. As Korzybski and many others have pointed out, consciousness of experience—that is, analysis—is an abstracting process.

Pollock adduces two major tendencies of language that are part of the working principles of linguistic theory: 1) the civilized use of language (versus more primitive uses) is notable for a "decreasing dependence of speech upon context of situation," and 2) languages tend toward increasing abstractness and generality. Pollock's authorities are Malinowski, Jespersen, Sapir, Bloomfield, de Laguna, and Head.

The first tendency has long interested linguists and ethnologists. On a primitive level, communication notably depends upon situation; the actual verbal language is relatively unimportant. This is Pollock's opinion. "The hearer's immediate awareness of the general situation which includes the speaker and his perception of the speaker's *non*-linguistic activity leaves comparatively little to be done by words." Much civilized use of language also depends upon situation, but to a lesser extent. In writing, the situation is almost completely obliterated, and sign usage is, to all intents and purposes, displaced. That is, the stimuli occur within the mind—"what the words do not communicate is not communicated." One must think carefully here about the meaning of "primitive"—e.g., primitive people, or primitive language? They are not the same "primitive."

The second tendency, toward increasing abstraction, leads to some subtle semantic problems. "As we have seen, it is often wrongly assumed that the meaning of a word is an external event or thing; as a consequence, it is often wrongly assumed that a perfectly concrete word is, or if it existed would be, the name of a perfectly concrete object." Simply stated, the fact is that truly concrete terms are evanescent. The meanings of most terms are abstractions and generalizations from many experiences. Pollock's discussion of the process of abstraction is interesting and fairly full. One of his quotations from Jespersen suggests, perhaps, the general tone:

> The world is in a constant flux around us and in us, but in order to grapple with the floating reality we create in our thoughts, or at any rate in our language, certain more or less fixed points, certain averages. Reality never presents us with an average object, but language does, for instead of denoting one actually given thing a word like *apple* represents the average of a great many objects that have something, but of course not everything, in common (Jespersen, 1924, pp. 63–64).

Pollock's own summary of these tendencies of language is pertinent here:

> As a result of these tendencies, the student of civilized communication must reckon with the following conditions: first, that many modern speech-transactions—including most of the uses of language called *literature*—are carried on without the support of nonlinguistic contexts of situation; and second, that most, if not all, of the conventional terms of language, when not narrowed by context of situation, refer to—and in this sense "mean"—abstract generalizations (pp. 73–74).

Pollock offers four considerations that are involved in these tendencies. First, normal utterance is a full-sentence statement. Second, "abstract and generalized linguistic forms are more useful than are concrete for making specific references." Third, most linguistic transactions are vocal, not written, and depend upon specific contexts of situation. Yet many people are not 'aware that linguistic symbols are generalizations from experience. Fourth, the symbols of language are generalizations not from one but from many human experiences—that is, they are universal. They are "most effective in communicating, not the living experiences (E) of human beings, but the relationships which are held to exist between elements abstracted from actual human experience."

Pollock describes the language of science to drive home his distinctions between the uses of language. It is a thorough explanation, the general nature of which is common knowledge. If the hearer's response, that is, his behavior as interpreter, is the "actual" meaning of the sign, how can one be sure that it is appropriate—that exact communication is possible? In many uses of language one cannot be sure. In the scientific use of language, called by some "man's greatest linguistic achievement," one can be certain. The process depends upon two things: the communicants must disregard all private connotations "except the reference to the referent agreed upon." Then, "they must choose as a referent a publicly discriminable stimulus, or reduce a more abstract referent to publicly discernable elements through a logical process." Enough has been said in the treatment of Richard's and Britton's ideas about the details of public meaning by definition. In "science-as-success," a term's meaning is specified by the operations of controlled experiments, within a publicly discriminable frame of reference. This lends linguistic significance to Bridgman's thesis of "operational meaning," as stated before. Mannheim's *Ideology and Utopia* is an attempt to supply the theory for the social studies whereby generalizations are controlled and public discrimination of referents is made possible.

The language of science, then, is referential symbolism:

> We are now in a position to understand more clearly the problem involved in the distinction between what De Quincey called the "literature of knowledge" and the "literature of power." That which the "literature of knowledge" communicates is not what is usually suggested by terms such as *matter, reality, fact,* or *truth,* but rather the relationship between generalizations which have been abstracted from the actual experience (E) of human beings. . . . To avoid for the present the ambiguous term *knowledge,* we may call this use of language *referential symbolism.* (pp. 90–91).

If scientific communication is one of the great achievements of men, it is both because of, and in spite of, the fact that it brings near to perfection the two prevailing tendencies of language—the tendency toward decreasing dependence upon situation context and the tendency toward increasing abstractness. In these terms, science is more obviously what Huxley called it—organized commonsense.

From this account of referential symbolism, Pollock proceeds to his discussion of what literature, as distinct from science, communicates, and how it communicates. Scientific language is the development of communication in one direction, literary language the development of communication in quite another direction:

> The key to an understanding of literature (L) lies in an awareness of the difference between a human being's actual experiences (E) and abstractions from these experiences. Psychologically, this involves the difference between the private discriminations of human organisms and the public elements therein. Linguistically, it involves the difference between the actual meanings of (or semantic reactions to) a symbol and symbol's referent (p. 95).

In science men direct the reader or hearer "to the relationships between particular referents." In literature men "express and communicate their own privately discriminable experiences." Literature is "the utterance of a series of symbols capable of evoking in the mind of a reader a controlled experience (E)." Literature attempts to communicate something like "the full richness of an author's actual psycho-physiological experience"—not abstractions.

These attempts at definition, Pollock admits, bring us to the pons asinorum of literary theory:

> We have come to the point where, if we are to advance, we must recognize clearly that the actual flow of life and thought in a human being is not the same as the factors, whether we call them "objects" or "ideas," which he abstracts from this flow. We must recognize that words in their ordinary referential use point at these abstractions and not at the human reality from which they are abstracted. The important point to emphasize is that the actual experiences (E) of human beings are different from—richer, fuller, deeper, more subtly discriminating than, *and inclusive of*—any abstraction or group of abstractions drawn from these experiences (E). With words in their referential use we point at these abstractions. If the reader has not already, as part of his own life-processes, undergone experiences (E) evoked by the patterned symbols we call literature (L), no words of mine in this book can make him experience what I am talking about when I write of evocative symbolism (p. 97).

These seem to be sound ideas. Britton no doubt aims at something like this sense of "evocative symbolism" in his phrase *dynamic intention,* but he never succeeds in expressing his meaning with anything like the insight displayed by Pollock. Britton's other category, like Richards's *symbolic use of language,* leads him so far off the track with its polarity of intellectual versus volitional activities that he is unable to do justice to literary communication. Pollock's thesis can be, and has been, expressed in many other ways. It has been held, for instance, that poetry (that is, poetics) demonstrates life in a way never to be approached by scientific reasoning. This I take to be the traditional humanistic understanding of the office of literature. The significance of Pollock's theory comes to this: he is interested, perhaps above all else, in resolving the antagonism, too much fostered among scientists and litterateurs, between two fundamentally different uses of language. Few men live through many days without using both, and if this theory of literature does no more than further a speedy dissolution of this antagonism, especially within educational theory, it will have made a notable contribution. One need only agree that scientific method and literary expression are, basically, linguistic phenomena— each is a phase of man's symbolic capacities. On this ground the scientific and literary uses of language together compose a whole that is obviously greater than its parts.

The significance of experience is the essence of evocative symbolism. A private experience is unique. Lewes's *Road to Xanadu* furnishes a choice illustration of the fleeting connnection between a writer's experiences and his expression of them. Coleridge's "stream of experience" was interrupted, and "Kubla Kahn" remains a fragment. Experience includes the activities of the imagination, as Coleridge said, but *imagination* is not always usefully defined. In Pollock's words, fiction enables a writer "to express through an evocative use of symbols his awareness of qualities and relationships of human beings which are too subtle to be pointed at by referential statement." This does not mean that the writer of fiction makes no use of referential statement, as one is sometimes led to believe. He does, of course. Pollock stresses the point expressed several times in the course of this work that literature is not limited to the communication of emotional states. "*What* literature (L) expresses and communicates . . . are individual human experiences."

Pollock adduces six methods that explain *how* this communication takes place. It is well to remember that his theory is based on two fundamental linguistic principles: 1) the meaning of a symbol is the response evoked, and, because of the traditional range of meanings, 2) a sign will be similarly interpreted by different readers. These are the individual and social factors of meaningness. This does not imply, however, that people respond in exactly the same way. There may be significant similarities of response without precise sameness in details. What has often been noted in terms of the greatness of literature—its lasting depth, acumen, and universality—can be expressed simply in linguistic terms. A skilled writer may respond in such a way to his own experience that he is able to produce a set of symbols capable of evoking a similar experience in the response of the reader. When the initial response retains its evocative power over many ages and over many minds, it is great literature.

Evocative symbolism, especially in poetry, may communicate experience by means of sound, suggestion, reference, stimulation, time-order, and creative power. Symbols are "original as well as conditioned stimuli." With the proper attention on the part of the reader, symbols are stimulative by their very sound. This is a point thoroughly discussed by literary critics, ancient and modern, and it needs no enlargement here.

Second, properly arranged symbols can "catch and direct the attention of the reader, thus helping to bring the course of the reader's experience (E) under the writer's control." That is to say, the use of symbols can foster suggestion. Rhetorical theory over a period of two thousand years could be quoted to support this idea. The popular term *spell-binding* is sharply expressive of the idea. Pollock prefers to talk about focusing the attention and receptivity.

Third, symbols as attention-getters point toward certain referents, "and thus help to evoke . . . the emotional and other psychological responses normally evoked by the referents." Reference is not the sole charge of scientific communication.

Again, another evocative trait of symbols is "their ability when skilfully ordered to arouse the 'imaginative cooperation' of the reader." Pollock simply means by this that the excellent writer will not try to express everything. He will allow the reader to complete the immanent experience himself. I doubt that this familiar point of "audience participation" needs further discussion.

Fifth, possibly most important of all, is that every linguistic sign holds a particular time-relationship to every other word. "As the time-order is determined by the writer, this characteristic gives him the power to arrange the time-patterns of the reader's experience (E) while reading." In conveying this idea, Pollock turns to Gestalt psychology with its laws of "good continuation" and "closure." The simple fact of the significance of word-order in literature is that, as the concert pianist depresses the pedal to develop certain effects of multi-tonal resonance, so the poet achieves a cumulative effect from the symbols. Here, if anywhere, resides the "logic" of poetry, the seeming lack of which has so disturbed Richards, Britton, and others of their school of thought.

> The writer may use prior symbols to prepare psychological settings for succeeding symbols. By so doing, he may give a symbol in its place in the symbol-series an evocative power which an examination of the symbol in isolation will not reveal (p. 126).

> The fact that linguistic symbols are received in a time-order predetermined by the writer makes it possible for the writer not only to prepare the psychological setting for the reception of the symbols, but also to concentrate on one particular type of effect, greatly increasing the normal power of the word in isolation so that unusually intense experience (E) may result. Because of this, the experiences (E) evoked by literature (L) are frequently, though by no means always, more intense than the experiences (E) evoked by the stimuli we meet in everyday life (p. 131).

Anticipation and guidance, then, are the subjective attributes of time-order as a method of controlling experience.

Last, among the characteristics of evocative symbolism is "the ability of a number of 'simple' symbols to evoke a more complex symbol." This, in translation, means that a literary artist can convey a complete personality or a total image. Some simple symbols call up in the reader's response the acquaintance with a person, or the "knowledge of a place." To put it differently—perhaps less accurately-the novelist can re-create reality. We *know* Becky Sharp, Mr. Pickwick, and Egdon Heath. This development of total impression is not achieved by abstraction, as, for instance, is the mathematical concept π, but by evocation.

Hence are the elements of evocative symbolism. Words—whether as original stimuli, as sounds, or as conditional stimuli—may be used as media to call up any pattern of experience of which the reader's biography and behavioral habits are capable. There is no need to emphasize here that this evocation of controlled experience is a cooperative process between the writer and reader. In this respect it is similar to all communicative situations.

What are the probable results of this evocative symbolism? "The pattern of experience (E) which the writer's words evoke," writes

Pollock, "may be one of many types." He suggests four. First, the evoked pattern may be "a reasonably direct transcript" of what the author has seen or heard or thought about (e.g., Melville's *Typee,* White's *They Were Expendable,* and the like). Second, it may be a counterpart of events that the writer has imagined (e.g., most adventure, mystery, and romance fiction). Third, it may be an allegory to teach a lesson. Fourth, and perhaps most important because it is the most subtle, the evoked experience may be what T. S. Eliot has called an *objective correlative.* Neither Eliot nor Pollock is quite clear in explaining this phenomenon, though the idea is well known. Pollock writes:

> The objective correlative is *objective* in the sense that in the evoked experience (E) the reader perceives "objects"—sees things or people, hears sounds, follows incidents. But it is *correlative* in the sense that the so-called "objects" (images, people, places, actions which the reader experiences *are not* the experience (E) the writer is attempting to communicate but are related to it in such a way that what the reader sees, the objective correlative, *itself acts as a complex evocative symbol and evokes the particular experience which the writer was striving to communicate* (Pollock, 1942, p. 139).

This seems to mean that the linguistic signs only initiate the total experience that the writer is trying to convey, a familiar attribute of much poetry and all tragedy. I believe the explanation becomes clearer with the application of some linguistic principles. What is at stake is the author's "promotion of purposes," and, as Stern makes clear, word-meaning is never the same as purposive intention, or the general meaning of a communicative situation. In this pattern of objective correlation, the individual symbols operate within any one of several of the six ways discussed above. Yet the controlled experience, here synonymous with purpose, can be explained only in terms of the composite experience—not in terms of several individual experiences. In Melville's *Moby Dick,* for instance, the reader follows Captain Ahab's adventures, but, fascinating as these are, they serve only to objectify the stuff of the total experience. The meaning of *Moby Dick* is not the fact of the pursuit, but the sense of understanding the thinking involved in the discovery of Captain Ahab. "In the end he comes to see that his sorrow is the secret of the power and poignancy of his joy." When we are able to appreciate and share Ahab's experience, we understand the meaning of *Moby Dick.* It is the revelation of his mind that is the desired experience. Any noteworthy poem or drama furnishes, in this sense, an interpretation of life that is the meaning to be evoked. This meaning is the author's purpose in communicating.

There is more to Pollock's book, but only by way of clipping loose ends. Chapter 8 is an analysis of some of Richards's writings. In Chapter 9 he recapitulates, and offers some definitive categories of the uses of language. Pollock develops this chapter with painstaking clarity, and includes a treatment of purpose, method, criteria of success, and limitations under each of his major uses of language. Inasmuch as the categories and the discussion of them are direct inferences from the foregoing theory, a brief summary serves here.

THE USES OF LANGUAGE

1. *Phatic Comm nion*
   This is a phr: se borrowed from Malinowski that suggests the use of language :imply to establish the bonds of social communion between indiv.duals" (e.g., conventional greetings, comments on the weather, and the like; small-talk).

2. *Referential Symbolism*
   Pure referential—". . . the writer's chief concern is to help the reader identify certain referents ('objects,' 'facts,' 'ideas.')." This is scientific communication.
   Pragmatic referential—". . . the writer's purpose is *both* to point the attention of a reader toward certain referents *and* to stimulate him to assume a certain attitude toward them or to act in relation to them in a specific way" (e.g., advertising, propaganda, political pleas).

3. *Evocative Symbolism*
   Literature—"In literature (L) the author attempts to express linguistically an experience (E) of his own in such a way that the experience may be communicated to a reader. His purpose is thus *both* to express *and* to evoke a human experience (E)."
   Pseudo-literature—". . . an author is primarily concerned, not with expressing an experience of his own, but simply with evoking in a reader an experience (E) which the reader desires or which for some reason, usually commercial, the author or a publisher wishes the reader to have" (e.g., "escape literature," detective stories, and the like) (p. 180).

With regard to this classification of the uses of language, it is evident that Pollock has satisfied his objectives very neatly. Here is the core of a critical methodology for student, critic, and educational theorist interested in the nature of literature. Here, too, is a neat balance between referential and evocative symbolism, a framework within which to fit the various communicative situations that are part of existence. Moreover, not only has Pollock evolved a neat literary theory, but he has effected a very happy wedding between poetics and rhetoric, two fences that have traditionally bounded presumably incompatible objectives of discourse. Set against the background of linguistic principles and tested according to the nature of the communicative situation, two of the classical rhetorical forms—deliberative and forensic address—make rather more use of referential than of evocative symbolism, but always with a pragmatic tone. The third classical type—epideictic speaking—moves over into the realm of evocative symbolism. Poetics principally employs evocative symbolism, but necessarily invokes reference for the purposive calling-up of the desired experience. There may be varying degrees of abstraction in public address,—on rare occasions, none. Poetic discourse abstracts but little, re-creates much.

In a chapter called "Postscript," admittedly a repository for casual observations and tentative conclusions, Pollock makes some interesting suggestions and reservations. He warns of the temptation constantly facing professional students of literature to concern themselves with the facts about literature to the neglect of the central experiences "which it is the distinguishing feature of works of literature to communicate." He offers an opinion frequently voiced in the privacy of the classroom but too infrequently printed:

> The proper conclusion which the student of literature should draw from an awareness that the communication made through literature (L) is essentially an experience (E) rather than a reference to referents is, I submit, that facts concerning literature, however interesting, useful or valuable in an ancillary way, are not the central subject matter for his investigation, and that the actual study of literature itself therefore becomes all the more difficult and the danger from loose thinking all the more pernicious. For in exact science, if a man adds two and two and gets a hundred, he can be shown to be wrong; but in the study of literature, he may, and sometimes does, add two and two and get at least a dozen, and then dodge the issue with urbanity, gentility, and a supercilious style (p. 199).

Neither the illness nor the treatment is new, of course, but it is a persistent ailment and needs regular attention.

Another idea stressed to good advantage is that the student of literature might well try to maintain the distinction between literary theory and literary criticism. Literary theory is preferably analytical, scientific classification, an "attempt to discover and to describe the characteristics of the pattern of experience (E) which a work of literature communicates." It is an objective analysis that "should be regarded as a critic's passport." Literary criticism, on the other hand, is evaluation—objective enough to be more than "merely a personal effusion," but in the main concerned with values. It goes almost without saying that this distinction is not easy to maintain.

In sum, Pollock's theory is adequate and interesting. It contains a generative idea that fits the modern concern with meaning into the traditional pattern of ideas. He is conservative in his judgments, extremely wary of overstatement. His theory, grounded as it is in linguistics and the psychology of communicative behavior, is timely. There is actually little to be said about *The Nature of Literature* that the author has not anticipated. Perhaps this is itself offers a significant commentary on his work—this theory of literature is extremely simple and very pat, and not without reason. Pollock stands in the stream of the humanistic tradition. His theory is grounded on what, in our present state of knowledge, appear to be unassailable assumptions. He keeps to a descriptive technique; he deals mainly in generalizations. His psychological doctrine of *experience,* admittedly an inadequately defined term, happily avoids some of the pitfalls that face associative or materialistic explanations of meaning. His linguistic authorities are unimpeachable. Nor can one reasonably object to his psychological documentation, because he is careful to depend in the main upon conservative interpretations of accepted experimental work.

The application of Pollock's own criteria of success or failure to his theory of literature is a task for the future. His system is readily available, and, in principle at least, has been followed for a long time, especially by those literary theorists who have been interested in the oral interpretation of literature. A critical acceptance or rejection of Pollock's general theory probably depends upon two points that are closely related. One may or may not agree with him that there is an urgent need for a theory of literature that "talks the language" of an "age of science," otherwise the reading and teaching of literature will suffer. Again, one may agree or disagree that the literary and the scientific uses of language are discernibly different but not competitive, and that human experience is not appreciably benefited when critical intelligence insists upon a divorcement into two camps, the literary and the scientific, which live at loggerheads with each other. I agree with Pollock on both counts, and find his theory constructive. His book might have been written in a style freer of technical jargon, but his usages are precise. *The Nature of Literature* is a systematic study that is rational. It is well organized, penetrating, conducted with care and with reserve. It is pleasant to continue this complicated consideration of modern theories of meaning with a sense of simple substance.

REFERENCES

Bloomfield, L. Language New York: H. Holt & Co., 1933.
Jesperson, O. The Philosophy of Grammar. London: Allen and Unwin. 1924.
Malinowski, B. "The Problem of Meaning in Primitive Languages." Supplement I. In, The Meaning of Meaning, edited by C. K. Ogden and I. A. Richards. 5th ed. New York: Harcourt Brace, 1938.
Myers, H. A. "Captain Ahab's Discovery." New England Quarterly (1942) XV: 15–34.
Paul, H. Principles of the History of Language. Translated by H. A. Strong. London: S. Sonnenschein, 1890.
Pollock, T. C. The Nature of Literature: Its Relation to Science, Language, and Human Experience. Princeton: Princeton University Press, 1942.

Chapter 11
THE COMMUNICATION OF MEANING
C. S. Peirce and A. G. Bell

Offhand, it may seem rather strange to bracket Charles Sanders Peirce and Alexander Graham Bell, in a consideration of the communication of meaning, but they were colleagues in several ways. In the terms of this book they contribute distinctive dimensions of meaning, each exerting tremendous influence that relates directly to the communication of ideas; the one in brilliant philosophical concepts, the other in brilliant electrophysical relationships—the core idea of which clearly holds modern civilization together. Peirce's *semiotic,* which inspired much of the thinking of C. W. Morris, involves refined verbal distinctions; this was Bell's primary point which he saw the need for teaching speech to the deaf. Both would agree that without speech, and its obvious relations to language, the mind would remain "narrowed." Bell thought of himself primarily as a teacher of the deaf, and his deep concerns and convictions in this field were often more primary in his thinking than his laboratory work on electromagnetic and variable induction modes of transmission. Finally, fortunately, the two came together. Peirce's commitment in these terms related to sign-symbol-logic-meaning as functions of intelligence. Both believed firmly that without verbal intelligence the mind's potentials could not develop to their fullest extent. This is an impressive dimension of meaning.

The "Collected Papers of Charles Sanders Peirce" were not published until 1931, hence many of his ideas, which were indeed fundamental, were probably not even known in any large aggregate to some of the thinkers on meaning to whom we have referred in this book. References in the following discussion that are taken from the

Collected Papers will be identified by chapter and paragraph (4, 62). The other major source has been the *"Selected Writings of Peirce"* (1955), selected and edited by Justus Buchler. These references from Peirce will be designated by (Buchler).

CHARLES SANDERS PEIRCE:
SOME HISTORICAL CONSIDERATIONS

Peirce offers many interstitial threads in this tapestry of meanings. Whether they belong in warp or woof, some critic may decide. This thought was generated by a remark of William James regarding Peirce, a fellow Harvardian, class of 1859. "He," said James, "is a goldmine of ideas for the coming generation." This might well read "generations," because it is doubtful that any other single person has better taught those who have followed him in the pursuit of meanings.

He was clearly an able man with words, as philosopher, scientist, dreamer, teacher, writer, whatever. He never did get around to writing a full expression of his thinking in an organized fashion; he was evidently undertaking this when he died in 1914. He surely must have been a delight in conversation. His observations in writing are pithy, sharp, succinct. He had little patience with vagaries of thinking that force their way into print. For instance, he is outspoken in his views of the field of metaphysics. The demonstrations of metaphysics, he wrote, "are all moonshine." Its work presents "so many systems of rummaging the garret of the skull to find an enduring opinion of the universe."

Several observations about Peirce as a person seem to be in order. There was usually a gentle humor associated with his critical generalizations. In the Buchler edition of *Selected Writings,* there is the statement: "Though infallibility in scientific matters seems to me to be irresistibly comical, I should be in a sad way if I could not retain a high respect for those who lay claim to it, for they comprise the greater part of the people who have any conversation at all" (p. 3). On the same page is a not unfamiliar plaint from a sensitive person, "I am a man of whom critics have never found anything good to say." Perhaps that is the price to be paid for having been not one, but several generations ahead of one's time.

He was profoundly concerned with an analysis of modes of inquiry, and as Goudge remarks, he was eminently prepared to undertake such a study:

His first-hand acquaintance with the procedures employed in mathematics and logic, his training in chemistry, his practical experience in astronomy, experimental psychology, geodesy, and optics, provided him with a wealth of material for examination. His great generalizing power enabled him to use this material for the formulation of principles exhibited in all types of inquiry. And his naturalistic orientation led him to insist that since inquiry does not take place in a void, it must be exhibited as a mode of human activity. The *raison d'être* of inquiry lies in the biological and social nature of man (1950, p. 11).

There is in Goudge's study of Peirce's thought a particularly sensitive and insightful treatment of the pitch of his mind; in particular, a nice distinction between "Peirce the naturalist" and "Peirce the transcendentalist." The latter aspect is quite beyond the scope of this book, although by no means unpertinent. It is with his range of thinking in and about the philosophy of science that he becomes the grandfather of much of later thinking about the dimensions of meaning.

PHILOSOPHY IN GENERAL

Perhaps as a kind of digression, a brief comment might well be made about Peirce's relations with formal philosophical systems. He was clearly not a joiner. On the other hand, he was surely not a "loner." He never produced a complete system of his own, although his many writings contain most of the ingredients. I do not pretend to have studied all his thinking in depth; that would take many years, and much of it is beyond ordinary comprehension. He makes brilliant statements, full of forceful analogy and striking metaphor, but in a general picture his attitudes become obscure and devious. He was clearly interested in many combinations of basic relationships, but not in the kind of follow-through that makes clear understanding possible. This is not a new thought. In the Introduction to the *Collected Papers,* there is a succinct statement of at least one aspect of Peirce's place in philosophy:

> Pragmatism, as it developed, followed the pattern of William James' thought and that of John Dewey, rather than the conceptions of Peirce; but it was Peirce, as James and Dewey magnanimously insisted, who defined the principle of the movement and gave it the first impetus. Never indeed a leader of movements, Peirce was an originator of ideas.

An obvious result of his approach to meaningful thought is a lack of formulation, or total system, that could be called Peircism. He did

not want that, and said much about "probable error" in the laboratory and about thought in general. "Humanum est errare." This
attitude involves both the objectives and the means of thinking. He
writes in the Preface to Volume I (1931):

> For years in the course of this ripening process, I used for myself to
> collect my ideas under the designation *fallibilism*; and indeed the first
> step toward *finding out* is to acknowledge you do not satisfactorily know
> already; so that no blight can so surely arrest all intellectual growth as
> the blight of cocksureness; and ninety-nine out of every hundred good
> heads are reduced to impotence by that malady—of whose inroads they
> are most strangely unaware (p. xi).

ON THINKING

This idea of "finding out" is closely linked with the entire scheme of
semiotic. Peirce was deeply concerned that there be a science of
philosophy with fresh and specific terminology, so that philosophy—
real inquiry—could share with mathematics—*abstract* inquiry—the
precision of expression and relative freedom from error that is
expected in the physical and biological sciences. In discoursing on
various reasons for concern with terminology, he wrote:

> Those reasons would embrace, in the first place, the consideration that
> the warp and woof of all thought and all research is symbols, and the life
> of thought and science is the life inherent in symbols; so that it is wrong
> to say that a good language is *important* to good thought, merely; for it
> is of the essence of it (2, 129).

Peirce was well aware that he was walking over relatively unex-
plored ground, at least in modern terms. He refers to himself as a
pioneer, "or rather a backwoodsman, in the work of clearing and
opening up what I call *semiotic*, that is, the doctrine of the essential
nature and fundamental varieties of possible semiosis [please refer
back to Locke]; and I find the field too vast, the labour too great, for
a first-comer" (5, 488).

It seems clear (and this point is recognized by various critics of
Peirce's work) that "sign" is for him an encompassing term, and that
when he refers to thought and learning he means not "sign" but
"symbol," particularly verbal symbols. His description of semiotic
(much more clearly expressed by Morris than by Peirce) is offered in
several aspects throughout his work. A basic description follows.

> In consequence of every representamen [sign] being thus connected with
> three things, the ground, the object, and the interpretant, the science of

semiotic has three branches. The first called by Duns Scotus *grammatica speculativa*. We may term it pure grammar. It has for its task to ascertain what must be true of the representamen used by every scientific intelligence in order that they may embody any meaning. The second is logic proper. It is the science of what is quasi-necessarily true of the representamina of any scientific intelligence in order that they may hold good of any *object,* that is, may be true. Or, say, logic proper is the formal science of the conditions of the truth of representations. The third, in imitation of Kant's fashion of preserving old associations of words in finding nomenclature for new conceptions, I call pure *rhetoric.* Its task is to ascertain the laws by which in every scientific intelligence one sign gives birth to another, and especially one thought brings forth another (2, 135).

SEMIOTIC

Within this triadic relationship, there exist the dimensions that are implicit and explicit for the conveyance of meaning. Peirce's extension of this thinking is highly verbal, but not very clear, because he does not consistently follow up his ideas with explanation. He does, however, follow his basic precept, the need for new language. Underlying the evolution of his various theses of semiotic are his beliefs that all reasoning is a function of the use of signs and symbols, and that logic is "philosophy of communication, or theory of signs" (Buchler p. xii).

According to Peirce, signs can be understood in terms of three trichotomies: "first, according as the sign itself is a mere quality, is an actual existent, or is a general law; secondly, according as the relation of the sign to its object consists in the sign's having some character in itself, or in some existential relation to that object, or in its relation to an interpretant; thirdly, according as its Interpretant represents it as a sign of possibility or as a sign of fact or a sign of reason" (Buchler, p. 101).

Through this discussion it might be well to keep in mind Peirce's meaning in his use of the term "sign." "A sign stands *for* something *to* the idea which it produces or modifies. Or, it is a vehicle conveying into the mind something from without" (Buchler, p. 80).

The language of these trichotomies is not simple to follow. The first includes Qualisign, Sinsign, or Legisign. A Qualisign is simply a quality, with no function "until it is embodied." A Sinsign is "an actual thing or event," usually a single thing or event. A Legisign is every conventional sign, such as a word in the formal structure of a language; it is in existence by law, if you will, which simply means by common agreement about the use of a common language.

The second trichotomy involves the sign as Icon, or Index, or Symbol. As "icon" suggests, it is in effect an image; it cannot act as a sign of an object until and unless there is an object. "Anything whatever, be it quality, existant individual, or law, is an Icon of anything, in so far as it is like that thing and used as a sign of it." An Index is, in Peirce's view, just that. It is a sign "which refers to the Object that it denotes by virtue of being really affected by that object." Examples include an index of a book (the object), or certain kinds of behavior that may offer an index to a person's particular ways of thinking. A symbol is a sign that refers directly to the object it denotes. All commonly understood words in a given "public" language are symbols. Inasmuch as Peirce regularly uses internal terms in his trichotomies to refer to or to define each other, explanations are frequently difficult to follow until one becomes accustomed to his special language.

In the third trichotomy a sign may be "a Rheme, a Dicisign or Dicent Sign (that is, a proposition or quasi-proposition), or an Argument" (Buchler, p. 103). A rheme is, or may be interpreted as, a sign of "qualitative possibility;" one may speak of "the idols of the marketplace." A dicent sign represents actual existence, some kind of thing or fact. An argument is a sign of law for its interpretant. "This is the way it should be said or done—this is the way we do it."

Clearly, any sign may be analyzed in terms of one or a combination of these trichotomies. Peirce was fond of emphasizing triadic relations, as opposed to diadic, and believed this to be the essence of phenomenology (*phaneron* was his term, "the collective total of all that is in any way or in any sense present to the mind, quite regardless of whether it corresponds to any real thing or not") (Buchler, p. 74). In sum, he asserts, "a sign is something A, which denotes some fact or object, B, to some interpretant thought, C. Peirce derives from his three trichotomies ten classes of signs, plus numerous subdivisions (Buchler, p. 115-119). His presentation is tightly reasoned, and it would be fruitless to try to paraphrase it in simpler terms; there are none. I suggest that the interested reader ponder the original presentation; it requires some pondering. Perhaps it is sufficient for our purposes simply to refer to his summary diagram (Figure 4). His description of it follows.

> The affinities of the ten classes are exhibited by arranging their designations in the triangular table here shown, which has heavy boundaries between adjacent squares that are appropriated to classes alike in only

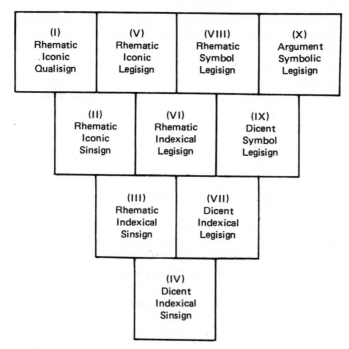

Figure 4.   Peirce's diagram.

one respect. All other adjacent squares pertain to classes alike in two respects. Squares not adjacent pertain to classes alike in one respect only, except that each of the three squares of the vertices of the triangle pertains to a class differing in all three respects from the classes to which the squares along the opposite side of the triangle pertains to a class differing in all three respects from the classes to which the squares along the opposite side of the triangle are appropriated. The lightly printed designations are superfluous (Buchler, p. 118).

PRAGMATISM

It would be unfair and unreasonable not to make some further reference to Peirce as at least one of the founders of *pragmatism*. Later, he becomes unhappy when "the word begins to be met with occasionally in the literary journals, where it gets abused in the merciless way that words have to expect when they fall into literary clutches" (Buchler, p. 255). Thereupon, he announces the birth of a new brainchild, *pragmaticism*, "which is ugly enough to be safe from kidnappers." Perhaps unfortunately, the kidnappers had enough hostages to protect themselves and the new term never caught on. In Peirce's lexicon it would have been the more precise of the two, in that it would require a highly precise vocabularly in conceptual extension, which the more common term does not (see Buchler, pp. 253–255 for an expansion of this idea).

In any event, Peirce had little use for the "metaphysical" terms *truth* and *falsity*. His basic idea of scientific hypothesis and procedure centered in his idea of the relations between doubt and belief in the inquiring mind. In an interesting pseudodialogue with "Mr. Make Believe," he states his case succinctly: "But if by truth and falsity you mean something not definable in terms of doubt and belief in any way, then you are talking of entities of whose existence you can know nothing, and which Ockham's razor would clean shave off. Your problem would be greatly simplified, if, instead of saying that you want to know the 'Truth,' you were simply to say that you want to attain a state of belief unassailable by doubt" (Buchler, p. 257).

He offers a profoundly simple explanation of the pragmatist's point of view in two papers in particular, the essence of which can be found in the Buchler edition (pp. 255–268). His indictment of loose thinking is sharp and clear:

> A theory which should be capable of being absolutely demonstrated in its entirety by future events, would be no scientific theory but a mere piece of fortune telling. On the other hand, a theory which goes beyond what may be verified to any degree of approximation by future discoveries is, in so far, meta-physical gabble.

Logic is careful thinking of terms of the theses of *semiotic,* the use of sign and symbol within a framework of scientific procedure (employing deduction, induction, and abduction), toward the end of establishing sound beliefs, unassailable by doubt. This portion of the chapter closes with a nice Peircean generalization:

> What . . . is the end of an explanatory hypothesis? Its end is, through subjection to the test of experiment, to lead to the avoidance of all surprise and to the establishment of a habit of positive expectation that shall not be disappointed. Any hypothesis, therefore, may be admissible, in the absence of any special reasons to the contrary, provided it be capable of experimental verification, and only in so far as it is capable of such verification. This is approximately the doctrine of pragmatism (Buchler, p. 267).

In the view of his colleagues and peers, Peirce without doubt should have a place among the most brilliant thinkers of the Western World through the period since his first professional writing, more than a century ago.

ALEXANDER GRAHAM BELL: SOME BACKGROUND

One of the reasons for including this chapter in a study of the dimensions of meaning is to bring together the thinking of two major creative minds, both steeped in laboratory procedures, each concerned with more than scientific experimentation, both dedicated to verbal-symbolic communication as the major foundation of reasoning, of thinking, and of knowing. Alexander Graham Bell, busy at many other kinds of things, both accepted and practiced Peirce's basic principles. He also went much further. Peirce is perhaps best known as a logician; Bell insisted that his deepest intellectual efforts and his deepest attachment to life and living was his utter devotion as a teacher of the deaf. Taking this into consideration, it becomes clear that it was this devotion that almost literally drove him to the invention of the telephone, thought of by his friend Edison as the instrument that "annihilated time and space, and brought the human family closer in touch."

Considering the fact that he was one of the geniuses of all time, and certainly outstanding in thought and accomplishment in modern times, I have found it difficult to believe that so little, aside from the obvious attention in the daily media, has been written about A. G. Bell. Even in the Library of Congress there is much more to be found about his father, Melville, than about "Aleck." This situation was remedied in 1973 with the publication of Robert V. Bruce's biography, *Bell: Alexander Graham Bell and the Conquest of Solitude.* It is a definitive book, written at the request of the family and with the family's full approval. Obviously, much of what follows is found in Bruce's work.

Without doubt, as happens in most families, many of Bell's proclivities, if not his achievements, had to do with his family. He was brought up in Edinburgh with his two brothers. His mother was severely hearing impaired; her speech and language were good, however, and Aleck seemed to be able to communicate with her more readily than could his two brothers. His father was both a teacher and a scientist in the field of phonetics and, perhaps with the inspiration of his wife's needs, he concentrated his attention on the classification of speech sounds and the development of a simple system of notation. This he called "Visible Speech," and both he and Aleck came to lecture extensively on this topic both in Great Britain and in the United States.

According to Bruce, Bell led a quite lonely life as a child:

The phrase "conquest of solitude" applies to be sure, to Bell's teaching of speech to the deaf and to his most famous triumph, the invention of the telephone. But it also applies to his own nature . . . something made him a rather solitary boy, given to the solemn Sabbath meditations and to long, lone musings on a hilltop near Edinburgh. Perhaps the tendency was inborn, perhaps it had to do with his mother's deafness and his father's rather overpowering eminence and sharpness of humor. . . . He developed the habit, which was also his father's of working alone long into the night and sleeping late the next day. . . . Throughout his life, he found it difficult to talk without reserve—except on such impersonal matters as science or technology—to anyone outside his family, and this inability distressed him (1974, p. 3).

He first taught in a boy's school in Scotland. He became interested in acoustics and experimented with tuning forks to study the vocal organs. In 1868 he began to teach the deaf at Miss Hull's school in London. She was a former student of his father and was interested in the use of Visible Speech. Thereafter, both his brothers died of tuberculosis, and his father emigrated with his family to Tutelo Heights, Brantford, Ontario. Aleck went to Boston to teach Visible Speech to the deaf. Here he was able to make some contacts at Massachusetts Institute of Technology (M.I.T.) that would lead to the laboratory facilities and professional stimulus that made possible the development of the telephone. He was successful with some private students, and worked with Sarah Fuller at her school in Boston. He taught Visible Speech at the Clarke School in Northampton, and worked long hours with Theresa Dudley, who eventually became a pupil at the new Clarke School for the Deaf; her father became a trustee. After some vicissitudes, which included work with George Sanders and a lasting relation with the Sanders family, he became a professor at Boston University. By 1873 he was working with Mabel Hubbard; this became a turning point in his life. In Bruce's words: "Along with his other roles during the 1873–74 school year—promoter, organizer, lecturer, tutor, professor, and occasional invalid—Bell played inventor in the fall and scientist in the spring" (1973, p. 104).

THE TELEPHONE

His electrical experiments were going along well, as he labored to develop his "harmonic multiple telegraph system." He had begun from a concept of Helmholtz with the use of tuning forks, then steel "reeds," but this could not produce speech. At this time, he was not even looking for a telephone. In early 1874, he was given access to M.I.T.'s apparatus and laboratories, and began experiments that turned him from telegraphy to acoustics. By mid-summer, while he was at Brantford, the concept of the telephone was born— approximately one month before a relatable statement by Elisha Gray of Chicago was published in the *Hartford Courant.*

The telephone was truly "born" on a hot summer day in 1875 in Boston, where Bell was at work with Watson; both heard the sound and timbre of voice through vibrating reeds. After many more vicissitudes, both with Mabel Hubbard with whom Bell was deeply in love (her father was his business partner), and with the U.S. Patent Office in Washington, Bell's telephone was finally patented on March 7, 1876, No. 174,465, three days after Bell's twenty-ninth birthday. In Bruce's words, this patent "would turn out eventually to be one of the most valuable patents ever issued." Within a reasonably short time, after triumphant demonstrations, more struggles with patents (a new one was issued to cover various revisions to "modernize" the instrument), and readying for commercial development, everything went well, with hundreds of telephones soon in operation. Bell and Mabel Hubbard were married, went to Niagara Falls on their honeymoon, and sailed on August 4, 1877 for a long stay in England.

TELEPHONE AND COMMUNICATION

There is no need at this point to go into the technical details of the development of telephonic circuitry that made the instrument work. If the reader wishes to delve into this, he will find it quite faithfully presented in Bruce's books. The basic point of it all is quite clear. Bell's charge was to convey speech over channels of wire—speech that would preserve the phonetic detail of vocal utterance with high fidelity in all aspects of the spoken message, so that the meaning of the message was clearly discernible—so that communication could take place. Thus there is added to our tapestry a psychophysical dimension of meaning without which much that we know and do these days in research, teaching, clinical work, and daily living would be impossible.

No doubt much of what has happened in fairly recent years in the field of electronics that concerns itself with communication would have happened without the foundation laid by Bell. Bell's work helped it to happen sooner, however, and gave a tremendous impetus to it. One has only to consider the ideas contributed by the Bell Telephone Laboratories and Westinghouse and the equipment contributed by

Western Electric to have some idea of what this impetus meant. What Bell did was to offer an intellectual synthesis—a more important accomplishment than the current, rather vapid term "innovative" could express. All the parts had been available for some time; it was for Bell to put them together with a set of drives and beliefs that were peculiarly his own. In many ways, he was a current, living example of Peirce's thesis of belief versus doubt in scientific thinking. Bruce clearly expresses the meaning of this:

> In the beginning Bell was driven by various pressures and perhaps by innate temperament to achieve something great—to make himself heard. The need for money on which to marry gave him added incentive. The specific goal of electrical speech transmission was latent in a number of simple, well-known physical principles; but these principls were in fields not usually conjoined, chiefly electricity, acoustics, and physiology. To bring these together and fuse them required imagination and a wide-ranging curiosity, both of which Bell had to the point of extravagance. Bell also chanced to be well grounded in the very assortment of special fields that converged at the crucial point. And with all these attributes, the inventor of the telephone needed to be armored by stubborn self-persuasion against the doubts and denials of supposed experts. Bell . . . had a full suit of that quality (1973, p. 365).

Although Bell always reported himself as "a teacher" (a designation that appears on his gravestone), he did little directly as a teacher in later years, but did much as a thinker and administrator, which concerns our dimensions of meaning. It might be pointed out that in 1879 Bell invented and used the first audiometer. This is an instrument employed in otology, audiology, and in experimental psychology to measure some of the limits of auditory acuity relative to frequency and intensity in response to stimulus by pure tones. One may suspect that many practicing audiologists have never heard of this instrument. It offered an incentive for Fletcher and his associates in the Bell Laboratories to develop the first electronic audiometer in 1922, the year of Bell's death. Bell demonstrated his audiometer for the National Academy of Sciences in 1885. He reported that more than ten percent of seven hundred pupils (source of group not specified) had some hearing impairment. More testing the next year suggested that one percent of those tested needed special classes (1973, p. 394). These are some of the earliest instances of which I am aware of what is now known as auditory (or hearing) screening. Presently, this is a general program undertaken under the aegis of public health and education, and is considered of major importance in determining an affected child's needs.

Perhaps it is unnecessary (but, on the other hand, it might be wise) to emphasize the importance of hearing for the development of language and speech by the infant and young child. Much of this is taken for granted, even by those who profess to be linguists or psycholinguists. It must not be taken for granted, because there have been many clear demonstrations that even a mild hearing impairment, let alone a severe or profound involvement, can interfere directly with these vitally important aspects of learning and knowing. Peirce's entire thesis of logic as the modus operandi of learning is based on symbolic behavior. Bell's most profound commitment was to the endeavor to help the deaf learn to speak. His work in telephonic circuitry clearly led the way to the development of the modern hearing aid and to a wide variety of classroom instrumentation in the training and education of children with impaired hearing. Inasmuch as language and speech are always learned normally through the auditory mechanism, when this mechanism is impaired almost any reasonably well balanced auditory aid is of service. The point, almost too obvious to warrant expression, is that the mind's meanings in terms of language, thought, and experience at root depend upon a variety of sensory perceptions, of which the auditory system is most important. Bell knew this, of course, which is why he dedicated so much time, energy, and money to the effort to teach the deaf to speak. The most important monument to this effort exists as the Alexander Graham Bell Association (For Teaching Speech To The Deaf) in Washington, D.C. This Association is a repository and disseminator of information in the field, and offers many services to parents, educators, and administrators whose interests relate to impaired hearing.

It is unnecessary in this setting to pursue the professional problems with which current activities in the education of the deaf are fraught. They would continue to interest Bell, as they did when he was part of the several controversies and discussions of methodology. They are not pertinent, however, to present considerations.

PEIRCE AND BELL

It is interesting to conjecture about how well Peirce and Bell knew each other; it is known that they were acquainted. That they had much in common except for deep concern with humanity and man's ability to communicate is doubtful. Peirce was preoccupied with his thinking, and Bell was profoundly occupied with his experiments. Ten years Bell's senior, Peirce was the iconoclastic thinker, supreme logician, brilliant philosopher of science who made a tremendous impact on his peers who had these interests. Otherwise, he was quite obscure, known only to a select few who could appreciate the meaning of his thought and writing. Bell, equally brilliant in a quite different range of interests, the synthesizer, doer, and promoter, achieved world-wide fame, fortune, and lasting reknown before the age of thirty. A sharp contrast, indeed! It is entirely possible that they would not have had much to say to each other, although this is scarcely imaginable between two men who had so many insights into the ways of mankind. A comment made by Bruce in connection with Bell as friend and benefactor of science is cited here as an envoi.

> And when, beginning in 1907, Bell and nine other well-wishers at William James's instigation joined in paying an annual pension of five hundred dollars to Charles S. Peirce and his wife, they did so anonymously. Peirce, who was not only old, sick, penniless, jobless, impractical, and eccentric, but also a scientist of ability and a philosopher of genius, was able in the seven years left him to produce some of his greatest work.

REFERENCES

Bruce, R. V. Bell: Alexander Graham Bell and the Conquest of Solitude. Boston: Little, Brown, 1973.
———.Alexander Graham Bell: Teacher of the Deaf. Alexander Graham Bell Lecture Series. Northampton, Mass.: The Clarke School for the Deaf, 1974.
Buchler, J. (ed.). 1955. Selected Writings of Peirce. New York: Dover Publications, 1955.
Goudge, T. A. The Thought of C. S. Peirce. Canada: University of Toronto Press, 1950.
Harshorne, C., and Weiss, P., eds. Collected Papers of Charles Sanders Peirce. Cambridge; Mass.: Harvard University Press, 1931.

Chapter 12
PHILOSOPHY AND SYMBOLISM
S. K. Langer

THE NEW KEY

Next, our attention turns to some of the thinking of Susanne K. Langer. A former student of Whitehead at Harvard, she has written widely on various matters of language, thought, and experience, but her major work on which we concentrate her is *Philosophy in a New Key,* first published in 1942. This book has gone through three editions and many printings. Her "new key" is verbal symbolism, and she concentrates on a truly remarkable discussion of the relations between sign and symbol in an unusual treatment of man's appraisal of himself and of his place in the universe.

Langer's approach to the study of ideas is indeed discerning. In her book she refers to "groupings of ideas," and writes, "It is the mode of handling problems, rather than what they are about, that assigns them to an age." Basically, this is a re-expression of a quite familiar mode of procedure: the way a question is asked, as well as the purpose for asking it, fairly well directs the nature of possible responses.

This concept is at the core of some of Langer's focal thinking. "In philosophy," she writes, "this disposition of problems is the most important thing that a school, a movement, or an age contributes. This is the 'genius' of a great philosophy; in its light, systems arise and rule and die. Therefore a philosophy is characterized more by the *formulation* of its problems than by its solution of them" (p. 4). This kind of observation may seem remote from the topic of this book, but it is not.

As was discussed earlier, this is an empirical age. Langer expresses clearly what has been referred to. "Genuine empiricism is above all a reflection on the validity of sense-knowledge, a speculation on the ways our concepts and beliefs are built up out of the fleeting and disconnected reports our eyes and ears actually make to the mind. Positivism, the scientists' metaphysic, entertains no such doubts, and raises no epistemological problems; its belief in the veracity of sense is implicit and dogmatic . . . It repudiates the basic problems of epistemology, and creates nothing but elbow-room for laboratory work" (p. 14).

There follows a remarkably succinct discussion of relations between philosophy and science, with some wry comments about confusions between fact-finding and thinking: "To the generations of Compte, Mill, and Spencer," she writes, "it certainly seemed as though all human knowledge could be cast in the new mold [scientific methodology]; certainly as though nothing in any other mold could hope to jell . . . The truth is that science has not really fructified and activated *all* human thought. If humanity has really passed the philosophical stage of learning, as Compte hopefully declared, and is evolving no more fantastic ideas, then we have certainly left many interesting brain-children stillborn along the way"(p. 17).

These are powerful words! She continues with a very interesting discussion of relationships that have occurred within the pursuit of laboratory science. In effect, she avers, it is passing strange that the scientific empiricists, often scornful of philosophical logic and reasoning, find it necessary to make so much use of "the ancient science of mathematics," which is based not at all on observation of events, but solely on pure reason. She points out that mathematicians themselves "give no set data their preference. They deal only with items whose sensory qualities are quite irrelevant: their 'data' are arbitrary sounds or marks called symbols." She points out that mathematicians are not very practical. "They are apt to be cloistered souls, like philosophers and theologians." Why, then, are they taken so seriously by the pragmatic scientists? "The secret lies in the fact that a mathematician does not profess to say anything about the existence, reality, or efficacy of *things* at all. His concern is the possibility of *symbolizing things,* and of symbolizing the relations into which they might enter with each other. His 'entities' are not 'data', but *concepts*" (p. 19). She goes on to emphasize the point that the essence of mathematics is symbolic, and makes a rather quizzical comment in leading into a summary of the topic. "The faith of scientists in the power and truth of mathematics [the science of pure reason] is so implicit that their work has gradually become less and less observation, and more and more calculation."

The point, Langer says, is that the age of science has almost forced the development of a new and profoundly interesting philosophy, the connecting link being the conceptualism of mathematics. She expresses this clearly: "all at once, the edifice of human knowledge stands before us, not as a vast collection of sense reports, but as a structure of *facts that are symbols and laws that are their meanings*. A new philosophical theme has been set forth to a coming age: an epistemologicial theme, the comprehension of science. The power of symbolism is its cue, as the finality of sense-data was the cue of a former epoch" (p. 21). Langer then goes on to refer to most of the innovators who are the subjects (or objects) of this essay. This is done, however, without any critical opinion, except that all this concern with symbolism and meaning is "in the air."

Thus, she leads her readers into the expression of her 'new key' in philosophy—into logic and the theory of knowledge, into the study of emotions, religions, and rites, indeed, of dreams and myths. Her summarizations are succinct.

> In the fundamental notion of symbolization—mystical, practical, or mathematical, it makes no difference—we have the keynote of all humanistic problems . . . The philosophical study of symbols is not a technique borrowed from other disciplines, not even from mathematics; it has arisen in the fields that the great advance of learning has left fallow. Perhaps it holds the seed of a new intellectual harvest, to be reaped in the next season of the human understanding (p. 25).

RHETORIC AND BELIEF

It is neither appropriate nor necessary to attend to all of Langer's ideas in this book: I shall concentrate on the tapestry. One trouble with this decision is that she has so many good ideas that there exist in her writing a plethora of quotable statements. I consistently concur with her basic point of view, that philosophy should largely be a study of meanings.

In another reference, there was some discussion of the three dimensions of meaning postulated by Morris from a background in Peirce. In that discussion, Miller's suggestion about the pragmatic dimension included some reference to relations between this dimension and belief. Some of this is rather old stuff to a classically trained rhetorician, but it is interesting that Miller, a psychologist, and Langer, a philosopher, come to quite similar observations. Langer has this to say in her consideration of "Symbolic Transformation":

> A changed approach to the theory of knowledge naturally has its effect upon psychology, too. As long as sense was supposed to be the chief factor in knowledge, psychologists took a prime interest in the organs that were the windows of the minds, and in the details of their functioning; other things were accorded a sketchier and sometimes vaguer treatment . . . But now, an epistemological insight has uncovered a more potent, howbeit more difficult, factor in scientific procedure—the use of symbols to attain, as well as to organize, belief. Of course, this alters our conception of intelligence at a stroke. Not higher sensitivity, not longer memory or even quicker association sets man so far above other animals that he can regard them as denizens of a lower world: no, it is the power of using symbols—the power of *speech*—that makes him lord of the earth. So our interest in the mind has shifted more and more from the acquisition of experience, the domain of sense, to the *uses* of sense-data, the realm of conception and expression (p. 28).

This is *logos,* in probably one of its best modern definitions. This the ancient Greeks knew well; their leaders in the heyday of Athens had to persuade them in ethical terms what was best for the state and for them. In all this, belief was paramount. Aristotle in his *Rhetoric* demonstrates this very clearly.

Langer continues with a quite learned discussion, supported by the opinions of various authorities, to support her contentions. These need not detain us here. In her consideration of the brain relative to symbolization, two comments warrant emphasis. She discusses the fact that symbolic activity is the starting point of most intelligence. "For the brain is not merely a great transmitter, a super-switchboard; it is better likened to a great transformer." Again, she generalizes, "The fact that the human brain is constantly carrying on a process of symbolic transformation of the experiential data that comes to it causes it to be a veritable fountain of more or less spontaneous ideas."

SIGN AND SYMBOL

Langer's third chapter is called "The Logic of Signs and Symbols." In her prefatory remarks for the second edition of the book (1951), she makes some statements that are most interesting and revealing (please refer back to the chapter on C. W. Morris in this book):

> If, however, I were writing it now [that is, *Philosophy in a New Key*] . . . that chapter heading would read "The Logic of *Signals and Symbols.*" Charles Morris, in his *Signs, Language and Behavior,*

employed a usage which I find superior to my own and have accordingly adopted since the publication of his book. Morris uses the word "signal" for what I called "sign" . . . The great advantage of Morris's usage is that it leaves us the word "sign" to denote any vehicle of meaning, signal or symbols, whereas in my own vocabulary there was no generic term, and the need of it was sometimes obvious.

This fresher distinction should be kept in mind as some of Langer's ideas are considered.

She reminds us that in psychological terms any thought that is verbally expressed must operate either as a sign or a symbol. Logically, there must be conveyance of meaning to someone about something. These two aspects of communication must always be present, if one is not talking nonsense, and the relations between them have been a source of contention over the years. Writes Langer: "The analysis of 'meaning' has had a peculiarly difficult history; the word is used in many different ways, and a good deal of controversy has been wasted on the subject of *the* correct way, *the* meaning of 'meaning'!" So be it! That is what the present essay is all about.

Langer emphasizes the need for general theoretical concepts regarding meaning. You will recall some of the problems encountered by Ogden and Richards and by Britton in undertaking to make theoretical distinctions simply too "pat." On the other hand, one can go to the opposite extreme. Langer refers to C. S. Peirce:

> Charles Peirce, who was probably the first person to concern himself seriously with semantics, began by making an inventory of all 'symbol-situations,' in the hope that when all possible meanings of "meaning" were herded together, they would show empirical differentia whereby one could divide the sheep from the goats. But the obstreperous flock, instead of falling neatly into a few classes, each according to its kind, divided and subdivided into the most terrifying order of icons, qualisigns, legisigns, semes, phemes, and delomes, and there is but cold comfort in his assurance that his original 59,049 types can really be boiled down to a mere sixty-six (Langer, 1942, p. 54).

This is sufficiently succinct to be noticeable. Yet once must doubt that Peirce was the first to take *semantics,* as a term and as a study, seriously. One might think that this honor, if it is an honor, would be assigned to Michel Bréal, who introduced the term in an article published in 1883. He referred to "la semantique," as "la science des significations." For an interesting treatment of the history of the term, I recommend Read's "An Account of the Word 'Semantics.'"

Be that as it may, Langer remains concerned about the diverse herds of sheep and goats. She does not approve the thought that meaning is a relation, because it is too simple. She generalizes, "It is better, perhaps, to say: 'Meaning is not a quality, but a *function* of a term.'" She continues, "Even in the simplest kinds of meaning there must be at least two other things related to the term that 'means'—an object that is 'meant', and a subject who uses the term." There follows a discussion of sign and symbol, her basic terms.

"The logical relation between a sign and its object is a very simple one: they are associated, somehow, to form a *pair*; that is to say, they stand in a one-to-one correlation" (p. 57). The remainder of the function involves the subject; that is signification. This is the interpretant. A man in a boat on the Chesapeake "reads" the sky, starts the motor, and drives hard to a shelter. Here is the combination of things that for an experienced boatman has *meaning*.

> The interpretation of signs is the basis of animal intelligence. Animals presumably do not distinguish between natural signs and artificial or fortuitous signs; but they use both kinds to guide their practical activities. We do the same thing all day long. . . . The logical basis of all these interpretations, the mere correlation of trivial events with important ones, is really very simple and common; so much so that there is no limit to what a sign may mean. . . . As for bells, the world is mad with their messages. Somebody at the front door, the back door, the side door, the telephone—toast is ready—typewriter line is ended—school begins, work begins, church begins, church is over-street car starts—cash box registers—knife grinder passes—time for dinner, time to get up—fire in town (p. 59).

This is a delightfully graphic definition. You will recall, in the opening remarks of this section, Langer's comment that she would have preferred Morris's term "signal" to her use of "sign." I believe it is clear from this passage why she stated that preference. All the events in reference here are indeed signals.

Langer goes on to discuss these signs (signals) and their interpretations as the simplest form of knowledge; the interpretations may be mistaken, but this is obvious. She likens the mechanism to an elaborated conditioned-reflex arc. Thus, in the use of these signals, laboratory science can set up generalizations among all sorts of mammals, including *Homo sapiens*. She writes:

> So it is not surprising that students of genetic psychology have seized upon sign interpretation as the archetype of all knowledge, that they regard signs as the original bearers of meaning, and treat all other terms with semantic properties as sub-species—"substitute signs," which act as proxy for their objects and evoke conduct appropriate to the latter instead of to themselves (p. 60).

"Symbols," on the other hand, "are not proxy for their objects, but are *vehicles for the conception of things*." This is the essence of her theory, and I doubt that any serious student of meaning would disagree with it. She continues, "In talking *about* things we have conceptions of them, not the things themselves; and *it is the conceptions, not the things, that symbols directly "mean."* Behavior toward conceptions is what words normally evoke; this is the typical process of thinking." This is, of course, the reason for the first part of the title of this book: language, thought, and experience—language (symbol) constitutes the essential function of thought relative to experience with conceptualization; thus the tapestry is woven—these are the dimensions of meaning.

Langer refers to a famous passage from the memoirs of Helen Keller concerning the day she discovered the conception of water, which Langer calls "the great advent of Language." "This passage is the best affidavit we could hope to find for the genuine difference between sign and symbol. The sign is something to act upon, or a means to command action; the symbol is an instrument of thought . . . Real thinking is possible only in the light of genuine language, no matter how limited, how primitive; in her case, it became possible with the discovery that 'w-a-t-e-r' was not necessarily a sign that water was wanted or expected, but was the *name* of this substance, by which it could be mentioned, conceived, remembered." This is the beginning of denotation, "the relation of conception to the concrete world."

Langer is specific in her differentiations:

> In an ordinary sign-function, there are three essential terms: subject, sign, and object. In denotation, which is the commonest kind of symbol-function, there have to be four: subject, symbol, conception, and object. The radical difference between sign-meaning and symbol-meaning can therefore be logically exhibited, for it rests on a difference of pattern, it is strictly a different function" (p. 64).

The association involved here is connotation, "the conception it conveys." This is the part of the symbol that makes it possible to think about an object that is not present and to which we do not, or need not, react. "Here, then, are the three most familiar meanings of the one word, 'meaning': signification, denotation, and connotation. All three are equally and perfectly legitimate, but in no possible way interchangeable."

THE LOGIC OF DISCOURSE

The next topic deals with meaning in discourse, in contrast with that for separate symbols. This naturally leads one to communication, which is the point of this work. This is a matter of propositions with a context, and, indeed, has much to do with the functions of "the com-municative chain" (Hardy, 1977). It is doubtful that Langer ever had an opportunity to think from phoneme (symbol) through the phonetic system and acoustic output of the speaker to the receiver of these acoustic events, through the sensory receptor system and on to the phonemic (symbolic) encoding system of the listener. This is the "communicative chain," a quite elaborate exchange in encoding on the part of the speaker and decoding on the part of the listener. This *is* human communication in terms of verbal-symbolic exchange.

Here in her discussion Langer gets to another of Morris's dimen-sions of meaning, the syntactical (grammar), the logical sequence of verbal-symbolic expression that makes possible the understanding of what is expressed in any given linguistic code. Langer expresses this in somewhat different terms, but with quite the same effect:

> Grammatical structure, then, is a further source of significance. We can-not call it a symbol, since it is not even a term; but it has a symbolic mission. . . . What the special constellation is, depends on the syntactical relations within the complex symbol, or proposition" (pp. 67–68).

I wonder if the reader is as fascinated as I am with the number of ways "the same thing" can be said by persons in quite different situa-tions, with different perspectives, different perceptions, and sometimes different objectives? This is one of the reasons I wanted to write this book. Over a long number of years as a student of verbal-symbolic meaning, I have been much impressed with the intellectual consistency of those who think clearly, according to their understanding of life and living. This has been going on in our ken for twenty-five hundred years!

With this verbal indulgence aside, the discussion of Langer's thinking proceeds. After some references to Bertrand Russell (who really did not discover all these various relations we have been refer-ring to), she offers a very succinct observation that, in her usual style, brings to life the meaning of patterns.

> It has become apparent that a proposition fits a fact not only because it contains names for the things and actions involved in the fact, but also because it combines them in a pattern analogous, somehow, to the pat-tern in which the named objects are "in fact" combined. *A proposition is a picture of a structure—the structure of a state of affairs.* The unity of a proposition is the same sort of unity that belongs to a picture, which presents one scene, no matter how many items may be distinguishable within it (p. 68).

That is a very nice expression of a thought that Ogden and Richards, and Britton, approached but never quite met. Langer goes on to discuss the wide varieties of technique and subject matter that might be included in any pictorial representation, all of which are acceptable. There is this much latitude, she says, because "*the picture is essentially a symbol, not a duplicate, of what it represents.*"

Immediately thereafter some astute observations are developed about various kinds of pictorial representations, most aspects of which are related to Morris's third dimension of meaning, the pragmatical. This is implicit in Langer's critique, but never specifically mentioned.

> Consider a photograph, a painting, a pencil sketch, an architect's eleva-tion drawing, and a builder's diagram, all showing the front view of one and the same house. With a little attention, you will recognize the house in each representation. Why?
>
> Because each one of the very different images expresses the same relation of parts, which you have fastened on in forming your conception of the house (p. 71).

THE POWER OF SYMBOLS

The symbol (perhaps best represented in phonological terms by phoneme) is, then, a concept, a function of the mind. It becomes per-sonalized, particularly in communication. Here I am referring to symbols in an extended sense—a sentence, a proposition, the totality of observation. This would be structure, in a linguistic sense. Langer generalized:

> The power of understanding symbols, i.e. of regarding everything about a sense-datum as irrelevant except a certain *form* that it embodies, is the most characteristic mental trait of mankind. It issues in an unconscious, spontaneous process of abstraction, which goes on all the time in the human mind: a process of recognizing the concept in any configuration given to experience, and forming a conception accordingly (Langer, 1942, p. 72).

This is what Korzybski was driving at, but he had to make his awareness of the idea "anti-Aristotelian." Langer does not feel this need. She says that this "is the real sense of Aristotle's definition of man as 'the rational animal'."

There is considerable further discussion of possible relations among situational combinations of words, with special attention to the speed with which extremely complicated creations of meanings can be developed. These are familiar concepts for the rhetorician, the psychologist, and the linguist. The remarkable thing about Langer's presentation of the complexity of verbal-symbolic relations is that it is done plainly, directly, without the usual professional jargon that ordinarily is employed in such discussions. She refers to the many logical refinements and extensions that may be adduced.

DISCURSIVE AND PRESENTATIONAL FORMS

It had been my original intention to include a discussion of the thinking of the radical logical positivists as a separate entity in this book. Langer has done it so well in her fourth chapter, however, that it would have been redundant; it is far better to react to her presentation. In reference here are Wittgenstein and his *Tractatus Logico— Philosophicies,* Carnap with the *Logical Syntax of Language,* and various others. Together they had formed what came to be known as the "Wittgenstein Circle," a group, it will be recalled, to which Korzybski paid much attention in formulating his own point of view.

The theorists were interested in a highly rigid logic of language, through which runs a highly puritanical strain with little intellectual leeway for the humanness of humanity. This is my comment, not Langer's. She writes that her entire logical theory is based on Wittgenstein's statement: "One name stands for one thing, and another for another thing, and they are connected together. And so the whole, like a living picture, presents the atomic fact." One cannot be sure about the meaning of a "living picture," and, taken quickly, this seems overtly to be a quite simplistic analysis of an extremely complex set of events. It is saved from this by Wittgenstein's "law of projection," whereby, for instance, the musician finds the symphony in the score (at least the director of the orchestra can do this). This involves translation. In Langer's words, "Projection' is a good word, albeit a figurative one, for the process by which we draw purely *logical* analyses."

There is a fairly extensive discussion about some of the possibly misleading aspects of syntax, the "what follows what" in linguistic form. "This property of verbal symbolism," Langer writes, "is known as *discursiveness*; by reason of it, only thoughts which can be arranged in this peculiar order can be spoken at all; any idea which does not lend itself to this 'projection' is ineffable, incommunicable by means of words. That is why the laws of reasoning, our clearest formulation of exact expression, are sometimes known as the 'laws of discursive thought'." Again, perhaps, if one considers that any statement has three dimensions of meaning, not one or two, this incommunicability would be dissipated. Even the most exacting laboratory scientists must believe in what he is doing or saying. He is not an automaton.

Wittgenstein protests against the way of words in ordinary conversation because the same word may signify in different ways. He would have this under control, because it leads to confusion in the proposition. "In order to avoid these errors," he writes in the *Tractatus,* "we must employ a symbolism which excludes them, by not applying the same sign in different symbols and by not applying signs in the same way which signify in different ways. A symbolism that is to say, which obeys the rules of *logical* grammar—of logical syntax."

Langer next introduces Carnap's extension into an analysis of Wittgenstein's philosophy and the development of demonstrations of what any given linguistic system can express. Langer generalizes this: "The distinctions between scientific language and everyday speech, which most of us can feel rather than define, are clearly illumined by Carnap's analysis; and it is surprising to find how little of our ordinary communication measures up to the standard of 'meaning' which a serious philosophy of language, and hence a logic of discursive thought, set before us" (p. 83). She then observes that Carnap's approach fully corroborates the point that symbolism is the key to epistemology and knowledge. One need not disagree with the generalization to observe that Langer becomes a bit starry-eyed in this treatment of discursive language. One must wonder if Wittgenstein and Carnap, among others, are socially speechless, or whether they tend to talk much the same way the rest of us do, when they are not discussing logical positivism.

It follows from what has been declared that any proposition that cannot be verified has no meaning; it is unthinkable. I wonder if such a generalization could stand up under its own verbal fire, so to speak. Suppose one were to propose that administrative attitudes toward the meaning of the term "democracy" in the Soviet Union are different from those in the United States. I suspect that most us *believe* that they are, but submit that verification would be impossible. I must submit that the proposition is by no means "unthinkable."

The charge from the logicians is that the "verbal combinations and other pseudo-symbolic structures" are really not significant. What are they? They are simply expressions of feelings and desires; they are expressive, not representative.

It turns out, as Langer continues, that most of this treatment of life and living has to do only with philosophical propositions and meanings, and therefore has to do only with the philosopher's laboratory of the mind. Sooner or later, what happens in that laboratory (this is Hardy, not Langer) must be communicated. Here I believe that one must agree with one of Wittgenstein's aphorisms—"Everything that can be thought at all can be thought clearly. Everything that can be said can be said clearly." One is almost forced to observe, however, that the logical-positivists seem quite devoid of a sense of humor, and that their own use of language produces a jargonic effect *ad extremis.*

Langer understands the general picture very well. "But if we consider how difficult it is to construct a meaningful language that shall meet neo-positivist standards, it is quite incredible that people should ever *say* anything at all, or understand each other's propositions." She then goes on to refute most of the limitations put upon symbolism by limiting its use to the discursive. She comments about things that in our experience are not part of the "grammatical scheme." "But they are not necessarily blind, inconceivable, mystical affairs; they are simply matters which require to be conceived through some symbolistic schema other than discursive language" (p. 88).

There follows a very nice analysis of sensory formulation and use, the net effect being that "the symbolism furnished by our purely sensory appreciation of forms is a non-discursive symbolism, peculiarly well suited to the expression of ideas that defy linguistic 'projection'." Her general point is that symbols imply meaning, and that there may be different types of symbolic expression—all of which involve conceptualizing what is expressed. The chapter concludes with the comment that signs are different from symbols and that discursive and presentational patterns are formally different. She suggests four outstanding types with which the rest of the book is concerned—language, ritual, myth, and music. This work deals only with the first of these modes.

LANGUAGE

In her treatment of language, Langer opens the discussion with a felicitous comment: "Between the clearest animal call of love or warning or danger, and a man's least, trivial *word,* there lies a whole day of Creation—or in modern phrase, a whole chapter of evolution" (p. 103). She continues with a general critique of casual and certainly uninformed statements that are heard and read recurrently about so-called primitive languages. The truth of the matter is that there are none. Every anthropologist who has brought back information about visits among the most primitive tribes on earth attests to this.

There have been many studies of different simian groups. They make sounds, without question, but these are at best signals of various feelings in their responses to situations. There is no denotation, therefore no speech. Langer refers to two of Yerkes's young apes who greeted their food with loud cries. "They are sounds of enthusiatic assent of a very specialized emotional reaction; *they cannot be used between meals to talk over the merits of the feast.*"

There follows a discursive inquiry into simian "talk" and wild-boy development, none of which leads very far toward an understanding of the onset of language in man. Langer shoots down some of the glib theories to the effect that children have linguistic intuition. This is, and always has been, a special brand of nonsense. She insists, and I certainly support the view, that language must be learned. The potential for this is present in all normally developing babies, but it must be nurtured. I am not sure that I agree with her that there is an "optimum period of learning" language. Rather, this is a serially ordered development that begins at birth and, so far as basic linguistic structures are concerned, extends at least into the fifth year. Most two-year-olds can learn a new word that interests them with one stimulus. A hearing-impaired child may need several hundred stimuli.

There is much more on language development, soundly based on firm authoritative ground. The general purport is well known. Langer then embarks on a trip with a thesis not so well known to students of child development or linguistics:

> The transformation of experience into concepts, not the elaboration of signals and symptoms, is the motive of language. Speech is through and through symbolic; and only sometimes signific. Any attempt to trace back entirely to the need of communication, neglecting the formulative, abstract experience at the root of it, must land us in the sort of enigma that the problem of linguistic origin has long presented! (pp. 126–127).

Well, one must ask, how *did* it happen? Langer's answer is specific and goes to the root of some of her reasons for writing her book:

> It could only have arisen in a race in which the lower forms of symbolistic thinking—dream, ritual, superstitious fancy—were already highly developed, i.e. where the process of symbolization, though primitive, was very active. Communal life in such a group would be characterized by vigorous indulgence in purely expressive acts, in ritual gestures, dances, etc., and probably by a strong tendency to fantastic terrors and joys (p. 127).

She further states: "It is not at all impossible that *ritual,* solemn and significant, antedates the evolution of language." All this, if the thesis is sound, happened a very long time ago, long before the known and recorded civilization of ancient China and Egypt—long before the Druids erected their fantastic monuments. How long ago?

Langer suggests that a background of voicing, eventually singing, with the ritualistic dancing and posturing, probably preceded speech. She refers to Jesperson's opinion suggesting that speech and song had the same source. This is a most interesting, imaginative part of Langer's projection, one that well warrants some profound thought. She refers in some detail to Donovan's ideas, presented in "The Festal Origin of Human Speech." I daresay this is well-known to anthropologists, but I doubt that it is to psychologists, li guists, or speech pathologists. The more one thinks about the idea, t e more engaging it becomes. Langer points out that the idea involves the emergence of naming, of conceiving objects, and of the early use of metaphor—the beginnings of story-telling about great events. L nger's insight is graphic:

> The utterance of conception-laden sounds at the sight of things that exemplify one or another of the conceptions which those sounds carry, is first a purely expressive reaction; only long habit can fix an association so securely that the word and the object are felt to belong together, so that the one is always a reminder of the other. But when this point is reached, the humanoid creature will undoubtedly utter the sound in sport, and thus move the object into nearer and clearer prominence in his mind, until he may be said to *grasp* a conception of it by means of the sound; and *now the sound is a word* (p. 134).

Thus sounds could have become representative. Obviously, all this is speculative, but it is intellectual, and offers as good an explanation as anything else that has come along the pike. Langer wonders how from such a beginning there could ever develop a system, which all language certainly is. She has an answer. Denotation of an object *holds* it. "This phenomenon of *holding on to the object* by means of its symbol is so elementary that language has grown up on it."

There follows an extensive discussion of the ideas of Philip Wegener, expressed in 1885. This is a complex treatment, and the highlights are briefly discussed here. "He recognized two general principles of linguistic development: *emendation,* which begets syntactical forms of speech, and *metaphor,* the source of generality." [Again, one may well wish that our philosophers would consistently differentiate between language and speech, and not treat the two as interchangeable, which they surely are not.]

Emendation is a process of building from one-word sentences (which are meaningful in themselves to the one-year-old) with the addition of vocables that relate to the situation. This involves a variety of auxiliary utterance (exposition) which eventually becomes verbal context. "When the speaker," explains Langer, "is fully aware of the context and the need of stating it, his speech is full-fledged." This is Langer referring to Wegener. These are interesting statements that I tend to accept as some kind of plausible theory, but do not accept as fact. This is not the way young children learn language. Nor do I believe, as Langer refers to Wegener, that the one-word sentence has only undifferentiated content. For the most part, when a twelve-month-old child says "ba" or "ookie" they are both context and content; more than that, there is intent.

Much of the remainder of this section in Langer's book develops the idea of metaphor as an active force in lexical development and change. "Metaphor is our most striking evidence of *abstractive seeing, of the power of human minds to use presentational symbols*," writes Langer. "One might say that, if ritual is the cradle of language, metaphor is the law of its life." This naturally involves slang, one of our most active metaphorical indulgences, much of which sooner or later becomes good usage in ordinary talk.

Perhaps one more fairly long quotation from this chapter might well be included, because, in a way, it offers a wide generalization of Langer's thinking and a reaching out for things to come:

> One more problem invites our speculation: Why do all men posses language? The answer, I think, is that all men possess it because they all have the same psychological nature, which has reached, in the entire human race, a stage of development where symbol-using and symbol-making are dominant activities. Whether there were many beginnings of language or few, or even only one, we cannot tell; but wherever the first stage of speaking, the use of any denotative symbol, was attained, there the development of speech probably occurred with phenomenal speed. For the notion of giving something a *name* is the vastest generative idea that ever was conceived; its influence might well transform the entire mode of living and feeling, in the whole species, within a few generations (p. 142).

ON MEANING

There are several subsequent chapters on ritual, myth, music, and art that I find fascinating, but I believe they must be foregone in this setting. They are much more than casually interesting and the ideas are put forward in Langer's usual incisive and engaging style.

In discussing possible relations between language and music, she is well aware of the sharp differences between them, particularly in terms of the logic of meaning. The essential point is that music, of however great worth as experience, can have no denotative function. Almost plaintively she writes that "it seems particularly hard for our literal minds to grasp the idea that anything can be *known* which cannot be *named*" (p. 232).

Her final chapter on "The Fabric of Meaning" is a gem of synthesis. The essentials of her thinking have been recounted in sufficient detail, so there is little need to repeat her recapitulation. On the other hand, I believe one must respect her capacity for generalization. The basic import of the chapter comes in her emphasis on "intellectual seeing, a primary capacity of the mind to deal with *gestalten* as the foundation of conception." She reviews some of the fundamentals of the mind's capacities for seeing:

> This dual operation of a datum as sign and symbol together is the key to realistic thinking: the envisagement of *fact*. Here, in practical vision, which makes symbols for thought out of signs for behavior, we have the roots of *practical intelligence*. It is more than specialized reaction and more than free imagination; it is the conception anchored in reality (p. 267).

A fact, she reminds, is by no means a simple thing, but it is always *there*. Fact-finding in modern terms has become common sense. Indeed, this is the essential point of this book, as a set of descriptors of long-term attitudes about meaning. In modern terms, this is an empirical age. She continues with the idea that it is the historian, not the scientist, who introduces "the standard of *actual fact*." "Not space and time, but a geographical place and a date, B.C. or A.D., anchor his [the historian's] propositions to reality. Science has become deeply tinged with empiricism, and yet its ideal is one of universality, formalism, permanence—the very ideal that presided over its long life since the days of Euclid and Archimedes."

Again, in astute observation of man's behavior when it is at its intellectual best, she writes, "Underlying these great intellectual structures—science, history, and the hybrid we call 'natural history'—is the dominant principle that rules our individual minds, the implicit belief in *causation*."

Indeed, had she paid more attention to the history of meaning in detail, and to the historical development and emergence of the many subtleties of the dimensions of meaning, Langer would have said enough so that this present book could not make much of a contribution. As it is, she chose to go other ways, always with intellectual grace and stylistic charm. Another of her "essences" is stated clearly:

The modern mind is an incredible complex of impressions and transformations; and its product is a fabric of meanings that would make the most elaborate dream of the most ambitious tapestry-weaver look like a mat. The warp of that fabric consists of what we call "data," the *signs* to which experience has conditioned us to attend, and upon which we act often without any conscious ideation. The woof is symbolism. Out of signs and symbols we weave our tissue of "reality" (p. 280).

A teacher of mine, a philosopher, said many years ago that a true philosopher always offers a system whereby his sense of reality, the nature of things, is held together in terms of apprehension and comprehension of some sort of a way to open a door. Langer's way is the study of symbolism, which gives philosophy a "new key," with many implications for other pursuits and concepts. The pursuit of meanings, she believes, is the whole idea of a systematic understanding of mental life. This pursuit is fraught with ups and downs, always with some sense of failure, or at least inadequacy. Mistress of metaphor, always concerned with the essentials of living, development, and change, Langer gives a provocative, thoughtful, colorful series of kaleidoscopes about the nature of the mind as it tries to solve its problems.

REFERENCES

Hardy, W. G. and Hardy, M. Essays on Communication and Communicative Disorders. New York: Grune and Stratton, 1977.

Langer, S. K. The Practice of Philosophy. New York: H. Holt & Co., 1930.

———. Philosophy in a New Key. Cambridge, Mass.: Harvard University Press, 1942.

Read, A. W. "An Account of the Word 'Semantics'." Word (1948) 4: 78–97.

Author's Caveat
LANGUAGE
AND SPEECH

Perhaps this is as good a place as any to express a strong caveat to those who are interested in the dimensions of meaning. There is a persistent lack of insightful differentiation between language and speech among those who concern themselves with language, thought, and experience, particularly among modern writers. This includes philosophers, linguists, psychologists, educators, whomever. A notable exception in the literature of the past sixty years is deSaussure, who makes some very nice distinctions between *langue* and *parole*. This is truly a notable exception, and one should be puzzled about this state of affairs. Perhaps a major pertinent point is that most writers in "the field" have had no, or at best very little, clinical experience as either diagnosticians or therapeutists in dealing with those who have, or are suspected of having, communicative disorders.

If one may reduce a broad complex to an almost simplistic explanation, language is an aspect of thought, while speech is a vehicle of language for communication. One can think in verbal-symbolic, linguistic, physically expressionless terms ranging from intuition to very difficult creativity. This does not require speech; it probably does require words. Words can be read—they do not require vocalization once a person has learned to read. Most of the large number of professionals who deal with those with communicative disorders of one sort or another have seen many, many persons with problems in speech, but none in language. With a large patient load, especially including young children, the obverse is commonly true—a language disorder (or lack, or delay) without apparent deficiency in articulation. These are simply day by day findings.

Considerable attention is currently being paid to Black English and, sometimes in the name of self-satisfaction, claims are made that it is a separate language from White English. This has not been demonstrated. Its structure is quite the same as that of most English, British, or American languages. It is different in several ways, concerned in the main with idiom, vocabulary, and pronunciation. However, these differences are not so great as some of the dialectal variations in Great Britain, and Black English clearly remains a cognate form of American English, which is what one would expect. Idiom is only one aspect of colloquial choice of words and phrases. Articulatory details and variations need not at all involve linguistic structure, and typically do not.

All of this makes it more difficult to understand why, among modern writers especially, no clear distinction is made between language and speech. In clinical terms, it is daily fare to test what are often called "levels of language" without recourse to speech, and it is obviously simple to test articulation without paying any attention to linguistic structure. So be it! This writer would have been derelict in this consideration of meanings not to insist on a distinction between two fundamental terms in verbal-symbolic communication.

Chapter 13
THOUGHT
AND LANGUAGE

L. S. Vygotsky

Through the often misty vistas of the study of meaning, Vygotsky's thinking produces some fresh air that blows away at least some of the mists that mask a clear view. He was 38 years old when he died in 1934; *Thought and Language* was published shortly thereafter. It was suppressed in 1936, reappeared in 1956, and was published in English in 1962 with an insightful introduction by J. S. Bruner. In Bruner's words:

> The present volume . . . ties together one major phase of Vygotsky's work, and though its principle theme is the relation of thought and language, it is more deeply a presentation of a highly original and thoughtful theory of intellectual development. Vygotsky's conception of development is at the same time a theory of education . . . looking at [his] place in world psychology, his position transcends either the usual functionalism of the Dewey-James variety or the conventional historical materialism of Marxist ideology. Vygotsky is an original (pp. v–vi).

In another passage Bruner points out Vygotsky's conviction that function is apt to determine structure, and comments that "if neither hand nor intellect alone prevails, the tools and aids that do are the developing streams of internalized language and conceptual thought that sometimes run parallel and sometimes merge, each affecting the other" (p. vii). The essence of Vygotsky's major thesis on the general topic of meaning is his consistent attention to growth and development, with which he concerns himself throughout his discussions. He is especially concerned with the meaning of change. There are preconceptual and prelinguistic states of affairs to be considered. As these mature to conceptual and linguistic functions, the new insights and new concepts of the child are not simply additive but are cumulative, and there is both feedforward and feedback in intellectual terms. The youngster who learns algebra changes his ideas about simple arithmetic, and so on and so forth (p. 115).

In terms of "levels of meaning," writes Vygotsky, "newer, higher concepts . . . transform the meaning of the lower."

> The ability to shift at will from one system to another [as in different forms of mathematical reference] is the criterion of this new level of consciousness, since it indicates the existence of a general concept of a system of numeration. In this as in other instances of passing from one level of meaning to the next, the child does not have to restructure separately all of his earlier concepts, which would indeed be a Sisyphean labor. Once a new structure has been incorporated into his thinking—usually through concepts recently acquired in school—it gradually spreads to the older concepts as they are drawn into the intellectual operations of the higher type (p. 115).

Vygotsky, as well as others, was quite indefinite in maintaining any distinction between the terms "language" and "speech." Without doubt the translators did their best; this is another instance, however, when one would appreciate the ability to read the original. He considers some of the effects of word meanings, and perhaps it is well to study some of his generalizations toward an understanding of what is usually meant by the term "language" in distinction from "speech." One should try to keep in mind that such discussions by Vygotsky are largely theoretical; there is no evidence that experimental observation was undertaken.

> What we want to show now is not how meanings develop over long periods of time but the way they function in the live process of verbal thought . . . we shall . . . consider the relations between thought and word in the mature mind . . .
> The relation of thought to word is not a thing but a process, a continual movement back and forth from thought to word and from word to thought . . . Thought is not merely expressed in words; it comes into existence through them. Every thought tends to connect something with something else, to establish a relationship between things (p. 125).

Vygotsky goes on to enlarge this concept of the development of thought in verbal terms, and considers various planes of this development toward the point of making a clear distinction between "the vocal and the semantic aspects of speech." "Grammar precedes logic," he writes, "and therefore syntactic forms can be well known long before a child makes detailed meaningful distinction among words" (pp. 126–127).

The first thing . . . is the need to distinguish between two planes of speech. Both the inner, meaningful, semantic aspect of speech and the external, phonetic aspect, though forming a true unity, have their own laws of movement (p. 125).

Perhaps, then, language and speech are not really indistinguishable in Vygotsky's ideas (some of this is related to his thinking about "inner speech," which is considered below). He clearly differentiates between semantic and syntactic aspects of thought and expression. He suggests that the very young child starts from a semantic whole, "from a meaningful complex"—a situation, if you will. Only later does he think of the meanings of words. "The external [spoken] and the semantic aspects of speech [language] develop in opposite directions—one from the particular to the whole, and the other from the whole to the particular, from sentence to word . . . The semantic and the phonetic developmental processes are essentially one, precisely because of their reverse directions" (p. 126).

THOUGHTS AND WORDS

It is time now to turn to some of Vygotsky's basic ideas about thought and words. It seems clear that he had no concept of the modern field of phonology, the business of which is the study of relations between sound and meaning. Rather, he thought of phonetics not as a science but simply as a record of vocal expression that "does not bring out the physical and psychological properties peculiar to speech but only the properties common to all sounds existing in nature" (p. 4). The separation of the study of sound and meaning, he remarks, accounts for the "barrenness of classical phonetics and semantics." There is an odd truncation in Vygotsky's thinking in this regard, yet one cannot know about the limits of his resources. He is quite specific. "The phonetic development has been studied in great detail, yet all the accumulated data contribute little to our understanding of linguistic development as such and remain essentially unrelated to the findings concerning the development of thinking" (p. 4).

He has a solution at hand, however—the treatment of the speech act (a term he does not use) by "*analysis into units.*" "By *unit* we mean a product of analysis which, unlike elements, retains all the basic properties of the whole and which cannot be further divided without losing them." He offers the analogies of the relation between molecules and water and between cells and the biological organism. The necessary unit of "verbal thought," he believes, "can be found in the internal aspect of the word, in *word meaning.*" "The nature of meaning as such," he writes, "is not clear. Yet it is in word meaning that thought and speech unite into verbal thought. In meaning, then, the answers to our questions about the relationship between thought and speech can be found" (p. 5). This is the very core of Vygotsky's thinking on *Thought and Language.*

Thought for him can be summarized in the capacity for generalization. Word meaning, with or without change of meaning as a product of time and environment, "belongs in the realm of language as much as in the realm of thought." Therefore, thought and speech (language) are inextricably related. Thus both analysis and synthesis are made possible. He agrees that the major function of speech is communication. Another is an intellectual quality that relates to thought. Word meaning is common to both. "Rational, intentional conveying of experience and thought to others requires a mediating system, the prototype of which is human speech . . ." (p. 6).

This point of view can be compared with that of Edward Sapir, with whose work Vygotsky was obviously familiar. Writing some ten-odd years prior to Vygotsky's book, Sapir says: "From the point of view of language, thought may be defined as the highest latent or potential content of speech, the content that is obtained by interpreting each of the elements in the flow of language as possessed of its very fullest conceptual value . . . At best language can but be the outward facet of thought on the highest, most generalized, level of symbolic expression" (1921, pp. 14–15). Obviously he and Vygotsky are in close agreement; they agree on many points. Sapir "is strongly of the opinion that the feeling entertained by so many that they can think, or even reason, without language is an illusion" (p. 15). Again, an aspect of all this that Vygotsky sometimes regrets (being a psychologist rather than a linguist) is that "language is primarily an auditory system of symbols. In so far as it is articulated it is also a motor system, but the motor aspect of speech is clearly secondary to the auditory" (p. 17).

These citations are offered simply to indicate how clearly, from a different point of view and a slightly different vocabulary, two extraordinary thinkers can come close together. One more generalization, taken from his Introduction, indicates what Sapir believed to be an extremely important idea. "We shall no doubt conclude that all voluntary communication of ideas, aside from normal speech, is either a transfer, direct or indirect, from the typical symbolism of language as spoken and heard or, at the least, involves the intermediary of truly linguistic symbolism" (p. 21). The weaving of the tapestry continues. In the terms of this setting, language, thought, and experience compose a truly remarkable trilogy.

With generalization comes conceptualization. The reason why communication with children is often difficult or impossible, Vygotsky wrote, is that they do not have the required concept. "There is a word available nearly always when the concept has matured."

Passing mention is made of some of the problems in the study of language. One is centered on the use of phonetics, with sound as an independent element. Vygotsky believed the more modern idea of phonemic analysis (with the phoneme as the irreducible meaningful unit of sound) to be much more useful as a unit of analysis, just as word meaning makes language analysis possible.

DIFFERENCES BETWEEN THOUGHT AND SPEECH

Vygotsky has much to say about the development of thought and speech, and places particular emphasis on the point that there is both merging and diverging in their progressive development. Considerable attention is paid to the study of apes by Kohler and Yerkes, and to the chimpanzees' use of at least some aspects of language that function apart from intellect. Their achievement in problem solving, Kohler observed, depended entirely on their ability to *see* the elements of a situation simultaneously. In other words, their intellect is a function of imagery, the source of ideation. Reference is made to the exhaustive but ineffectual efforts by Yerkes to teach chimpanzees to speak. In general, their vocalizations are emotional expressions, fulfilling a need, but in no way intentional or informative. (All this is very much in synchrony with current work with apes in teaching them to communicate, not with speech but with simple sign language.)

From this study several conclusions are drawn. For example, thought and speech have different roots and independent developmental courses; they are not correlated in apes, and the close correspondence between them in man is not found in apes. Finally, Vygotsky found that "in the phylogeny of thought and speech, a prelinguistic phase in the development of thought and a preintellectual phase in the development of speech are clearly discernible" (p. 41). Further comparisons between ape and human baby are undertaken, and attention is called to Buehler's phrase, *chimpanzoid age* (approximately 10–12 months in infant development). Vygotsky refers to Wilhelm Stern's emphasis on the sudden emergence of "demonstrable speech" (Bloomfield's term in *Language*) and the discovery of naming. This becomes important in that it "becomes possible only when a certain relatively high level of thought and speech development has been reached." In current terms, from more than sufficient evidence, this spurt in development usually occurs as a "one-word sentence" between the ages of 10–14 months—rather younger than Vygotsky records.

The argument continues with a discussion of inner speech. Watson's mechanical thesis is dismissed, but there remains to be found a suitable link between overt and inner speech. Vygotsky, like Piaget, found it in *egocentric speech,* although he differed from Piaget in the detail of relationships and final description. Egocentric speech is in effect only self-communicative, in contrast with social or overt speech. The meaning of egocentric speech, and its place in the differentiation between thought and language, is dealt with in sharp contrast of opposites by Piaget and Vygotsky. With Piaget it simply "dies off" with the development of logical thinking and social communication. In Vygotsky's view it leads to the development of inner speech, a rather different kind of "language" that the adult uses the rest of his life. This is a sufficiently important divergence (indeed, it is at the very core of linguistic development) for us to attend to Vygotsky's analysis:

> Egocentric speech as a separate linguistic form is the highly important genetic link in the transition from vocal to inner speech, an intermediate stage between the differentiation of the functions of vocal speech and the final transformation of one part of vocal speech into inner speech. It is this transitional role of egocentric speech that lends it such great theoretical interest. The whole conception of speech development differs profoundly in accordance with the interpretation given to the role of egocentric speech. Thus our schema of development—first social, then egocentric, then inner speech—contrasts both with the traditional behaviorist schema—vocal speech, whisper, inner speech—and with Piaget's sequence—from nonverbal autistic thought through egocentric thought and speech to socialized speech and logical thinking. In our conception, the true direction of the development of thinking is not from the individual to the socialized, but from the social to the individual (pp. 19–20).

So be it! A genuine problem in an attempt to be a sensitive historian and a fair critic lies in an apparent need to accept dichotomous thinking as *the* way of life. The "either-or" that seems ingrained in much of the thinking of the Western World may be treacherous. Why is it not possible to respect a series of additive generalizations derived from careful observations that are not dependent on, nor directed by, some conclusive theory—one that by some inadvertent pressures must go this way or that? How about both ways, or on occasion, a third way? The human brain is without doubt the most remarkable computer system ever wrought. Why cannot an intelligent youngster from the ages, say, of two to seven, undertake a quite wide variety of observations and functions all at once, or at least in almost breathtaking sequence? It seems clearly apparent, from a long-term clinical viewpoint about sequential development, that children who are developing normally, or otherwise, are quite individual. If they are not, then they usually are not because of controlling familial, cultural, or social forces that interfere or direct.

We have all seen 30-month old children "playing together" in a highly individual fashion, talking contentedly with themselves and their toys. Is this autistic speech? In a way, perhaps, it is. It surely must also represent a social milieu that is part of the child's world. These toys are people—they have names and respond as their host wishes (he or she sees to that). Where, then, does the autistic begin and end, and wherein is not all this a social enterprise?

This was the sort of approach adopted early by Piaget, who was interested more in observation than in theory. However, it would not quite satisfy Vygotsky, who clearly required unified conceptualization and theoretical confirmation of his basic thesis. It is entirely reasonable that one might well accept the best of both approaches, the theoretical and the specific, as well as the social and the individual, in order to understand a little better the workings of the mind with respect to language and thought.

INNER SPEECH

Particular attention should be paid to Vygotsky's concern with inner speech, because it offers a key to his thinking about the relations between thought and language. (One should try consistently to keep in mind the point that Vygotsky did not leave a systematic, fully mature scheme of things. His translators surely did a stellar job of putting things together, but there was much more he wanted to do, for which there was not time.) He takes sharp exception that egocentric speech, so important in the child's early habits, simply dies out. This is, he says, an illusion. It no more dies out than does a child stop counting when he stops using his fingers and "counts in his head." What actually happens, insists Vygotsky, is that one kind of speech succeeds another.

> The decreasing vocalization of egocentric speech denotes a developing abstraction from sound, the child's new faculty to "think words" instead of pronouncing them. This is the positive meaning of the sinking coefficient of egocentric speech. The downward curve indicates development toward inner speech (p. 135).

Vygotsky conducted a series of experiments based on Piaget's study of situations relating to egocentric speech, that is, a series of collective monologues. Each confirmed the point that when the child employing egocentric speech was forced by different devices to lose the illusion of a social audience, the coefficient of egocentric speech dropped drastically. In other words, with the elimination of the situation wherein egocentric speech is very similar to social speech, it always dwindles. "Both subjectively and objectively, egocentric speech represents a transition of speech for others to speech for oneself. It already has the function of inner speech but remains similar to social speech in its expression" (p. 138).

Inner speech becomes not "speech minus sound," but a separate function with its own "peculiar syntax." This involves changes from nomination to predication, with the omission of subject and all subject-modifiers and reliance on predication. "This tendency toward predication appears in all our experiments with such regularity that we must assume it to be the basic syntactic form of inner speech" (p. 139).

Vygotsky believes this sort of thing happens in overt speech only when the subject is known and understood by two people in conversation; the exchange rarely includes a sentence—only a word or short phrase. Sometimes these shortened forms cause confusion, especially when the topic is shifted and the responder says what is in his mind, not what is in that of the speaker. In general, Vygotsky believes, "If the thought of two people coincide, perfect understanding can be achieved through the use of mere predicates, but if they are thinking about different things they are bound to misunderstand each other."

Abbreviation, condensation, reduction of number of words, predication—these are the marks of exchange relatable to inner speech. When this kind of understanding does not exist, the result is confusion. This is illustrated with a delightful little poem, Russian in note. Again, one wishes to be able to appreciate the original:

> Before the judge who's deaf, two deaf men bow.
> One deaf man cries: "He led away my cow."

"Beg pardon," says the other in reply,
"That meadow was my father's land in days gone by."
The judge decides. "For you to fight each other is a shame.
Nor one nor t'other, but the girl's to blame."

Country justice in the presence of such disabled communication is probably much the same the world over. It is most interesting that in all his treatment of thought and language in theoretical terms, and in all the experimental work that is described (much is not), Vygotsky consistently centers on effective communication and the communicative act. We have been considering inner speech with its rather special predicative syntax—a form of language, if you will, but with self-expressive connotations that seem to be relatable to an earlier egocentric speech. It is also a form of external speech, quite similar to inner speech, that can exist in a very much shortened form of expression when two persons in conversation know each other and their topic well. This entire communicative structure, which Vygotsky makes believable, does in effect add another dimension of meaning to the tapestry.

Because this is an important idea in Vygotsky's thinking, some expansion may be in order. Inner speech is predicative and is concerned with semantic, not phonetic, aspects of communication. Three semantic subdimensions are adduced. First is the prevailing "of the *sense* of a word over its *meaning*," sense being "the sum of all the psychological events aroused in our consciousness by the word." Quite naturally this kind of thought processing, involving both decoding and encoding in modern psycholinguistic terms, is extremely complex. Meaning may well remain stable, but sense is a variable function of context. This may lead to extremes that relate directly to Morris's *intentional* dimension. Vygotsky, after Paulhan, expresses it this way: "A word derives its sense from the sentence, which in turn gets its sense from the paragraph, the paragraph from the book, the book from all the words of the author" (p. 146). This is surely a form of Gestalt Psychology.

There are two other "peculiarities" of inner speech. There is a tendency toward agglutination—combination of words—that has been referred to; combined words better express complex ideas. People tend to do this regularly, if ungrammatically, in American English even in professional writing. It is managed by stringing six nouns together, the first five of which are intended as modifiers of the sixth. The Germanic habit of doing all this in one word seems cumbersome, but it probably is not, because it saves the spaces between the words.

"The third basic semantic peculiarity of inner speech is the way in which senses of words combine and unite—a process governed by different laws from those governing combinations of meanings" (p. 147). This produces a kind of verbal opacity that almost defies description because it is intensively individual. This is a kind of personalized idiom "that is difficult to translate into the language of external speech."

It can be better understood, Vygotsky believes, by paying attention to the next plane of verbal thought, which turns out to be thought itself. Again, the essence of the idea is that we think in the form of gestalten that become a kind of nonverbal, pictured experience of totality. We see and recall an experience as a whole event. In terms of some form of decoding experience it is probably a multisensory, multiprocessing, multirepresentational sequence. It is not unitary, like speech is. It is only when we try to express this in words that we have problems. Vygotsky employs a felicitous phrase to express this:

> A thought may be compared to a cloud shedding a shower of words. Precisely because thought does not have its automatic counterpart in words, the transition from thought to words leads through meaning (p. 150).

Some principles that have a basis in rhetoric are next considered. Communication cannot be direct: it involves thought, meanings, and words. Thought is engendered by needs of all kinds; it is motivational. Furthermore, it cannot well be understood without an understanding of the affective-volitional tendencies that engender it. "To understand another's speech, it is not sufficient to understand his words—we must understand his thought. But even that is not enough—we must also know its motivation" (p. 151).

All of this leads to some historical comments and refutation of various psychological generalizations of the different schools—association, gestalt, behaviorist, idealist—in that they paid no attention to inner speech, which is part of the essential means in the individual's development of thought. "The relation between thought and word is a living process; thought is born through words. A word devoid of thought is a dead thing, and a thought unembodied in words remains a shadow" (p. 153).

I take leave of Vygotsky on inner speech with his own summary. Interestingly enough, it presents a somewhat different topic, a perspective opened up by his study and, one suspects, a set of ideas he intended to pursue, had there been time.

We studied the inward aspects of speech, which were as unknown to science as the other side of the moon. We showed that a generalized reflection of reality is the basic characteristic of words. This aspect of the word brings us to the threshold of a wider and deeper subject—the general problem of consciousness. Thought and language, which reflect reality in a way different from that of perception, are the key to the nature of human consciousness. Words play a central part not only in the development of thought but in the historical growth of consciousness as a whole. A word is a microcosm of human consciousness (p. 153).

CONCEPTUAL THINKING AND LEARNING

There remains one more topic, actually a set of topics, that he treated at some length and about which he felt very strongly. One chapter considers concept formation in general; a second is concerned with the development of scientific concepts in childhood, which he believed to be a basic aspect of learning and of reaching intellectual potential.

He relates much of his thinking to Piaget, whose first book had been translated into Russian and which he knew well. A fundamental point, Vygotsky believed, was the fact of major differences between the groups of children involved. He refers to Stern's comment that the speech of children in a German kindergarten tended "to be predominantly social at a very early age." Stern had chided Piaget for neglecting to take sufficiently into account the social and environmental aspects of child development, particularly in terms of language and speech. Vygotsky also felt this way. "We, too, are convinced that the study of thought development in children from a different social environment, and especially of children who, unlike Piaget's children, work, must lead to results that will permit the formulation of laws having a much wider sphere of application" (p. 24).

Although ostensibly he admired Piaget for his fundamental work in the study of child development, he and Piaget were poles apart in some of their basic approaches, and in some of the things that each took for granted. Vygotsky summarizes an aspect of this in his discussion:

> The basic framework of Piaget's theory rests on the assumption of a genetic sequence of two opposite forms of mentation which are described by the psychoanalytic theory as serving the pleasure principle and the reality principle. From our point of view, the drive for the satisfaction of needs and the drive for adaptation to reality cannot be considered separate from and opposed to each other. A need can be truly satisfied only through a certain adaptation to reality. Moreover, there is no such thing as adaptation for the sake of adaptation; it is always directed by needs. That is a truism inexplicably overlooked by Piaget (p. 21).

CONCEPT FORMATION

In Vygotsky's view, concept formation is the basic function of the mind. It does not involve simply association, but involves what might be called elementary or fundamental operations of the mind in a very nice combination of activity. Here, especially, word and thought come together. "This operation is guided by the use of words as the means of actively centering attention, of abstracting certain traits, synthesizing them, and symbolizing them by a sign" (p. 81). The processes of conceptualism are relatable to two prinicipal objectives, complex formation and what are called "potential concepts;" each has several possible stages. "In both, the use of the word is an integral part of the developing processes, and the word maintains its guiding function in the formation of genuine concepts, to which these processes lead" (p. 81).

Vygotsky does not have much use for what he refers to as traditional modes of studying concepts, particularly in children. These largely involve definition and abstraction, and give an idea only about what has been accomplished, nothing about how it is done, which is his main point in investigation. His major complaint is that traditional psychological approaches separate the word from the mind's perceptual matter. He refers to Ach's experiments with nonsense words, and a focus on "the functional conditions of concept formation." Without doubt this was the forerunner of the "Vygotsky blocks," which are well known to most serious students of child development. A basic point in the study of concepts that seems to be quite fully agreed upon is that the development of new concepts, or the capacity to do so, takes place at puberty or thereabouts. Before that, Vygotsky's group believes, there exist "thinking in complexes" and "pseudo-concepts."

BASIC DEVELOPMENT

"The ascent to concept formation," as Vygotsky calls it, has three phases and several substages. The first phase has to do with the gathering of disparate, unrelated objects into "heaps." This is a putting together of what Vygotsky calls "a vague syncretic agglomeration of individual objects which somehow have a sort of quite unstable togetherness assembled under one word meaning." This has been called "incoherent coherence" in the child's thinking. It apparently has three stages: 1) trial and error (random guessing about meaning),

2) organization of visual field (some sort of perception of contiguity), and, as a result of this two-stage operation, 3) the putting together of "elements taken from different groups or heaps that have already been formed by the child." This gives meaning of sorts to a new word. (It should be mentioned parenthetically that these observations were based on the performance of 300 subjects with the "method of double stimulation;" this involved the use of blocks of different colors and shapes, each marked on the bottom with one of four nonsense "words." The task was to conceptualize the possible groupings.)

The second phase has to do with a quite variable activity called "thinking in complexes." The sense of unity in the child's mind is derived from genuine relations between or among objects. The result is a kind of familial structure, a complex whose bonds are concrete and factual. This is a function of direct experience and suggests in communicative terms a subsidence of strictly egocentric values. The child is shown the sample object with the "name" exposed and proceeds to make combinations. The first type is *associative*; the word is not a proper name but a family or group name. However, among many kinds of ways, the child chooses to construct his groups.

A second type is *collections,* in which grouping is controlled by selection of an aspect that makes them different; this is association by contrast. It is a functional operation, a grouping from experience (articles of clothing, the names of objects in a place-setting at meals, and so forth). Then comes the *chain complex,* a dynamic linking of one object to another. Once in the chain, each link may lead to others—blue, triangle, tall, thin, crescent, round. There may be about as many links as there are blocks. All attributes are equal in function. This Vygotsky calls "the purest form of thinking in complexes," because there is no nucleus, only relations between single elements. "A complex does not rise above its elements as does a concept; it merges with the concrete objects that compose it" (p. 65).

A fourth type of complex is labeled *diffuse.* This is "marked by the fluidity of the very attribute that unites its simple elements." Concrete groups come from indeterminate bonds. Link one is a yellow triangle, then: triangle → trapezoid → squares → hexagons → semi-circles. Color is "equally floating and changeable." These complexes are limitless, and involve almost endless combinations in terms of transition and generalization.

The last type of complex is the *pseudo-concept.* This happens every time the child surrounds the sample triangle with all the other triangles. This could have been done by the concept of a triangle, but

Vygotsky and his associates believe this is not so. "Experimental analysis shows . . . that in reality the child is guided by the concrete, visible likeness and has formed only an associative complex limited to a certain kind of perceptual bond. Although the results are identical, the process by which they are reached is not at all the same as in conceptual thinking" (p. 66). The status of the pseudo-concept is exceedingly important.

> Psuedo-concepts predominate over all other complexes in the preschool child's thinking for the simple reason that in real life *complexes corresponding to word meanings are not spontaneously developed by the child: The lines along which a complex develops are predetermined by the meaning a given word already has in the language of adults.* (p. 67).

The adult cannot pass to the child his own mode of thinking; the child must learn to do his own thinking in complexes. There are many mutual relations in word meaning between child and adult; meanings are shared, but the concept is by no means ready made—it must be developed, and it usually takes until puberty for this to happen. The content of the pseudo-concepts often coincides with that of adult concepts, and verbal exchange with adults is a major factor in conceptual development in the child. In fact, Vygotsky believes, the child begins to use conceptual thinking before he really knows what he is doing.

Vygotsky applies some logic to all this that is both remarkable and, at first glance, somewhat startling.

> The child's acquisition of the language of adults accounts, in fact, for the consonance of his complexes with their concepts—in other words, for the emergence of concept complexes, or pseudo-concepts. Our experiments, in which the child's thinking is not hemmed in by word meanings, demonstrate that if it were not for the prevalence of pseudo-concepts the child's complexes would develop along different lines from adult concepts, and verbal communication between children and adults would be impossible (p. 68).

Shades of the slow-developing, multiply involved child for whom meanings are evanescent and pseudo-concepts possibly nonexistent!

In his early development of word meanings, the young child mixes two forms, the associative complex and the syncretic image. "Each new object included [in his grouping relative to his own term] has some attribute in common with another element, but the attributes undergo endless changes" (p. 70). Vygotsky then refers to participation, a faculty of primitive thinking, and thinking that has a concrete reference in terms of complex grouping. "Since children of a certain age think in pseudo-concepts and words designate to them complexes of concrete objects, their thinking must result in participation, i.e., in bonds unacceptable to adult logic" (pp. 71–72).

In a particularly interesting section that follows up some of these ideas (pp. 72–75), the point is re-emphasized that the history of language "clearly shows that complex thinking with all its peculiarities is the very foundation of linguistic development." He refers in modern terminology to relations between meaning and referent. "Using this terminology, we might say that the child's and the adult's words coincide in their referents but not in their meanings." He refers to a variety of instances of change of meaning and identity of referent with samples from Russian, French, and German, and with examples of metaphor in developing idiom. He mentions one in particular, in terms of complete thinking, as a rule rather than as an exception: the Russian word *sutki,* meaning "day-and-night."

> Originally it meant a seam, the junction of two pieces of cloth, something woven together; then it was used for any junction, e.g., of two walls of a house, and hence a corner; it began to be used metaphorically for twilight, "where day and night meet"; then it came to mean the time from one twilight to the next, i.e., the 24-hour *sutki* of the present. Such diverse things as a seam, a corner, twilight, and 24-hours are drawn into one complex in the course of a word, in the same way as the child incorporates different things into a group on the basis of concrete imagery (pp. 73–74).

What does *sutki* mean? When were you alive?

The third stage of concept formation (the first two being the predominance of the syncretic image and of the complex in thinking) is abstraction, the singling out of elements that can be thought about apart from the concrete experience that initiates them. This means synthesis combined with analysis. This is also done with the blocks, no two of which are identical. "The attributes which, added up, make an object maximally similar to the sample become the focus of attention and are thereby, in a sense, abstracted from the attributes to which the child attends less . . . the global character of the child's perception has been breached. An object's attributes have been divided into two parts unequally attended to—a beginning of positive and negative abstraction" (p. 77).

The next stage in abstraction is that of *potential concepts*— grouping is done on the basis of a single attribute. "Only the mastery of abstraction combined with advanced complex thinking, enables the child to progress to the formation of genuine concepts" (p. 78). This kind of generalization is almost the opposite of Korzybski's on abstraction, without the atomization and without normative values. Vygotsky notes that words serve important functions in complexes, and comments that "we consider complex thinking a stage in the development of verbal thinking." Finally, Vygotsky writes in terms of concepts:

> A concept emerges only when the abstracted traits are synthesized anew and the resulting abstract synthesis becomes the main instrument of thought. The decisive role in this process . . . is played by the word, deliberately used to direct all the part processes of advanced concept formation . . . [and in adolescence] when the process of concept formation is seen in all its complexity, it appears as a *movement* of thought within the pyramid of concepts, constantly alternating between two directions, from the particular to the general, and from the general to the particular (p. 78, 80).

This is indeed a remarkable presentation of sequential development of the processes that enable the human mind to become distinctive and creative in the adaptation to environment that is intelligence.

SCIENTIFIC CONCEPTS IN CHILDHOOD

The last concerns with Vygotsky's penetrative thinking on matters pertaining to concept formation are questions he asks and answers with regard to childhood education, learning, and intelligence. These inquiries have both practical and theoretical significance. What happens in the child's mind as he is taught scientific concepts? What happens as information comes in to the child's consciousness of such concepts?

Vygotsky is quite abrupt in his treatment of the two then contemporary answers from psychologists. One represents the school of thought committed to the idea that scientific concepts are simply absorbed and understood. This is simple drillwork with which Vygotsky has no patience. He has made it clear that conceptual thinking is an act of thought that "can be accomplished only when the child's mental development has reached the requisite level." Otherwise one deals only with parrotting. He lists the intellectual attributes necessary for this development: deliberate attention, logical memory, abstraction, the ability to compare and differentiate.

The second "school" Vygotsky objects to holds that the child's use of scientific concepts is no different from what he does with ordinary concepts. This he denies. He notes that Piaget goes further than most with his use of *spontaneous* (the child's own mental efforts) and *nonspontaneous* (influenced by adults) concepts. However, Piaget seems to insist that only the first of these offers real insight into the workings of the mind. With this Vygotsky disagrees, and herein lies one of the major differences between them. If Piaget's insistence on the progressive development of "the social" is sound, then he is inconsistent with his insistence on the primary of spontaneous conceptualization. So it goes. Each author to his own works! More of this is considered in the discussion of Chomsky's contributions below.

Clearly, Vygotsky does not share Piaget's thinking about the child's "replacement" of his own thought-patterns with those of adults, a kind of constant internal state of conflict. Instead, Vygotsky believes that "the two processes—the development of spontaneous and nonspontaneous concepts—are related and constantly influence each other. They are parts of a single process . . . not a conflict of antagonistic, mutually exclusive forms of mentation" (p. 85). Vygotsky's goal was to develop a methodology that might utilize the best of current thought toward the study of scientific concepts, and therefore toward progress in classroom curriculum and method.

Experiments were carried out (largely in the social sciences) to try to determine the child's understanding of relationships that may become a foundation for verbal understanding, for the use of verbal-symbolic operations instead of concrete experiences. This requires some revised thinking about the "law of awareness" (we are more aware of what we have difficulty adapting to) and the "law of shift" (whereby consciousness involves a gradual change from the concrete to imaginative expression in words). Vygotsky is not satisfied with this. The law of shift, like the law of awareness, may at best answer the question of why the schoolchild is not conscious of his concepts; it cannot explain how consciousness is achieved. (Incidentally, Vygotsky's children were 7 to 8-years old; Piaget's were 7 to 12-years).

The key to all this, according to Vygotsky, is found in some principles that have already been considered here—"perception in terms of meaning always implies a degree of generalization." Once generalization of "inner forms of activity" is accomplished, higher and higher levels of activity are involved. "In this way, becoming conscious of our operations and viewing each as a process of a certain kind—such as remembering or imagining—leads to their mastery" (pp. 91–92). In effect, this means that consciousness and control become part of a system, "a system of relationships of generality." "It is our contention," avers Vygotsky, "that the rudiments of systemization first enter the child's mind by way of his contact with scientific concepts and are then transferred to everyday concepts, changing their psychological structure from the top down" (p. 93).

INSTRUCTION AND DEVELOPMENT

Next considered is Vygotsky's critique of three general attitudes about education, and a fourth from him and his colleagues. He writes, "The interrelation of scientific and spontaneous concepts is a special case within a much broader subject: the relation of school instruction to the mental development of the child" (p. 93). As he indicates, this was a major concern of Soviet psychology in the early 1930s, a kind of concern that had to be a major spur for any psychologist.

The first of these views considers instruction in the schools and child development to be quite separate, different aspects of a child's life. Attempts had been made to analyze the separate "products." Vygotsky comments that this had never been achieved; the net effect is mere reduplication of speculative efforts. His observation is clear-cut. "Learning depends on development, but the course of development is not affected by learning" (p. 94). This he rejects.

A second view indentifies development with instruction—they are synonymous, both based on association and the formation of habits. This was Jamesian theory, revived by Thorndike, and further expressed by the contention that a child is simply a bundle of conditioned reflexes. It is still preached today. Vygotsky gives it short shrift—if they are identical there can be no question about relationships between them.

Vygotsky believes that the third, primarily the viewpoint of Gestalt psychology as represented by Koffka, is an improvement over the others. There is interdependence between maturation and learning; new operations are introduced with the idea that education involves "the formation of new structures [of thinking] and the perfecting of old ones;" and finally, instruction "can transform and reorganize other areas of child thought." "The admission that different temporal sequences are equally possible and important is a contribution by the eclectic theory that should not be under-estimated" (pp. 95–96).

The theory held tentatively by Vygotsky and his group is based on findings from four investigations in definite areas of school instruction—reading and writing, grammar, arithmetic, natural science, and social science. The first involves the developmental level of learning in terms of basic school subjects. At the start of school the functions are naturally quite immature. Vygotsky uses writing as a kind of typical example of differences among various relationships. Why the lag, the large difference (several years) between the child's "linguistic age" in speaking and in writing? There are several reasons. Writing does not go through the developmental history of speaking. It is a separate function, differing "in both structure and mode of function." It requires high abstraction, and requires that words (speech) "be replaced by images of words." It is to speech as algebra is to arithmetic. The relation of written language to inner speech is different from that of oral speech. "One might even say that the syntax of inner speech is the exact opposite of the syntax of written speech, with oral speech standing in the middle" (p. 99). Detailed written speech "requires what might be called deliberate semantics—deliberate structuring of the web of meaning." That is a most interesting and insightful phrase. The endpoint is that intellectual development "unfolds in a continuous interaction with the contributions of instruction."

A second inquiry was coincidental; it had to do with temporal relations between instruction and development. Atlhough the relationship is complex, the conclusion was that instruction usually precedes development. The relationship, however, is individual. "The turning point at which a general principle becomes clear to the child cannot be set in advance by the curriculum" (pp. 101–102).

The third question had to do with transfer of training. It was found that this is not atomic, but unitary. There is not compartmentalization according to topic; instead, there is much interaction. Consciousness of system and mastery of tools are at stake here. "It follows from these findings that all the basic school subjects act as a formal discipline, each facilitating the learning of others; the psychological functions stimulated by them develop in one complex process" (p. 102). In short, the child does not simply "learn a subject he learns how to learn.

The fourth set of studies is probably the most important, because it has to do with developmental measurement and some important aspects of intelligence. The usual method involves the use of "standardized" tests. The problems the child can solve on his own, so to speak, presumably indicate his intellectual development at any given time. This group tried a different approach. For instance, two children were found to have a "mental age" of eight according to norms. Each was offered problems more difficult than he could manage by himself and was provided "some slight assistance," e.g., the first step in solution, a leading question. "We discovered that one child could, in cooperation, solve problems designated for twelve-year-olds, while the other could not go beyond problems intended for nine-year-olds" (p. 103). The difference between mental age and problem-solving capacity can be treated in "zones." The first child is in "zone 4," the second child in "zone 1." "This measure gives a more helpful clue than mental age does to the dynamics of intellectual progress" (p. 103).

This is, indeed, creative education. It comes complete with useful aphorisms. "What the child can do in cooperation today he can do alone tomorrow," "it must be aimed not so much at the ripe as at the ripening functions," "instruction must be oriented toward the future, not the past," and so on. All this has been called the *sensitive period* by various outstanding educators.

A basic hypothesis was tested and retested: a child becomes conscious of his spontaneous concepts rather late, and his ability to use words to define concepts, and to become conscious of them in operational terms, comes long after he has developed the concepts. On the contrary, the scientific concept begins with verbal definition and functional use in "nonspontaneous operations." "It starts its life in the child's mind at the level that his spontaneous concepts reach only later" (p. 108). One more generalization is indicated, although it is obvious from Vygotsky's discussion. "Scientific concepts grow down through spontaneous concepts; spontaneous concepts grow upward through scientific concepts" (p. 109). For solid learning of subject matter, *which* should lead *which* seems clear.

In summary of this treatment of conceptual thinking, Vygotsky believes the focal problem to be "the interrelation of concepts in a system." The phases and stages in the development of this system include syncretism, complex, preconcept, and concept. He believes that the studies cited "reaffirm on a sound basis of data that the *absence of a system* is the cardinal physiological difference distinguishing spontaneous from scientific concepts" (p. 116). He makes two more generalizations:

> Studying child thought apart from the influence of instruction ... excludes a very important source of change and bars the researcher from posing the question of the interaction of development and instruction peculiar to each age level ... A future investigator may well find that the child's spontaneous concepts are a product of preschool instruction, just as scientific concepts are a product of school instruction (p. 117).

It would be simple to indulge in a variety of encomiums about Vygotsky's presentation. His contemporaries and colleagues, Luria and Leontiev, have won world rekown. It is interesting to imagine what Vygotsky's accomplishments might have been, had he had the opportunity to complete his work. His ideas are presented with great economy, and with redundancy sufficient to make his teaching effective. He worked in depth with intensity and with a freshness of analysis that has lost little in more than forty years. Some of his thinking was revolutionary at the time he wrote. In terms of certain aspects of educational methodology, it still is. His forward thinking about language and thought, with no recourse to the statistical analyses that are currently apt to be dull and thoughtless, and his refreshingly empirical point of view, put many new figures and tones in the tapestry. They are unique contributions.

REFERENCES

Bloomfield, L. Language. New York: Henry Holt, 1933.

Ginsburg, H. and Opper, S. Piaget's Theory of Intellectual Development. Englewood Cliffs, N.J.: Prentice-Hall, 1969.

Piaget, J. Judgment and Reasoning in the Child. New York: Littlefield, Adams, 1959. (Routledge and Kegan Paul, London, 1928.)

Sapir, E. Language: An Introduction to the Study of Speech. New York: Harcourt, Brace and World, 1921.

Vygotsky, L. S. Thought and Language. Translated and edited by E. Hanfmann and G. Vakar. Cambridge, Mass.: M. I. T. Press, 1962.

Chapter 14
GENESIS AND DEVELOPMENT AS DIMENSIONS OF MEANING

"In the beginning was the Word" according to the New Testament (John 1:1). Relative to our general topic, one must doubt very much that the beginning is a word, or a sentence. This is not a desecration in any sense, because we are discussing the genesis of language in young children. New Testament relators to the contrary notwithstanding, very much has to happen in terms of language development before the emergence of the first word. Some of what must happen is perceptual, some is physiological, much is social, and even more is rudimentary learning—particularly the kind of learning that makes possible the change from reflexive to controlled responses.

Perhaps it is important to suggest again that this book is concerned mainly with dimensions of meaning as they are relatable to language, thought, and experience. The concern is not with linguistics, the study of ways in which a sentence comes into being, nor with what some of us have had to deal with clinically—what goes wrong when a sentence does not come into being? Nor is the concern with psycholinguistics, a quite modern term that refers to the behavioral aspects of linguistic relationships in communication. Perhaps there is a genuine connection with what might be called biolinguistics, but this at best would be only partially relatable to the dimensions of meaning. There have been many long discussions in the past twenty-odd years—for the most part theoretical—about the genesis of language. Vygotsky, Luria, Piaget, and others have had much to say about learning and meaning in child development, but for the most part these were older children of school age. Only quite recently has attention been directed more sharply toward the state of affairs during the pre-speech months of development. Interestingly enough, much of this concern has been whetted by the emergence of a clinical and educative concept known as "learning disability." Children with this problem are notoriously different in various perceptual activities, in learning language, and in functions of attention and memory. Interest in their problems and the need to do something about them has encouraged much concerted attention to various features of pre-speech development.

EARLY DEVELOPMENT

Much consideration has been given in recent years to developmental phases of the first year of life, particularly, relative to acoustic cues, the progression from reflexive activity (observable at birth) to orientation in the environment. Relationships between responses to sound and the perceptive and receptive operations that eventually lead to language have only quite recently been addressed in detail. "It is clear that language development is a direct derivation from hearing. What needs much more study are the relations among listening, attention to those sounds in the environment that become increasingly important (like the sounds of speech), and the connections between these experiences and the general process of phonologic and linguistic development" (Hardy, 1975).

There has been a veritable deluge of ideas about ways and means to test hearing from the immediate neonatal period, through infant development, and then on into preschool age. The general point of this burgeoning interest is the conviction that if a child were to be found with a potentially handicapping condition, he could be treated as early as possible. Inasmuch as most children do not have such a condition, an increment of this kind of searching has been a much clearer understanding of normal development than had been known.

One basic point has been mentioned recurrently: in normal development, children have a tremendous capacity to learn the rules of language. Indeed, for the first several years, children are "language learning machines." This has been expressed succinctly by a psychologist in whose laboratory the study of these various capacities and related achievements has been going on for many years:

> Whether the capability is innate or learned (if, indeed, that distinction is valid) babies do acquire the ability to recognize speech as they become

increasingly sophisticated at deriving relatively constant properties of highly variable acoustic signals. By some process of selecting, rejecting, filtering, and transforming inputs which are often very crude and indistinct, babies make the transition from receiving acoustical sounds to perceiving informational language.

It is hard to imagine any aspect of subsequent linguistic and psychological development more formidable than that (Friedlander, 1972, p. 2).

HISTORICAL POINTS OF VIEW

DeSaussure

There have been influential precursors of the modern deluge of interest in language and linguistics. The thinking of deSaussure, with his insistence on a differentiation between *lange* and *parole*, has already been referred to. Early in his professional attention to the general consideration of language, he broke off from the traditional aspects of etymology and philology and concentrated his attention, and that of his students, on language as a system. "Language," he said, "is a self-contained whole and a principle of classification. As soon as we give language first place among the facts of speech, we introduce order into a mass that lends itself to no other classification" (1915 p. 9).

The *Course in General Linguistics,* the only record of deSaussure's thinking in general, was published posthumously in 1915, and is actually a compilation of students' notes from a series of courses he gave in Geneva at the University. Without doubt these lectures were the product of many years of profound study. Indeed, in Bloomfield's opinion, they provided "a theoretic foundation to the newer trend in linguistics study" (1915 p. xi). DeSaussure makes some basic principles very clear. "In separating language from speaking we are at the same time separating: (1) what is social from what is individual; and (2) what is essential from what is accessory and more or less accidental" (p. 14). There is consistent differentiation between the code and the message. The description of the "characteristics of language" is most interesting:

(1) Language is a well-defined object in the heterogeneous mass of speech facts. It can be localized in the limited segment of the speaking-circuit where an auditory image becomes associated with a concept. . . . Moreover, the individual must always serve an apprenticeship in order to learn the functioning of language: a child assimilates it only gradually.

(2) Language, unlike speaking, is something we can study separately. Although dead languages are no longer spoken, we can easily assimilate their linguistic organisms.
(3) Whereas speech is heterogeneous, language, as defined, is homogeneous. It is a system of signs in which the only essential thing is the union of meanings and sound-images, and in which both parts of the sign are psychological.
(4) Language is concrete, no less so than speaking; and this is a help in our study of it. Linguistic signs, though basically psychological, are not abstractions; associations which bear the stamp of collective approval—and which added together constitute language—are realities that have their seat in the brain (1915, pp. 14–15).

A major contribution, in deSaussure's thinking, would be a *"science that studies the life of signs within society;. . . .* I shall call it semiology" (p. 16). It is almost inconceivable that deSaussure would have been unfamiliar with Locke's ideas, yet there is no reference to them. The general scheme would be a science of signs, of which linguistics would be a part. For deSaussure, the linguistic sign is a combination of a concept and a sound-image; but then he would like to remove some of the ambiguity that is apt to result from the use of these terms.

I propose to retain the word *sign* [*signe*] to designate the whole and to replace *concept* and *sound-image* respectively by *signified* [*signifié*] and *signifier* [*signifiant*]; the last two terms have the advantage of indicating the opposition that separates them from each other and from the whole of which they are parts. As regards *sign,* if I am satisfied with it, this is simply because I do not know of any word to replace it, the ordinary language suggesting no other (p. 67).

Two fundamental principles govern the sign. First, it is arbitrary; it is part of the code of the linguistic community. Second is the "linear nature of the signifier." "The signifier, being auditory, is unfolded solely in time from which it gets the following characteristics: (a) it represents a span, and (b) the span is measureable in a single dimension; it is a line" (p. 70). This is perhaps one of the earliest specific references to what is popularly known nowadays as "the speech chain" or "the communicative chain." Obviously, there is much more to be considered about deSaussure's thinking and work. Perhaps this is sufficient to serve the general principles sought after in this chapter.

Edward Sapir

The only book written by Edward Sapir, *Language: An Introduction to the Study of Speech,* was published in 1921, only six years after deSaussure's *Course*. It has exerted considerable influence and contains some rich kernels that are pertinent to this inquiry. In the Introduction, Sapir makes an interesting biosocial point. He discusses a child's predestination to walk without instruction, and comments that "walking is an inherent, biological function of man." Not so with language.

> It is of course true that in a certain sense the individual is predestined to talk, but that is due entirely to circumstance that he is born not merely in nature, but in the lap of a society that is certain, reasonably certain, to lead him to its traditions. Eliminate society and there is every reason to believe that he will learn to walk, if, indeed, he survives at all. But it is just as certain that he will never learn to talk, that is, to communicate ideas according to the traditional system of a particular society (p. 4).

Then, after dismissing various possible instinctive aspects of communication, he continues with a definition of language. It is "a purely human and non-instinctive method of communicating ideas, emotions, and desires by means of a system of voluntarily produced symbols" (p. 8). He goes on with the comment that these symbols are auditory and are produced by the organs of speech. Language, in terms of the mind's meanings, grows "with the mind's general development." "From the point of view of language, thought may be defined as the highest latent or potential content of speech, the content that is obtained by interpreting each of the elements in the flow of language as possessed of its very fullest conceptual value" (pp. 14–15). Language is the "outward facet" of thought. On the other hand, Sapir is firm in his belief that one cannot think nor reason without language. Again, in terms of definition, he remarks that language "is primarily an auditory system of symbols." The motor aspect of speech "is clearly secondary to the auditory."

The basic stuff of the book has to do with a careful treatment of various kinds of linguistic analyses, with the emphasis always on relations among language, thought, and culture. This discussion takes leave of Sapir with reference to two of his basic ideas.

> Once more, language, as a structure, is on its inner face the mold of thought. It is this abstracted language, rather more than the physical facts of speech, that is to concern us in our inquiry. . . .
>   The fundamental groundwork of language—the development of a clear-cut phonetic system, the specific association of speech elements with concepts, and the delicate provision for the formal expression of all manner of relations—all this meets us rigidly perfected and systematized in every language known to us (p. 12).

This is a somewhat different approach from that of deSaussure, but the main points are clear: language and thought are intimately related; language is learned on the bosom of a society whose codified rules are already set for each next learning effort.

Otto Jesperson

A third outstanding figure among the professors of language fifty-odd years ago was Otto Jesperson, whose book, *The Philosophy of Grammar*, was published in 1924. In this work he refers to communicative exchange; this pervades most of his treatment of grammatical forms and combinations. He writes:

> The essence of language is human activity—activity on the part of one individual to make himself understood by another, and activity on the part of that other to understand what was in the mind of the first. These two individuals, the producer and the recipient of language, or as we may more conveniently call them, the speaker and the hearer, and their relations to one another, should never be lost sight of if we want to understand the nature of language and that part of language which is dealt with in grammar (p. 17).

One wonders how different some of the outpourings of the last twenty years in linguistics and semantics might have been had this simple set of descriptors been kept in mind! The point is entirely clear. The most important aspect of language is sound (speech) in communication between at least two people. Jesperson is recurrently fretful about the history of limiting the study of language to the written word, a tendency that now frequently recurs in full flux. He makes the point sharply. "Quantity, stress, and intonation, which are very inadequately, if at all, indicated in the usual spelling, plays important parts in the grammar of the spoken language, and thus we are in many ways reminded of the important truth that grammar should deal in the first instance with sounds and only secondarily with letters" (p. 18). In somewhat more modern terms this is the burden of phonology, a subject that has been studied in considerable depth in recent years.

Jesperson is succinct in his concluding remarks on "living grammar."

> My chief object in writing this chapter has been to make the reader realize that language is not exactly what a one-sided occupation with dictionaries and the usual grammars might lead us to think, but a set of habits, of habitual actions, and that each word and each sentence spoken is a complex action on the part of the speaker. The greater part of these actions are determined by what he has done previously in similar situations, and that again was determined chiefly by what he had habitually

learned from others. But in each individual instance, apart from mere formulas, the speaker has to turn these habits to account to meet a new situation, to express what has not been expressed previously in every minute detail; therefore he cannot be a mere slave to habits, but has to vary them to suit varying needs—and this in course of time may lead to new turns and new habits; in other words, to new grammatical forms and usages (p. 29).

This is not a bad presager of modern psycholinguistics, a term Jesperson did not know. He does, however, refer to grammar as "a part of linguistic psychology or psychological linguistics." One wonders how many current psycholinguists realize by how much Jesperson preceded them fifty-odd years ago. His name is rarely mentioned in the current literature.

He devotes much attention to his ideas about "systematic grammar," and they are indeed modern. He adopts Bréal's term "semantics" in general reference, but chooses to leave the topic alone. The discussion closes here with the friendly advice to young students of language to consider him well.

THE LANGUAGE LEARNING SYSTEM

It is time to return more directly to the main topic of the chapter, the child's language-learning system as an aspect of the dimensions of meaning. What has immediately preceded represents a kind of ethical appeal to the reasoning of some of the best twentieth-century thinkers who devoted a lifetime of interest to the portrayals that concern this work. Some of the principal ideas with which one is left seem quite clear. Language is by all means a human activity that is learned. By nature, other things being equal, a child has an extraordinary capacity to undertake this learning. How well he does this (which is in large part a social activity) depends mainly upon his environment; how rapidly language-learning develops is related, in turn, to a variety of biosocial aspects of self, of life, and of living. Without exception, the oldsters of the modern study of language believe that auditory capacity (perception, function, integration) is the foundation of language learning. Living language, so to speak, is sound—not written words. Inasmuch as most children have arrived at their basic language system long before they can read, this seems obvious. What is not so obvious is that most linguists take all this for granted and, with some few exceptions, do not wish to be troubled to have to think about how it all comes about. This writer believes that these early stages of what eventually is called language development are most important—as the acorn is to the oak. There are those who are in agreement:

> Judging by the theoretical and speculative literature as it stands today, receptive language development in infancy is a minor topic of marginal significance. Issues related to infant listening and receptive processes are virtually ignored in the literature of the new wave of language studies that assumed torrential proportions in the early 1960's. . . . They [authorities] seem to suggest that auditory perception in general and language perception in particular are topics on which thoughtful observers would hardly need to spend much time. There is little in this literature to suggest that the problem of how babies come to recognize the phonological, lexical, semantic, and grammatical systems in the language that they hear represents a psychological, linguistic, and developmental problem of the greatest magnitude (Friedlander, 1970).

Amen! Indeed, in the favorite term of one of the modern leaders among linguists, this sort of attention is usually dismissed as trivial, despite the fact that the problem is fully describable and circumscribable, and that the means to study it exist. Obviously, the addressing of these developmental aspects of infancy is simply not the thing with which most linguists wish to spend their time. One must doubt, however, that this point of view automatically reduces the topic to trivia. The discussion now turns to some rather more positive thinking.

In a recent book, of which this writer was senior author, an attempt was made to outline some aspects of "the cohesiveness of hearing, language, and speech." This was a reduction of some material that had been presented over the years. One is reluctant to continue a current trend toward redundancy in publication, but the ideas fit well into the present discussion.

There are several generalizations that can be made about the young child's capacity to communicate verbally, all of which seem pertinent to the development of language. First, every normally developing child does acquire a language learning system. Some aspects of this, such as elementary auditory pitch discrimination, exist from birth and are much refined within the first year of life. It is eminently clear that the features of development that are pertinent to the subject are functions of growth, of mind and body, and of learning. This observation, about which most thoughtful observers agree, brings into question the use of the term "innate," which has become popular in the past twenty years. Perhaps a definition, or explanation, offered at a conference in 1966 on the genesis of language would be helpful here.

> Not even Leibnitz would have said that an innate idea was in any sense known prior to the time that experience had caused it to appear in the organism. It would be more accurate to say the innate components were simply potentialities that would develop if the environment presented the occasion for them to do so; they were the things that an organism would learn easily, quickly, and immediately, the way it would structure its experience in order to profit from it (Miller, 1966).

Well and good! Yet one must doubt that this is quite the way to describe how a four-month-old infant deals with his world. Moreover, one may find some fault with Chomsky's often repeated remark regarding language acquisition, to the effect that a "normal child acquires this knowledge on relatively slight exposure and without specific training" (Chomsky, 1975). He does not identify the age-range of the children he refers to. The normal child requires several months to learn to hear, in any refined sense of the term "hear," and several more months before the emergence of the first word. During this period (let us generalize it at one year plus) he has received a barrage of language stimulus from mother and siblings. He does not go to school, but the "training" is quite specific. It has to do with communication, wherein verbal expression is only one aspect of several probabilities. It usually takes him another year to achieve control and use of a very short sentence. (One-word sentences, which are not admitted into the factory by many linguists, occur much earlier. When baby points with determination from his playpen and says "ba," he has committed communication in a verbal form that has many of the ingredients of a sentence. When he smiles at mother in eager expectancy and asks "ooky?," she knows what he means.) One might hope that in the often repeated generalization from contained linguists many of them would be constrained to identify ages and stages of development in children, as is required in most scientific procedures, and not simply lump together children as "children." The question of when an "infant" becomes a "child" is wide open for exploration; so much for this author's bias.

A second generalization, or postulate, involves almost universal agreement that hearing and auditory feedback are fundamental in this learning process. One observer states:

> When one takes away the auditory side of language and is forced to present it in the visual domain, the innate processes that make language acquisition such a speedy and impressive performance operate extremely poorly (Jenkins, 1966).

This clearly suggests that linguistic theory cannot account for the finesse with which the very young accept *this,* reject *that* in terms of acoustic stimulus, and gradually learn to refine what is useful and rewarding. Input usually outstrips output in the early stages of playing the language game, although the two are almost inextricably connected. "In the language learning process," writes Dennis Fry, "the production of speech is inseparably connected with the reception of speech, and the learning of both go forward in the young child" (Fry, 1966). In all of this, listening is fundamental, and habits of listening are closely related to attention and memory. There is much of all this in developmental terms that requires most careful study.

A third point relates to much that has already been expressed; it relates to what is often called the "critical period" in young child development. "Between the ages of two and three years, language emerges by an interaction of maturation and self-programmed learning" (Lenneberg, 1966). This last phrase is not explained in detail; possibly it is looked upon as part of the fruition of innate capacities. In any regard, however, one might question the restriction to "self." What about social influences—even those limited to the familial surroundings? One may grant that all early language learning is in part a function of maturation. Yet it does not happen in a communicative vacuum, and there are almost infinite variables from child to child. One simply cannot ignore motherhood and its contributions to childhood. In the same chapter on "the natural history of language," Lenneberg offers an extension. "Language is an activity that develops harmoniously by a necessary integration of neuronal and skeletal structures, and by reciprocal adaptation of various physiological processes." Obviously, these activities do occur. One would appreciate access to the details of function that make this possible. This has been the burden of investigation by Vygotsky and Luria, and more recently among American psychologists and inquirers in the communicative sciences. Clearly, there is a long way to go before relations between structure and function in language learning can be fairly well delineated.

Fourth, "a major reason for the existence of the brain is an exquisite ability to feedback and feedforward in the communicative act, and thus make possible in each next child the development of a symbol system especially tuned to capacities of cognition and intent in order to establish and maintain a pertinent relationship with his environment" (Hardy and Hardy, 1977). The concept of feedback is well known to anybody versed in electroacoustics or bioacoustics; it is also the sine qua non of learning verbal language and speech. Among other things it involves self-hearing, and is therefore a monitoring function.

This capacity, together with feedforward, may possibly be the essence of intelligence in man; together they could well account for a child's ability to generate a sentence he has never heard before.

There has been discussion of Jesperson's views on what is nowadays thought about as psycholinguistics. In his treatment of the "building up of sentences," he makes this most perceptive statement: "Apart from fixed formulas a sentence does not spring into a speaker's mind all at once, but is framed gradually as he goes on speaking" (p. 26). For better or worse, this is an aspect of feedforward, a concept that is receiving more and more attention these days relative to neurophysiology and information theory. It involves refinements of temporal sequencing in communication and in adaptive behavior in general. It also involves extensive neural populations as spatio-temporal patterns of organization, with much of the organizational control centered in the limbic system of the brain, which in these terms has been described as "a planning station which activates a variety of substations and organizes their functions in space and time according to determined sequences, processing at the same time information which interplays with the organization of the response" (Smythies, 1970). Indeed, one might subsume much of language learning within the general developing picture of the neurochemistry of the brain. Some of these relationships called "feedforward" have been treated more fully in several recent works (Smythies, 1970; Hardy, 1972; Hardy and Hardy, 1977) and in a veritable host of laboratory reports too numerous to list.

Perhaps if one wishes to study in detail an important aspect of brain function, one would do well to concentrate not on the detail of the sentence, but on the communicative act. We all know how to communicate verbally, and have since childhood. How do we "know" about feedforward?

> What directs us forward to what we say next? Aside from various emotive inspirations, "the next" should be finite in choice of topic and language. A major strength of generative grammar is that its professors do indeed study a major aspect of the communicative act. A plausible foundation for a definition of the next step in the communicative act leads to another generalization—verbal communication is concerned primarily with meaning (Hardy and Hardy, 1977).

In terms of language use in communication, feedback and feedforward are profoundly significant aspects of the ways and means with which we deal with verbal symbols.

AUDITORY PROCESSING

Much concern with early infant auditory testing has been expressed in recent years, yet very little information has been forthcoming from neonatal screening tests. The details of this are not of concern here. Perhaps it is unnecessary to emphasize the point that there is a vast difference, relative to the study of very early infant auditory behavior, between what can be found out in wide-sweeping screening tests and what can be learned from carefully controlled laboratory observations with similar groups of children.

The number of studies of this latter sort is mounting rapidly. Perhaps two kinds of approaches might well serve in treating the dimensions that are dealt with in this chapter, one psychological, the other social.

First is Friedlander's work on "Receptive Language Development in Infancy." He is largely interested in issues and problems. "In studying language development in infancy," he writes, "it is wise to remain aware that one is concerned with the primary stages of what may be the most intricate growth process in the world of nature." After a reference to language decoding in terms of genes and enzymes, he continues:

> But in language studies we do not yet know what processes guide the relationships among the organism as a whole, the structure and function of its parts, and the environment, in the emergence of verbal meaning and symbolic adaptive intelligence before its organization begins to become explicit and externalized in speech. Without a decent regard for the intricacy and majesty of this problem it is doubtful we can ever begin to solve it (Friedlander, 1970).

He then refers to data that tends to support this view. Each of the topics is expanded only sufficiently to make the point. Only an outline, in Friedlander's terms, is necessary for the present purposes.

These data fall into five principal categories:

1. The relatively finely tuned status of neonates' auditory sensitivity
2. The status of auditory stimuli as functional reinforcers for operant performance in neonates
3. Discrimination of purely isolated phonetic stimulus cues in the first six months
4. Involvement of listening responses in complex central nervous system and perceptual-cognitive functioning in infants

5. Discrimination of complex linguistic properties and high output operant responding for complex natural language feedbacks by babies under the age of 18 months.

The point is that babies under eighteen months do respond in these terms, and with very considerable consistency. They require several months to learn to "hear" in the sense of clear localization of sound and general responses to acoustical stimuli. Then, babies apparently learn to listen and, in terms of the accomplishments referred to in 5 above, seem to move rapidly along in a language learning situation. There can be little doubt that these are clear demonstrations of auditory processing—sometimes called "auding"—which is fundamental for language learning. (Frequent references are made to the work of Eisenberg and her associates on neonatal observations, and, more recently, on cardiotachometry. The reader is referred to Bradford's book on the audiovestibular system for an expansion of physiological observations of the young baby.) Friedlander makes an important point about this aspect of development:

> Whatever these data ultimately may be interpreted to signify, there can be little quarrel with the evidence that listening to sounds and voices seems to have hitherto unsuspected potency as a desirable form of activity to babies whose own speech has barely advanced to the stage of one and two word sentences (p. 19).

RECEPTIVE LANGUAGE

One may well insist on the need to pay special attention to receptive language functions as a separate entity. They have not been well studied because they are rarely included in linguistic and psycholinguistic overviews. The core of this is the infant's interest in, and capacity for, listening. There can be little question that this is the essence of early language development; without it, verbal language does not develop.

Friedlander divides the general approach into three aspects:

1. The primacy of listening over speech in infant growth and communication
2. Psychological differences between reception and production
3. Possible differences in neural substrates.

It is scarcely pertinent to the general objective to go deeply into the detail of Friedlander's arguments, but, simply because the general topic has been treated so skimpily in professional discussions of language and meaning, a rapid review seems to be in order. A fundamental idea is that receptive language is processed, and grows much more rapidly than does productive speech. This needs no discussion; it is apparent from every baby's calendar. Even without much facility in motor expression, many children (those with various forms of cerebral palsy are obvious examples) learn to listen and to "communicate receptively." This is what Friedlander has in mind when he states: "To focus investigation only on the emergence of expressive functions, or to wait two years or more until the baby can begin to use his own speech to offer what is at best highly restricted evidence of what he comprehends, is to neglect what may be one of the most important stages of developmental organization in all of the child's growth" (p. 20). Furthermore, "the fact remains that the infant's experience at hearing language spoken is an indispensable prerequisite for his own eventual ability to speak it." So be it! This happens to be true, despite some of the dubious theoretical vagaries of Chomsky, Lenneberg, McNeil, and others. There are direct ways to accout for a child's obviously superlative capacity to manage most language functions by three to four years of age (Soviet psychologists tend to put it at five years, but that may simply reflect problems with the language). Unfortunately, most students of language pay little attention to what has been going on before the emergence of full sentences. Accordingly, they overlook the foundations of a child's appreciation of and experience with a major dimension of meaning (author's bias). For the most part, one may assume that it makes little difference which language or speech dialect is considered; the fact of the primacy of language reception seems obvious and generally agreed upon by those who think about it.

A next section of this address to developmental features relates to "psychological differences between reception and production"—more specifically to matters of control in communication, and to what Friedlander calls the "problem of divergence and convergence." In verbal communication, the speaker has full control over the message; the listener must adapt to whatever the speaker chooses to include. For the infant listener this must involve an inordinate amount of selecting this, ignoring that, sorting out what is not understood, remembering something that has been heard before—all this long before the capacity to use full sentences. Indeed, this sort of thing surely accounts for the obvious communicative intimacy between infant and parents and siblings. They all have the password for a very special club. Good teachers of the young become expert in this matter of control. In fact, any speaker who wishes to control his audience must pay sharp attention to his listeners' reactions and convey his message accordingly. It seems that, without recognition of this factor of control, communication with a young child (infant?) might well break down completely.

Discussion continues with observation that as a process listening is "highly convergent," while speech is "highly divergent."

> Speech is generative, egocentric, essentially unconstrained in the possibilities over which it may range, unlimited in its options, and subject to continual branching off in new directions. Listening is fundamentally reconstructive, constrained to processing the speech of others, operates toward the progressively more limited options of interpreting inputs, often must select among inputs from two or more message sources at the same time, and is directed toward the attainment of specifiable objects. Speech is open-ended in its possibilities, while listening is closed-ended in its constraints (p. 22).

Another topic has to do with "neurological substrates," and refers to Lenneberg's general principle that "there is no evidence for an 'absolute' language area." It is scarcely necessary to pursue this topic very far. Close to the time when both Lenneberg and Friedlander were considering this issue, several articles appeared, offering evidence that fairly well settled the general question (these articles were followed by various others). Masland wrote on "Brain Mechanisms Underlying the Language Function" (1970), and he and others have followed the findings. The evidence is quite clear that the left hemisphere prevails in most aspects of language management; its functions have largely to do with temporal events and, the reasoning goes, inasmuch as language learning is largely an auditory function, the left hemisphere leads the way. Much evidence from stroke patients who are aphasic corroborates the idea. The right hemisphere is more largely concerned with the differentiation of spatial and tactile events. Some of the details of this require much further investigation, but the general patterns of findings and thinking are now quite readily accepted in the field of neurophysiology.

There is considerably more in Friedlander's presentation, all interesting in terms of the communicative act, but not particularly pertinent to this inquiry. At the end of a long discussion on "dimensions of variability," he refers to Colin Cherry's observation in his *On Human Communication* that each perception or recognition induces an association with some concept or class or universal, some aspects of which may be entirely private. Friedlander picks this up in terms of his essential argument:

> The essence of receptive language growth is the setting up of an enormous number of new classes—in a relatively brief time and with only the most primitive powers of critical cross-checking, validation, flexible assignment of members to classes, and constant re-assignment (pp. 48–49).

One must agree with Cherry and Friedlander that this represents genuine creativity and does indeed present the potentials of the very young mind operating at its best. Given a chance, children are language learning machines.

SUMMARY

What do these various points of view and sometimes different perspectives teach in weaving the tapestry of the dimensions of meaning? Several matters seem apparent.

First, in terms of genesis and early prespeech development of language, there can be little question of the fundamental importance of hearing and of auditory integration in activity of the brain. This is the essence of early receptive language learning. Second, there can be no question about the fact that language intake is a learned activity. Obviously—so very obviously—the potentials must be present in the small brain. The development, however, takes months and years of loving tuition with a scarcely finite number of successes and failures, trials and errors. This is by no means an automatic set of occurrences. Third, this is clearly a creative activity on the part of the baby, driven largely not by a desire to design sentences but by an almost fervent groping to communicate, to understand and to be understood. This is a development through time; it does not just happen, nor flash upon the consciousness like Athena's delivery from Zeus' brain. Fourth, there is accountability plainly apparent. Given a normal system of brain function, there is nothing vague and mysterious about what takes place. Unfortunately, with each next child, much of this development is covert and does not lend itself to ready observation and analysis. Fortunately, most of our children are little language learning machines, and for the most part their mechanisms work well.

REFERENCES

Bradford, L. J., ed. Physiological Measures of the Audio Vestibular System. New York: Academic Press, 1976.

Chomsky, N. Language and Mind. New York: Harcourt Brace Jovanovich, 1972.

————. Reflections on Language. New York: Random House, 1975.

deSaussure, F. Course in General Linguistics. Edited by C. Balky and A. Sechehaye. Translated by W. Baskin. New York: McGraw-Hill, 1915.

Friedlander, B. Z. "Receptive Language Development in Infancy. Merrill-Palmer Quarterly (1970) Detroit.

————. "The Screening and Assessment of Young Children." Paper presented before the President's Committee on Mental Retardation, Boston, 1972.

Fry, D. B. "Development of the Phonological System." In The Genesis of Language: A Psycholinguistic Approach, edited by F. Smith and G. A. Miller. Cambridge, Mass.: M.I.T. Press, 1966.

Hardy, W. G. "Feedback and Feedforward in Language Acquisition. Acta Symbolica (1972) III, 2: 70–82.

————. "Reflex and Conditioning Audiometry." In Physiological Measures of the Audo-Vestibular System, edited by L. J. Bradford. New York: Academic Press, 1975.

———— and M. Hardy. Essays on Communication and Communicative Disorders. New York: Grune and Stratton, 1977.

Jenkins, J. J. "Reflections on the Conference." In The Genesis of Language: A Psycholinguistic Approach. edited by F. Smith and G. I. Miller. Cambridge, Mass.: M.I.T. Press, 1966.

Jesperson, O. The Philosophy of Grammar. New York: W. W. Norton, 1924.

Masland, R. L. 1970. "Brain Mechanisms Underlying the Language Function. In Human Communication and Its Disorders: An Overview, edited by R. Carhart. N.I.N.D.S. Monograph No. 10, U.S. Government Printing Office, pp. 85–109.

————. Unpublished address. Testimonial Dinner for Hardy, Hardy, and Haskins. Baltimore Hilton Hotel, Baltimore, Md., 1974.

Miller, G. A. "Comments in General Discussion." In The Genesis of Language: A Psycholinguistic Approach, edited by F. Smith and G. A. Miller. Cambridge, Mass.: M.I.T. Press, 1966.

Sapir, E. Language: An Introduction to the Study of Speech. New York: Harcourt Brace and World, 1921.

Searle, J. R., ed. The Philosophy of Language. London: Oxford Univ. Press, 1971.

Smith, F. and Miller, G. A. (eds.) The Genesis of Language: A Psycholinguistic Approach. Cambridge, Mass.: M.I.T. Press, 1966.

Smythies, J. R. Brain Mechanisms and Behavior. New York: Academic Press, 1970.

Chapter 15
SPEECHWAYS AS A DIMENSION OF MEANING
Henry L. Mencken

It seems entirely fitting to include in this book a dimension that has to do with the American language—with some of the ways people express themselves in a reasonable effort to communicate. An obvious master of this is H. L. Mencken, trenchant essayist, blower-up of already inflated politicians and quacks of all voices, expert at poking a firm finger into overstuffed shirts, and commonly known in the past as "the sage of Baltimore." This aspect of the man is largely forgone here; this chapter concentrates on him as a scholarly authority on language in use.

The best approach in this writer's opinion is the excellent *The American Language* (1963), edited by Raven I. McDavid, Jr. with the assistance of David W. Maurer. This includes the fourth edition (1936) and the two Supplements, with considerable abridging, annotations, and some new material. Inasmuch as Mencken was forever changing and adding to his own book, originally published in 1919, and inasmuch as he always wanted to keep it alive and fresh, he would have had only warm interest in what McDavid has done. Mencken sustained his first stroke in 1948; it left him with a semantic aphasia from which he never recovered, despite all the efforts that several of us made in his last eight years. From that time on he was not able to read a word, nor a note of music, and was naturally quite bereft. This was scarcely a fitting finale for one of the great newspapermen and litterateurs of the twentieth century.

THE CHANGING MIND

McDavid writes in his Introduction, "Mencken always insisted, with what seems to most linguists an excessive modesty, that he was not a scholar himself, but one who pointed out the quarry for others to bag." Through the time of the first three editions (the fourth, which is best known, was published in 1936) Mencken received such a spate of informational detail and suggestions that he was hard put to manage it. He writes in his Preface, "The present book picks up bodily a few short passages from the third edition, but they are not many. In the main, it is a new work." The point is that he was not a linguist in the usual academic sense, but a student of Americana who played some most interesting chords in speechways, an interest that consumed a tremendous amount of participation, at home and abroad.

He writes in a very gentle fashion about this appetite:

> When I became interested in the subject and began writing about it (in the Baltimore *Evening Sun* in 1910), the American form of the English language was plainly departing from the parent stem, and it seemed at least likely that the differences between American and English would go on increasing. This was what I argued in my first three editions. But since 1923 the pull of American has become so powerful that it has begun to drag English with it, and in consequence some of the differences once visible have tended to disappear. The two forms of language, of course, are still distinct in more ways than one, and when an Englishman and an American meet they continue to be conscious that each speaks a tongue that is far from identical from the tongue spoken by the other. But the Englishman, of late, has yielded so much to the American example, in vocabulary, in idiom, in spelling, and even in pronunciation, that what he speaks promises to become, on some not too remote tomorrow, a kind of dialect of American, just as the language spoken by the American was once a dialect of English (1963, p. vi).

Inasmuch as this was written only forty-odd years ago, we are not yet quite at that "some not too remote tomorrow," and, even if we were, most educated Englishmen would not admit it. This is an aspect of language and speechways about which one must just "wait and see." Some of our younger colleagues have wondered about the bulk of the fourth edition. Obviously this is an information-bearing function of which Mencken was clearly aware.

> At the risk of making my book of forbidding bulk I have sought to present a comprehensive conspectus of the whole matter, with references to all the pertinent literature. My experience with the three preceding editions convinces me that the persons who are really interested in American English are not daunted by bibliographical apparatus, but

rather demand it. The letters that so many of them have been kind enough to send me show that they delight in running down the by-ways of the subject, and I have tried to assist them by setting up as many guide-posts as possible, pointing into every alley as we pass along.

In any event, McDavid has chosen wisely in his continuance of Mencken's design and has even managed to expand it in terms of his own textual extensions, all of which are clearly marked.

THE EARLIEST ALARMS

"The Earliest Alarms" was the subtitle of Chapter 1, obviously chosen with a newsman's eye. It took two wars and years of verbal intercourse to convince some of the British gentry that the United States really existed as an independent nation, and that, perforce, some new aspects of the language were required. As Mencken states it, "The first American colonists had . . . to invent Americanisms, if only to describe the unfamiliar landscape, weather, flora and fauna confronting them." One must try to keep in mind that for a century and three quarters these Americans were mostly Englishmen in their roots, and the language they engendered—vocabulary and idiom—was often ridiculed and scorned in the parent country. Changes and additions began to occur as early as 1612 and were reported extensively by 1735, by which time the English had lived through another revolution internally and had pretty well settled down with the House of Hanover. British visits to and complaints about "America" were not yet in style. "Nevertheless," writes Mencken, "as Allen Walker Read points out, the legend of American speech as something exotic and difficult to understand—reflecting the manners of a new and barbarous society— had been established before the Revolution" (p. 4). British verbiage about all this, commonly led by the distinguished Dr. Samuel Johnson—who deplored everything American—usually included the terms "vile" and "intolerable" with the arrogant selfindulgence that was typical of most British gentlemen of the 18th Century when discussing the boondocks of the United States.

Mencken spends time and some amusement in considering one John Witherspoon, once president of Princeton, later a participant in the Continental Congress and a signer of the Declaration. A Scottish clergyman in the land of the infidels ("in partibus infidelium"), he was devoted to the country and its politics, but not to its language. Mencken quotes his remarks about Americanisms:

I understand a use of phrases or terms, or a construction of sentences, even among people of rank and education, different from the use of the same terms or phrases, or the construction of similar sentences in Great Britain. . . . It does not follow in every case that the terms or phrases used are worse in themselves, but merely that they are of American and not of English growth. The word *Americanism,* which I have coined for the purpose, is exactly similar in its formation and significance to the word Scotticism (p. 6).

In Mencken's words, his few actual criticisms were rather prissy, and, although he consorted with politicians, one must doubt that he ever understood the language of politics and an "appeal to the people" in a language that the people understood.

There has never been an Academy in this country, as there has been in Europe, and one may believe it is safe to say that there never will be a nationally recognized organization that dictates precepts of language usage. Mencken records the point that John Adams was for it in 1780:

This I should admire. England will never more have any honor, except now and then that of imitating the Americans. I assure you, Sir, I am not altogether in jest. I see a general inclination after English in France, Spain and Holland, and it may extend throughout Europe. The population and commerce of America will force the language into general use.

How much prescience may a person have, to have written those words nearly two hundred years ago! This was to be an Academy "for refining, improving and ascertaining the English language" in America. Fortunately, such an institution was never brought about. An attempt as made in 1820, with John Quincy Adams in the chair. Various bigwigs were interested, but, as Webster wrote, it "would be of little use until the American public should have a dictionary which should be received as a standard work." Quite in the course of events, this was already well in progress and Webster's first edition was published in 1828. The British scholars who were approached would have none of this, however, and Jefferson refused the presidency of the Academy. He later wrote:

There are so many differences between us and England, of soil, climate, culture, production, laws, religion and government, that we must be left far behind the march of circumstances, were we to hold ourselves rigorously to their standard. . . . Judicious neology can alone give strength and copiousness to language, and enable it to be the vehicle of new ideas (p. 13).

Noah Webster became the lion uncaged relative to the American language. He expounded and declaimed, argued and insisted. He knew that language development was bound to go its own way, but was sharp and firm enough to record the directions in which it went. Mencken offers an excellent disquisition on Webster's contributions. He quotes the dictionary-maker on English writers on language. "They seem not to consider that grammar is formed on language and not language on grammar." To this Mencken observes, "Here he might have been preening himself on his own wide acquaintance with languages, at least twenty in all. Even if we concede that his knowledge of most was rather superficial, the number is staggering" (p. 15).

Webster's "Dissertations on the English Language" (1789), and "A Compendious Dictionary of the English Language" (1806) are now available in facsimile and are well worth reading. Mencken reminds us in an amusing passage that "among Englishmen and Anglomaniacs" the language needed no enrichment. One Basil Hall visited Webster and launched a frontal attack:

> "But surely," argued Hall, "such innovations are to be deprecated."
> "I don't know that," replied old Noah. "If a word becomes universally current in America, where English is spoken why should it not take its station in the language?
> "Because," replied Hall loftily, "there are words enough already."

Oddly, enough, there are some among the British today who still hold to this view; fortunately, there are not too many.

This situation was different throughout much of the nineteenth century, and most American writers—usually biographers and historians—were excoriated in British magazines and journals for their lexical atrocities. The list includes Jefferson, Webster, Adams, Marshall, Bancroft, Barlow, and several others among the most notable persons of the day. Even now some of the then objectionable words are in good usage in England. However, as Mencken points out, "to the English reviewers of the time words so unfamiliar were not only deplorable on their own account, but also proofs that the Americans were a sordid and ignoble people" (p. 19). It is unnecessary to explore further what Mencken calls "the English attack;" he treats it thoroughly and his observations are warmly recommended for attention. This aspect of "the other" English language is brought to a close with one more comment of Mencken that is penetrating but expressed without acerbity:

> To this day English reviewers are generally wary of American books and seldom greet them with anything properly describable as cordiality. In particular, they are frequently denounced on the ground that the Ameri-

canisms which spatter them are violations of the only true enlightenment (p. 25).

So be it! On occasion, in this regard, one has to think well about whether one is an Anglophile or an Anglomaniac. (One is reminded of a bit of Scottish-English folklore of the early seventeenth century known as "The Beggar's Benison." Some British critics would no doubt deny its existence, but that is their stuffiness, not ours. This topic is not pursued; one need only to pursue the literature.)

INQUIRY

I do not believe it is necessary to follow the form of Mencken's book, but some material that follows sharply on what we have been considering is quite intriguing. It is called "The Materials of Inquiry." Mencken had discussed the point that although several European countries had been deeply concerned with "correct speech forms," it was the "feeling of many American philologians that the serious study of the common speech of their country is beneath their dignity." This was despite the fact that disparity of dialectal and some idiomatic variants were the main points of concentration of "the British attack."

In addressing "the hallmarks of American," Mencken is precise:

> The character chiefly noted in American English are, first, its general uniformity throughout the country; second, its impatient disregard for grammatical, syntactical and phonological rule and precedent; and third, its large capacity (distinctly greater than that of the English of present-day England) for taking in new words and phrases from outside sources, and for manufacturing them of its own materials (p. 98).

Without doubt American English is the most homogeneous spoken by any major group of people in the Western World. Mencken speaks for himself on its content:

> The characteristic American habit of reducing complex concepts to the starkest abbreviations was already noticeable in colonial times, and such typical Americanisms as O.K.. N.G., and P.D.Q. have been traced back to the early days of the Republic. In so modest an opeation as that which has evolved *bunk* from *buncombe* there is evidence of a phenomenon which the philologian recognizes as belonging to the most lusty stages of speech (p. 99).

As for rhetoric and its appurtenances, Mencken has other ideas than the classical ones of this writer. To be fair, however, let us have Mencken speak for himself:

The American, from the beginning, has been the most ardent of recorded rhetoricians. His politics bristles with pungent epithets; his whole history has been bedizened with tall talk; his fundamental institutions rest far more upon brilliant phrases than upon logical ideas (p. 99).

Indeed, all aspects of English—British or American—went through quite the same stages of development. It is just that people have forgotten. Language, especially in its speechways, is a bursting state of affairs; it is never *there*—it is always coming into being. One must agree with Mencken that our pedants have never quite understood this. He refers to "the yoke of grammarians and lexicographers," and observes with some trenchant discernment:

> Standard English, in the Eighteenth Century, succumbed to pedants whose ignorance of language processes, was only equaled by their impudent assumption of authority: Swift, Horace Walpole, Thomas Gray of the oft-misquoted "Elegy" and, above all, Samuel Johnson. No eminent lexicographer was ever more ignorant of speechways than he was (p. 100).

One simply must believe that the speechways (and thus the language) of the market-places and the multitudes is an active, changing thing, quite fully responsive to the needs of the day and the tenor of the times, in either plush or earthy phrases. Note has been taken that the written language and the speechways are by no means "the same thing." There is apt to be a sort of ritual in each that can be understood only by the initiated. In formal writing, English English is apt to be stuffy, while American English tends to be multisyllabic in an owlish way. Mencken expresses it thoroughly well. He had been referring to Johnson, Quiller-Couch, and Gowers, when he wrote:

> American has so far escaped such suffocating formalism. Of course, we have our occasional practitioners of the authentic English jargon and have seen some weird mutations develop under the green thumbs of federal bureaucrats, educationists, literary critics and the gray-flanneled admen of Madison Avenue (p. 101).

He refers, however, to some of the plaints expressed years ago by Jacques Barzun, who deplored the lost "racy, colloquial creations" that have been supplanted by "the flaccid polysyllable." "Pioneer," he wrote, "has yielded to pedant." Mencken rounds out the topic with a penetrating opinion. He discusses the "Dogberrys in and out of office," and continues:

> we incline toward a directness of statement which, at its greatest, lacks restraint and urbanity altogether, and toward a hospitality which often

admits novelties for the mere sake of their novelty, and is quite uncritical of the difference between a genuine improvement in succinctness and clarity, and mere extravagant raciness (p. 101).

THE CHANGING LANGUAGE

Few persons have written with more perception of the human being-in-language-action than Mencken. With his newsman's aplomb, a nose for discovering quickly where the action is, and a tremendous capacity for understanding both human foibles and accomplishments, he never fails to be entertaining in his judgments. He had a particularly sharp and resourceful set of insights about what was going on in the eighteenth century relative to American English. This capacity led him into a most remarkable examination of what happened *when* in the creation and definition of a quite new language and, more important, why it happened. Even as a small boy he had begun to pay detailed attention to what he heard people say about events that he had observed, and then started to think carefully about why they used the words they did. His father was a prime example for him; and although he did not like his family's business, which was selling tobacco, he did pursue it through his father's lifetime and smoked cigars through almost all of his own.

What he was able to clearly understand was the function of language as a way of life and as a means of living. *The American Language* is a truly monumental work, a monument to him and to the language of which he was a master. If one were to have access to only one book about the language spoken by most of the English-speaking people of the world, this book would be the choice for guidance, and, in a scholarly way, for inspiration. The Bible is commonly referred to as a masterpiece of the English language, and well it might be! Along with the acceptance of "The Beggar's Benison," King James I caused to be assembled the most remarkable gathering of biblical scholars ever known. He paid them very well, and they wrought in his name. The results are well known to most literate persons.

There is a social aspect of Mencken's major work that simply must be respected. The world sat for too long near the feet of stuffy litterateurs like Samuel Johnson, who did not really know what was going on. He was entirely able to work his way through a skein of words—glot and polyglot—to figure out where they came from, and to fit them into a really maginificent frame of reference that helps us all to comprehend and be better able to use the language. The more one reads of Mencken, the more one becomes aware of the profound regard he had about the many whats, whys, and wherefores of American English. He was such a thoroughly sufficient scholar that he well knew the differences between the two kinds (or composites) of *the language* that had the same parentage. With due regard for professional colleagues who have sought far and long for insights into the linguistic nature of things, one must doubt that anybody has done the job better with regard to American English.

One might well refer to a most perceptive article (speech) written by Theo Lippmann, Jr., editorial writer for the Baltimore *Sun,* which was Mencken's long-time love and verbal conveyor. Here one will find a very thoughtful reference to the honing of the *Sunday Sun* under-taken by Mencken, Johnson, Kent, Owens, and others. One statement among many others contains some special information for writers:

> Of an afternoon I devoted myself to a long signed article for the next day. It was printed in the column next to the editorials, and was set in such crowded type that it consumed a great many words. When I under-took this job it seemed easy enough, for I was busting with ideas in those days, and eager to work them off. But in a little while I found that writ-ing 2,000 or 3,000 words a day was really a killing chore, and one day I remember especially, when sitting at the typewriter became suddenly unendurable, and I turned to pen and ink for relief (Lippmann, 1976, p. 6).

This is perhaps the best advice one can give a writer, young or old, newsman, or simply an observer of life and living. There is much more to be said about Mencken, but perhaps it is better to leave it with this much, and leave some more for another time.

REFERENCES

Lippmann, T. Jr. "H. L. Mencken and Press Criticism." Menckeniana: A Quarterly Review, Fall (1976) pp. 2–13.

Mencken, H. L. The American Language: An Inquiry into the Development of English in the United States. 4th rev. ed. New York: Alfred A. Knopf, 1919.

———. In The American Language: Fourth Edition and the Two Supple-ments, Abridged, With Annotations and New Material, edited by R. I. McDavid, Jr., and D. W. Maurer. New York: Alfred A. Knopf, 1963.

———. The American Language, Supplement I. New York: Alfred A. Knopf, 1966.

———. The American Language, Supplement II. New York: Alfred A. Knopf, 1967.

———. Newspaper Days. New York: Alfred A. Knopf, 1968.

———. Happy Days. New York: Alfred A. Knopf, 1973.

———. Heathen Days. New York: Alfred A. Knopf, 1975.

SUMMARY

One may assume that anybody who does much personal telephoning at long distance has repeatedly heard the phrase, "We cannot complete your call as dialed; please check the number; this is a recorded message." The simple fact about all this verbiage is that the machinery does not work fast enough to keep up with the digital facility of an old-time fly caster. The group will not admit it, but that is the truth of the matter. This has been checked personally many dozens of times. Dial the same number within a few minutes, but at a much slower pace, and the call goes through. The foregoing example is presented in this book simply as a kind of demonstration of how far things can go wrong in the workings of a major system in our society. The dimensions of meaning are both great and small.

What is at stake, of course, is programming. That introduces the human factor, as usual. Regardless of the astuteness of a computer, somebody, sometime, somewhere has to put together its organization, and make this relate with what some other humans—not machines— think is important. A computer is not a substitute for thinking; only for an arrangment of somebody's idea about something in a very simple binary structure. If there are only two parties in an election, which do you vote for? This is a quite simple-minded mode of procedure so far as dimensions of meaning are concerned. Somebody, somehow, must put in the right kinds of information in order to get out of the system what might be further productive.

These are only mathematical concepts that may or may not be valuable relative to any important dimensions of meaning. The pocket calculator is another example of non-thinking. It is without doubt of tremendous help to those who have to count, but these are for the most part merchants who have little more to do with dimensions of meaning than to organize their prices for their own benefit. So it goes! How those prices are set becomes a very important dimension for the user of whatever is involved, and, in a way, this does relate to meaning.

An interesting aspect of this kind of discussion is a consideration of what universities are presented by way of students who presumably become "higher learners," and of what these universities accomplish by way of helping these students to become mature readers (and perhaps writers) of the language known as American English. One can be sure that in the long run the general result is apt to be all right. There remain some reservations, however, because after observing and working with graduate students for more than forty years, I am quite certain that there are gaps to be closed.

Precisely how to close these gaps presents problems that are open for conjecture. There remains always a considerable difference between education and training. One—at least this one—would like to see more emphasis on education (perhaps in the sense that Isocrates would have thought of the idea), and go on to assume that there are various ways to earn a living. As one chooses one or another of these ways, which dimensions of meaning need to be of concern should become quite obvious. This is a personal matter.

There has been undertaken here a review of a variety of ideas about some dimensions of meaning expressed over a considerable range of time. As was suggested in the introductory chapter, a reasonable question about this sort of effort relates to choices of inclusions and exclusions. This is not an easy matter to deal with. Within only the past two or three years there have been several hundreds of articles, chapters, and books that could be related to dimensions of meaning. The great majority are not sufficiently fundamental to be so related, for they deal only with obvious leaves on the tree with little attention to the roots.

The topic is in general subject to a wide variety of opinions about verbal-symbolic meaning. In times long ago the major effort consisted of attempts to understand "who we are" and "where did we come from?" Sometime later came the question, "where are we going?" The historical aspects of these ponderings have been quite well managed (although one may be certain that there will forever be more such management). One may well suspect, however, that the last question will never be answered to any reasonable degree of satisfaction. This, according to an aphorism about life on the Mississippi River boats of an older time, is simply "in the cards."

Some have recurrently suggested that much of what is being considered here has to do with exchanges of messages between people, not simply the exposition of an idea.

The main point of the communicative act is communication, not only the construction of sentences for the sake of talking or the use of references that may or may not be shared, . . . but also the very practical matters of motivation, intention, appealing to and interesting others, and expressing the point that what we think is important and pertinent in a communicative exchange. Such an exchange is clearly related to how we think. This is a matter, in terms of the communicative act, of rhetoric, not of linguistic theory. When all is said and talked about, the study of people called *psychology* is a study of behavior. The dimensions of meaning refer to human behavior, not to linguistic theory. How a person believes, or thinks about, or otherwise reacts to his needs in his environment is very much a part of himself, of the person he believes himself to be, and, not in small degree, closely connected with the way he looks at himself within the frame of his life's picture (Hardy and Hardy, 1977, pp. 4–5.

There is no reason to try to summarize everything in this book. One can pick and choose topics according to one's interests. A few personal remarks are of interest to the writer. The nature of meaning in terms of verbal-symbolic development and function is largely the nature of mankind and its ways. Language is a communicative mode of behavior. It is not a "science" on the part of the person who uses it. Indeed, most college freshmen do not know syntax, nor most of the basic "rules" of language, and could not care less about this lack of knowledge. They simply talk, and very few write well. No doubt this reflects one aspect of our educational system. Despite the number of publications available, the habit of general reading seems no longer common among the younger generation. There seems to be too much "doingness" that is more important than simply being contemplative about the reasons for life and living. These observations without doubt express a point of view that is out of style. So be it! The style will change.

REFERENCES

Hardy, W. G., and M. Hardy. Essays on Communication and Communicative Disorders. New York: Grune and Stratton, 1977.

Index

Date Due